D0285342

Small-Fly Adventures

SMALL
Fly
Adventures
in the West

A Guide to Angling for Larger Trout

NEALE STREEKS

ILLUSTRATIONS BY ROD WALINCHUS

PRUETT PUBLISHING COMPANY
BOULDER, COLORADO

Printed in the United States

10 9 8 7 6 5 4 3 2 1

Library of Congress Cataloging-in-Publication Data

Streeks, Neale.
Small-fly adventures in the West : a guide to angling for larger
trout / Neale Streeks ; illustrations by Rod Walinchus.
   p.   cm.
Includes index.
ISBN 0-87108-870-3 (pbk.)
1. Trout fishing—West (U.S.) 2. Fly fishing—West (U.S.)
I. Title.
SH688.U6S77 1996
799.1'755—dc20
96-3315
CIP

Contents

Illustrations

Tables and Charts

Chapter Opening Photographs

Page 1: A tailwater rainbow inspects a *Baetis* mayfly dun just before eating it. The fly can be seen directly in front of the trout's nose.

Page 9: What looks like a sip from a distance is actually an engulfing of the fly.

Page 23: As the fish goes down after a rise, a swirl is left, along with a bubble or two of air. The air was taken in with the fly and is vented out the gills upon the descent. Bulging fish release no bubbles.

Page 59: Dense weedbeds often line the edges of rich rivers in summer. Here a trout comes out from beneath cover to sip a leftover spentwing. Observant anglers can target such fish throughout the day.

Page 71: This trout is easing forward to capture a fluttering dun. Such scenes promise excitement for match-the-hatch anglers!

Page 95: As the trout sinks back down after a rise, he creates rings on the water's surface. I often use these rings to mask my presentation, casting quickly after the last rise in hopes of capitalizing on the next one!

Page 125: Trout can often be spotted by vigilant anglers even between hatches. Nymphing trout in clear, shallow water make excellent stalking prospects!

Page 143: A rainbow drifts downstream while scrutinizing a natural. The *Baetis* dun is but inches from the trout's nose and unaware of its fate!

Page 167: This trout's nose is in the air and is what the angler sees on the water. The size of the trout can often be predicted by the look of its riseform.

Page 217: A small stream of water shoots from this trout's mouth as it takes the fly. This shot captures the moment that little "pop" is heard when a trout is gobbling spentwings.

All photographs are by the author.

Acknowledgments

Special thanks to Jim Pruett for instigating this project; to Orvis, Daiichi, Umpqua, and Just Reels for information and products; to a host of guides and writers who, over the years, have taken the time to give me bits of insight, including: George Anderson, Mike Lawson, Randall Kaufmann, Rick Hafele, Dave Hughes, Skip Morris, John Goddard, Peter Shutt, and others; and to Clearwater Photo of Great Falls, Montana, for the black-and-white processing.

Introduction: Thinking Small

Grey days, sullen, dank
Swallows circle over Mayfly's ranks . . .

Languid swirls on steel grey flows
Midges buzz in hatching droves.

River rushes, musty in dew
lay a mirror image of russet, yew . . .

Reflections broken by pulsing Trout
circling wider near eddy's bank.

Anonymous

There he was, nose and shoulders clearly discernible above the gray spring flow, slow bulging wakes pushing off his weaving torso. The mist-shrouded mountains, rushes, cattails, and willows were peripheral realities, moving out of focus as the eye and world wrap around the rise of a trout. An endless parade of midges danced lightly on the water, as if afraid to get their feet wet. Of this, the trout was wholly aware. And there I stood, hunched in olive drab, motionless in waders, feeling the river's pull, knowing what to do yet hesitating. The hunter's thrill, the trickster's doubt; will I spook another one, or feel the frantic race and pull on a vibrating load of graphite?

Check the 6X for frays. Examine the tiny fly, again. Work line out fast and away from the watchful trout. Drop a third of the twelve-foot leader ahead of and just outside his lane. Play it safe, make him lean over a bit for it.

There! A splaying of the fins, the rhythmic head surge, the merest tightening of the line . . . a wallow, a head-thrash, a fleeing run. Leader cuts water. Reel feeds line. Oh, for the song of the Hardy! The slightest of flies, a mockery of nature, has once again connected me to my inexcusable passion!

Sublime moments and settings when the river world is perfect and the trout tell you what they want are not everyday affairs. They must be waited for and waited out. In this windscape called Montana, such moments might come once a day, once a week, or once a month. One must be ready for them.

The last three times I went fishing, I forgot clippers, having lost them weeks ago. When the windless days come, I forget I forgot them. What trouble on-stream! Once I went without a reel, but did have an extra spool. Try playing hot edgewater trout with your spool in your pocket! But I always try to go with a good load of flies and tippet.

More and more fly-box space seems to be reserved for an outlandish number of small flies, tiny flies, productive flies. Cheap and easy to tie (with the right eyewear and lighting), they only require a light tippet and an exacting cast to do business—oh yes, and a degree of confidence that can take some experience in building. But you might find, as many have, that days of chucking big Royal Wulffs and getting smashing takes are diminishing on many waters. The fish have seen *those* before. Fishing pressure is sufficient now that trout must think twice before taking, even in the more remote waters of the world. He looks for the familiar, the dependable, the numerous, which often means the small. I would love to fish big dry flies as much as the next fellow with bad eyesight, but I would also like to catch a few fish!

Here one tempers his reality with that of the trout, learns new ways (new to him, anyway), and toys longer with each watery encounter. He learns the river, its trout and hatches. In knowledge alone some pleasure is found. But the angler puts this knowledge to work for the sake of added sport. Fly fishing makes one look closer at his riverine world and thus understand and appreciate it more. In the process techniques can become more refined, and the catch rate usually goes up.

When a young angler begins his long journey down streamside paths, he might initially think big: famous hatches of big flies, big-time rivers, and big fish. Surely this must be the pinnacle of the sport. More experience and time spent on-stream develops a more enlightened view. For on a seasonal basis, large flies are oddities, quickly passing phenomena that often leave the angler grasping for straws. Those low-water months of steady sipping trout feature small flies all across the West. The sooner one learns this, the more trout he's apt to catch.

And just what is small? I am going to use pale morning dun mayflies as an artificial dividing line to mark the upper limits of "small." This will mean that flies from #16 down to #28 will pass as small in this volume. And whereas East Coast anglers have a habit of generalizing any small fly as a "midge," regardless of species, we will keep things on a hatch-oriented basis. This puts the amateur entomologist-angler on surer footing.

The pale morning duns (PMDs) make an excellent dividing line, for they and everything smaller comprise the real "super hatches" of the West. Although there are numerous hatches of larger aquatic insects that are of great interest to anglers and exciting to fish, none approach the density and duration of the small-fly super hatches discussed here.

It only takes a brief look through a fisherman's fly box to see where his path has led. Even a decade ago it wouldn't have been unusual to find the casual angler's box filled with stoneflies, hoppers, and attractor patterns. The odd wet ant and small Adams might have been in there, too, but his notions and understanding of river life would have been laid bare by the contents of his vest. And the rivers he fished may have had so little pressure as to allow these flies to catch all the fish he wanted.

Today's well-traveled fisherman will have more exacting patterns on hand, and most of them will likely be small. He'll still have some attractor patterns but may spend more time wishing he could use them successfully, while tying on the latest PMD emerger. Terms and flies like "cripples," "sparkle-duns," "CDCs," "Tricos," "BWOs," and "PMD" will no doubt be heard, and instead of having a handful of "old favorite" flies, he'll probably sport several variations of each locally important hatch.

This is a trend that took over slowly in the West, picked up steam in the sixties, seventies, and eighties, and ended up as a steamroller of realization. Famous rivers, guides, and authors helped it along, and the new tailwater rivers kicked it into high gear. Awareness of small-fly hatches and fishing is now a highly polished skill. Beginners can walk right into what took their predecessors decades to know. Their realization of stream realities can come at the beginning of their fishing careers rather than at the end. Perhaps this volume will help put that trout-fishing reality in focus for the beginner and help further refine the midlevel angler's skills. Each fisherman's reality will vary with the water he chooses to fish, but once fishing the small hatches is mastered, everything else seems to come much more easily.

A History of Small-Fly Fishing

I am not overfond of small flies, except when they work. That seems to be often these days. I would rather have large dumb trout that smash a Royal Trude on the first drift. But that kind of trout is getting harder to find worldwide.

I like tying small flies because most are cheap and easy. As a guide giving away many experimental patterns every year, for me this becomes important when looked at on a decade-by-decade ledger. A tier can rattle off a dozen midge pupae in nothing flat, and catch as many or more fish than with an intricate and time-consuming tie.

Matching hatches of minutiae has become an obsession with some, an art form, and sometimes a lofty plateau that the occasional angler uses to look down his nose at the commoners below, who might still be casting Goofus Bugs on seven-foot leaders. In my mind, when I've had a lot of coffee anyway, I figure it's easier to catch "selective trout" (a Ray Bergman expression from the thirties) by imitating what they're eating, which is thus less sporting than trying to fool them with something they're not eating. When was the last time you skated a Hewitt Spider or Bivisible over a Trico-feeding trout to try to garner an explosive take? That is sport. No, most of us high-tech types go small and match the hatch for one reason and one reason only—to catch more fish, period. Matching the hatch is the easiest way to instant gratification.

Fishing small flies has always had a following. Its limitations have always been defined by the hooks available in any given era. Centuries ago, the

British were fishing midges and matching a number of "smut" naturals on their chalkstreams. Turn of the century Yanks were using them, too. The availability of small hooks marked the bottom line.

Today's hooks are smaller and better, but manufacturers are still juggling designs for the tiniest flies. It's a trendy market. Straight, upturned, or enlarged eyes are used; short shanks, wide gapes, and mini-barbs have become prominent. Manufacturers offer "chemically sharpened" hooks, and barbless options are, after five-plus centuries, becoming more available. Going small is still being defined by the suitable manufacture of hooks.

Tiny hooks need fine tippets, and these too have improved. Without these improvements in leaders, it would be hard to get drag-free drifts of #20 to #28 flies. Rod manufacture has surpassed its needs in some ways. Ultra-rigid rods are too stiff to set hooks delicately with 6X to 8X tippets and hot fish. There has been a swing back to softer-tip rods for small-fly work, and some anglers add a "bungee butt," an extra-stretchy leader butt section to absorb further shock.

The tricks used to make fishing small flies easier are old hat too, having been around for decades. Using a dry fly for an indicator, or a piece of visible material of some sort were practices used by a now-deceased and much less populated generation of anglers. Certainly today's fishermen, with their free time, mobility, and numbers (a relatively new thing in the world of sport fishing) have taken these practices to new heights, and along every imaginable avenue. In many cases they have to, for the fish have seen so many flies and fishermen and are used to eating small stuff. One cannot help but be a little sad when realizing that the world's population will likely be doubling every forty years or less from now on, and imagining where fishing pressure and natural resources will stand in fifty years. Size 36 flies will no doubt be needed to fool the tentative fish of the future, the few that remain anyway.

Perhaps the biggest single factor in the development of small-fly use on a mass scale is the advent of tailwaters, or dam-controlled trout fisheries. These slower-paced, gravel-bottomed, and steady-flowing rivers produce more small naturals than big. Zillions more. Anglers soon realized that much of the fishing to be had was on the small-fly end of the spectrum, as is true of many spring creeks. Since tailwaters offer the most consistent fishing conditions, highest trout populations, and largest average fish sizes, it's no wonder that anglers flock to them. It is there that most have been quickly educated on the fine points of fishing small, casting with precision, and fighting big fish on light tippets. It is a modern phenomenon, linked to the populating of the West and the "taming" of rivers for human use.

I still find a great pleasure in blind casting large dry flies on bouncing riffles. There is a satisfying athleticism in walking all day and punching out perfect casts to pocket, bank, and feeding lane, an intrinsic oneness with the rod,
and joy in placing the fly just where the eye looks. One can fish with a relaxed mind and take in the grandest of scenery. Casting skills are thus honed
along the way. Every now and then a gaping mouth will come lunging at the
fly, and the happiness there is of the lighthearted and innocent sort.

But more and more we find ourselves fishing small because it works. More
and more often I might be dangling a tiny Brassie under that Royal Wulff,
and find more trout taking it. And when trout are rising steadily all the year
long and making sure targets of themselves, it's likely that small flies will be
possessing both trout and anglers' minds.

The western trout's landscape is immense, perhaps a million square miles
of jumbled mountain ranges and river-carved valleys. Its domestication by European types is very recent. There still live homesteaders who dwell, in fact,
just as Scandinavians did hundreds of years ago. Their tools and lifestyles
were of the Iron Age in a new Stone Age world of bison and grizzly bear.
Their great-grandchildren wouldn't be caught dead without a twenty-five-
thousand-dollar pickup truck, hard-rock CD, and satellite dish. Things have
indeed changed quickly!

The trout's world has changed, too. Where before he was little accosted,
the same "sporting types" that exterminated buffalo plucked them from lake
and stream for pleasure and meat. When Lewis and Clark "discovered" cutthroat trout at the Great Falls of the Missouri, a new page of western history
was turned.

The earliest sport fishermen used fly rods with British salmon and trout
flies. Little note was made of "selectivity," for they could hardly shoulder the
bulging bags of trout back to camp. Trout waters near Denver and Yellowstone saw such wilderness sporting parties, and then the ax-ring of civilization. Some rivers were scoured for gold and left nearly lifeless. The western
United States witnessed on a tremendous scale the wholesale destruction of
wildlife and natural resources in a short time. Conservation practices are not
a value of industrial society, especially where there are seemingly endless
frontiers of richness. Even today, when we deem ourselves so educated and
clever, salmon and steelhead are rapidly disappearing from Pacific drainages.
Acid rain is destroying eastern U.S. and European salmonid populations.
Saltwater fisheries are disappearing too. Remember the craze for blackened

redfish some years back? It almost decimated redfish populations in many areas as spawning schools were spotted by aircraft and netted en masse! This is how resources are destroyed by thoughtless consumerism.

As time went on and gold lust settled, more homesteaders and cattlemen came, and thus more sportsmen. An observant few even fostered a conservation ethic. Yellowstone was made the first U.S. National Park in 1872. A very few quality stretches of trout river were privatized and protected, for instance Colorado's South Platte. Elsewhere, trout held their own in cattle-trounced streams, timber-raped drainages, and irrigated bottomlands from New Mexico to British Columbia and Colorado to California. Some races of trout, steelhead, and salmon were lost forever.

Trout were still there for the taking, though, and some newfangled East Coast dry-fly patterns began to be seen. On the whole, it was flies like the Royal Coachman and Rio Grande King that were most used by western fishermen. A 1910 article from *The Outing Magazine*, which touted Saratoga, Wyoming (on the North Platte—the trout were not native, all were stocked in the late 1800s), as the "greatest trout fishing town in the world," speaks of Silver Doctors, Royal Coachmen, and Jock Scotts being skittered across the surface. Westerners were quick to develop patterns to suit their independent lifestyles, though. (Perhaps buffalo dubbing was used—who knows?) Deerhair wings were used as early as the 1930s.

While large and numerous fish were being duped and anglers explored and exploited the golden age of western trouting with standby producers, civilization "back east" and in England was already taking a closer look at their more fastidious rising trout. One cannot help but look at England first, where clear-water chalkstreams, dependable hatches, and visible trout gave early birth to hatch-matching and the smallest of flies, those well-known cornerstones of fly fishing (or should we say *trout* fishing, because that was the prevalent sporting method for centuries. Spinning gear is the newfangled apparatus and only became available in the post–World War II era. It really compounded fishing pressure and popularity, though bait fishing without a reel was always an option through the ages.) The *Book of St. Albans* first included the "Treatise of Fishing with an Angle" in 1496. It is suspected that earlier writings, dating to at least 1450, influenced this book, which presents the first English accounts of trout fishing that still exist and can be positively dated. The "Treatise" depicts match-the-hatch fly fishing as an already full-blown and intricate sport, noting insects and fly patterns on a month-by-month basis and even suggesting stomach autopsies to help in deciding what fly to use. Now this paints a rather amusing scene when such a refined country sport is viewed in its proper light. Knights in armor are still running around lopping off enemy and peasant body parts, criminals are being drawn and quartered, plagues are rampant, America is yet to be "discovered," and Shakespeare is not yet even a twinkle in his father's eye (indeed, his father is not yet a twinkle in his *own* father's eye).

In J. W. Hill's book, *A History of Fly Fishing for Trout*, he quotes a few aspects of the "Treatise" worth reporting here: He writes, "the hooks were not large, measuring 2 or 3 to 15 on the modern scale . . . but they were shorter in the shank and thicker in the wire." Then: "Hooks are the most subtle and hardest part of your craft. . . . For small hooks, use the smallest square-headed steel needles that you can get . . . heat your needle red hot in a charcoal fire, cool it, make the barb with your knife, and sharpen the point. Then heat it again and bend it into the shape of the very excellent figure which is given; test the temper of the point, flatten the shank, and file it smooth so that you can lash your line to it. Heat it again and plunge it in water; thus will it be hard and strong." One can see some obvious bottom lines here for the average angler making small hooks for himself!

Rods then were long and limber, twelve to eighteen feet in length, which was necessary to battle larger trout with no reel (it had yet to be invented).

"The line is to be of horsehair, white and round, the longest you can find. Stain it different colors for different waters . . ."

It is becoming clear here that the match-the-hatch fishing of the day to selective trout entailed much more than strutting into your local fly shop for its thousands of consumer-oriented products.

The "Treatise" recommends that "the trout is to be fished for with a line of nine hairs [which were twisted together] and the great trout with one of twelve." A hundred years later angling authors wrote suggesting lines of three hairs, and one states that "you can kill the greatest trout that swims on a single hair, if you have sea room, and that a single hair will kill five trout to one taken by a line of three hairs twisted." This has a modern ring to it.

Another great quote derides, "with a double hair a man who could not kill a trout twenty inches long deserved not the name of an angler." Fishing fine seems to have had its early devotees, but remember that medieval flies were dapped and skittered, and the line was kept off the water as much as possible, often with an assist from the wind. Anglers stayed low and out of view of the trout, so as not to spook them. An early twentieth-century Frenchman noted that "you could tell an English angler by his kneepads."

Many English anglers not only stayed low and out of view to fool the trout when casting, but often during the entire battle, too. Not being able to "give line" (that is, fishing with a relatively short fixed line and no reel) called for tempering the trout's panic and fight as much as possible. Staying completely out of view helped.

Fly fishing continued to develop in England, where the chalkstreams, or spring creeks, demanded higher skill levels. Many trout were in the two- to four-plus pound range. In many cases anglers recorded every trout they ever caught, noting its weight, the weather conditions, fly pattern, time and date of capture. This systematic record-taking, which has come to seem so very British, has helped document England's ongoing fishing history.

In 1836, *The Fly Fisher's Entomology*, by Alfred Ronalds, was published. It is an interesting and beautiful work, with color plates of naturals and fly patterns. It is very modern in all regards. Of the forty-eight naturals and fly patterns listed, it is interesting to note that seven were midge or Diptera patterns, three were beetles, plus ants, houseflies, leaf hoppers, caddisflies, stoneflies, and mayfly spinners and duns. The fact that seven were midges, or "smuts," shows that the recognized need to match the smallest aquatic insects had long been noted. By now, "gut" was the established leader material. Ronalds suggested the "kirby" hooks for small flies.

It is interesting to note here that the "buzz" style of tying used for some of these old flies was simply a hackle palmered over a dubbed body, like a Griffith's Gnat, though the hackle is usually shown lying back, wet-fly style. There is no doubt, however, that buzz patterns were often floated and skittered on the surface. As early as 1590 dry flies were suggested, to be fished "aloft on the water." Some had cork foundations. The line was kept off the water, and the angler hid behind streamside foliage. Ronalds in the early 1800s speaks about his "Black Gnat" and the naturals: "This insect skims the brook all day long in immense crowds . . . The stomachs of trout have been found nearly gorged with this fly. To make it Buzz, a light dun hen hackle may be wound upon the body above [black ostrich herl], and thus made, it kills decidedly best." He made winged patterns, too: "These black flies resemble many small beetles, and may be ranked among 'general flies.' In fine low water, after midsummer, they are most useful." Here in the early 1800s then, is a good reference for using one pattern as a midge or small beetle for picky midsummer spring-creek trout. Sound familiar?

At the turn of the twentieth century, midge and midge pupa patterns were being touted by a few skilled angling authors. J. C. Mottram's most interesting book, *Fly Fishing: Some New Arts and Mysteries,* was published in England in 1921. Among his many observations and fly patterns are included midge pupae and drys. One of his pupal patterns is nothing more than a bare hook with black floss built up near the eye as a thorax, and in front of that, half a turn of the tip of a starling's hackle. These were tied on the "smallest and lightest hooks made." He noted that "it is many times the size of the natural smut, but the fish often do not notice its size, and like its shape." Other pupal patterns were tied with thin wedges of cork to make them float vertically, as emerging midges do.

Some of his midge drys are similar to Griffith's Gnats but use black and gray wool or silk for the body and white or gray hackle. Other patterns use black ostrich herl for the body, with a collar of white hackle and a thorax (more like a head) of black wool. These were tied on #16 to #18 Allcock hooks, decidedly small for that day. On some patterns he left half the hook shank bare to further the effect of diminution. A last note of interest from his book states that, "The season of 1913 was remarkable for the dearth of ephemeroptera and the abundance of smuts, and on referring to my log, I find that almost as many chalk stream fish were killed on smuts as on duns."

Back in the eastern United States, simplistic brook trout had historically obviated any need for small-fly specialization. The introduction of the more fastidious brown trout in 1883 was to change that. In 1933, the great American angling author Edward Hewitt wrote of midge fishing, suggesting flies as small as "18's or even 20's." He noted that "when trout are feeding on the surface and will not take any kind of dry fly, they are almost always feeding on midge larvae and midges." He also noted that, "I have never been able to buy any good midge flies, either here or in England, and have been obliged to tie them myself. Those bought are always much too large and heavily tied to take our trout." He suggested anglers have on hand "a few lengths of gut four to six feet long, about 5/1000's of an inch in diameter" to be added to the usual leader for midging trout. Here again, the manufacture of hooks, leaders, and flies defined the bottom line, the smallest limitation of available fly patterns.

Ray Bergman, in his thoughtful and well-researched classic *Trout* noted that, "The real need for the small flies is when midges are on the water, and the smaller your 16's and 18's are tied, the more chance there is that they will be effective. When you buy small flies, insist on the right size hackles," because most were found with oversized hackle, which rendered them less effective. His second edition of *Trout,* in 1952, included flies down to #20, an Adams, and a Black Angel or "other black pattern."

Vincent Marinaro's 1950 book, A Modern Dry-Fly Code, speaks of using #22s to imitate light floating minutiae, preferably with offset or "Sneck" design hooks. He also notes that, "The problem of obtaining small hooks in the finest wire with good temper is a vexation at all times . . . the search for the finest gut in good quality is equally or more vexing." He speaks excitedly of finally finding some 8X gut testing with a four-ounce breaking strength. This he thought necessary for the proper drag-free float and minimum disturbance to the surface film. It is interesting to note that he mentions the testing strength of 5X gut to be but eight ounces. To those of us now used to modern 5X advertised with breaking strengths of over four, and even five, pounds, it becomes apparent that fishing small in past generations was challenging indeed.

By the time 1958 rolled around, Joe Brooks, globe-trotting angler and inspiration to many, wrote about anglers on the Yellowstone using #18 to #20 hooks with 5x short shanks. These were to imitate "snow flies," or winter midges, on these year-round western fisheries. Size 20s seemed to be the bottom line for suggested flies, though he mentioned #22s. He also wrote that "the smallest nymph I have ever been able to find was tied on a #16 hook, but certainly there are naturals which would be matched with a size 18 or even 20 if these were available on the market." His ant and beetle patterns, by the way, products of Pennsylvania spring-creek fishing, ranged from #8s to #20s.

Perhaps no other book so shaped the modern fly fisher's course as did Selective Trout, first published in 1971 by Doug Swisher and Carl Richards. Here, the tiniest hatches were scrutinized across the country, and new pattern ideas down to #28 were suggested. A major mental shift had begun, on a widespread scale, away from the traditional (if it didn't make sense) and on to the practical and productive. More anglers looked forward to small-fly challenges (which often translates into more rising fish for more hours of the day, and more days of the year), and faced them with less trepidation. Just as important, manufacturers kept producing smaller hooks and better leader material and came to notice this growing specialized market. The corner was finally turned.

Big Versus Small

The more one looks at a river—into it, under it, over it, and around it—the more there seems to be to discover. All is intertwined. A river is a good indicator of the health of an ecosystem, something which, unfortunately, mankind has made a habit of ignoring til the very last second.

When it comes to aquatic insects, their many and varied forms can be intimidating for a novice to comprehend initially. Once one begins to understand them a bit, he actually finds himself enjoying them. He likes looking at them, at their silhouettes as they ride the currents, at the way they fly and their mating dances, at their various colors and forms, and he finds meaning in their life cycles as part of a whole.

I look at aquatic insects the way most people look at big-game animals—as things to be admired and understood. And there are many more varieties to comprehend than there are mammals! Most intriguing of all is how trout feed on them. On waters clear enough to see into, such feeding is obvious. I have been fortunate enough to spend many years fishing New Zealand, where trout behavior is shockingly clear at times. There, lessons are to be learned. I've also been guiding on Montana's Smith and Missouri Rivers for over eighteen years, and also on the Blackfoot, Big Horn, South Fork of the Flathead, and other regional waters. It is interesting to see how trout-insect relations vary from drainage to drainage. While trout the world over have certain similarities, they also show noticeable differences.

"Prerunoff" conditions feature low, clear rivers, many with rising trout. Midges predominate here.

The more one observes rivers, the more patterns in insect-trout behavior begin to emerge. Some patterns are universal. There are always more prey than predators, whether wildebeests and lions, plankton and whales, or flies and trout. There are usually if not always higher numbers of small species than of large. Predators will feed most often on the most common and numerous prey. This line of thought has obvious parallels in trout fishing.

In the trout's world on most rivers, small insects greatly outnumber large ones, except at certain and relatively brief times of year. This is where the generalizations become interesting! Let's look at a typical western freestone river and its seasonal fluctuations.

Throughout the Rocky Mountain West, perhaps the largest and most diverse trout arena in the world, a labyrinth of waterways are forever gnawing at the mountain's roots. Winter snows pile high. Early spring can see ice-free waters as yet unaffected by high-mountain snowmelt. I call this the prerunoff period. This can last from February to late May, depending on the year, location, altitude, snowpack, temperature, and what have you. From May into early July the high-altitude snowfields melt off, bringing most rivers a rush of silted, gushing runoff water. By mid-July, most rivers have come down and cleared out. A proliferation of insects can occur at this time. Mid- to late summer can often overheat waters, with some lulls in fishing. Fall generally sees a continuance of low flows, hatches, and reinvigorated fish till subzero temperatures take over. Coastal temperature influences, altitude, snowpack depth (or lack of it), and those always-varying continental weather patterns, sometimes extreme, can affect "normal" seasonal fluctuations and hatch dates on a year-to-year basis.

During this seasonal progression hatches aren't just different, they adjust to water levels and temperatures in surprising ways. Generally speaking, their size and color changes en masse to match conditions, an evolutionary step to ward off a variety of troubles. This is the kind of thing that keeps fishing interesting.

First let's look at general size trends in aquatic insects as they relate to water levels. In early spring, before the runoff and when waters are still low, the few species of emerging insects tend to be small. These include the little winter stoneflies (black and brown) and droves of midges. In some places where waters warm earlier, such as low-altitude, southern, coastal, and spring-fed streams, *Baetis* mayflies might put in an early showing. These are smaller flies, ranging from #28s (the smaller midges—some are bigger) to #16s.

As the runoff period first begins (varying with circumstance), the size of some emerging flies begins to go up with the increased water flows. Stonefly species become larger (#14 to #8), as do mayflies, including the western march brown, *Rhithrogena morrisoni* (#16 to #14). Caddis (a mid-sized family of flies on the whole, #18 to #14, though there are very small and large ones) begin their mind-boggling array of seasonal hatches. *Baetis* mayflies (#20 to #16) become widespread and especially important on tailwaters and spring creeks. Beetles, too, become active at this time, though most anglers consider them only as late-summer options.

During the maximum runoff period, from late May into early July, the largest insects hatch. These include the giant salmon flies and golden stoneflies (#4 to #8, 3x long). In the mayfly arena, the big green and brown drakes put in their seasonal showing (#10 to #14). Many other medium-sized species begin hatching in this time, some carrying over into the lower water flows of the post-runoff period—midsummer. Notable here are the pale morning duns (PMDs) and various caddis species; also some *Epeorus*, *Paraleptophlebia*, *Ephemerella*, and *Heptagenia* species. These range in size from #12 to #18.

As waters drop and clear to summer lows, insect size decreases, with some exceptions. Stonefly species drop off quickly in size to #14—the little yellow, green, and brown stones—and then give out completely for the year. Tricos

Generalized Seasonal Water Fluctuations
and Aquatic Insect Size

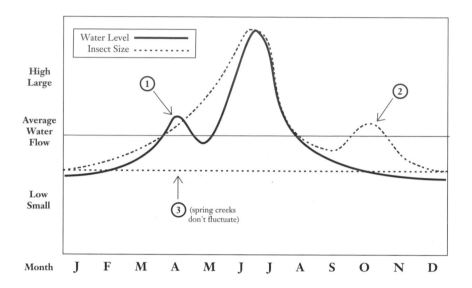

1. Early-season rain or high temperatures can cause early runoffs.
2. There is an upward trend in size for some autumn insects, though smaller midges and *Baetis* can dominate dry-fly action in many quarters.
3. Small insects, primarily midges and *Baetis*, continue to be important, especially on tailwaters and spring creeks, where flows are controlled.

Small insects are on the water for more of the season and hatch in better fishing conditions than large insects tend to do. Actual timing of runoff and hatches can vary with altitude, weather, and snowpack across the West.

circumstances. Come the hot and dry months, they tend to push their hatching and mating hours into early morning and late evening, avoiding the arid sun. Tricos (*Tricorythodes minutus* mayflies) would be the big exception here, for they fearlessly linger into late morning. This brings us to another trend, that of timing.

When weather is cold in spring and fall, aquatic insects tend to hatch at the warmest time of day—midafternoon. Come the heat of midsummer, a noticeable trend toward A.M. and P.M. hatches occurs, with flies avoiding the heat of midday.

A big exception here are the midges, or *chironomids*. I have found that these will hatch at any time of day, if conditions are ideal, throughout the season. Since this is by far the most populated family of aquatic insects, and in many cases the most important to trout, this hatching pattern is of great importance to anglers.

It seems to me that midges prefer calm, humid days or hours to hatch and mate. Most aquatic insects prefer humid conditions, for a dehydrated fly has a hard time molting its final skin. Midges will hatch morning, midday, or evening, and any time of year when weather conditions are right. Locally in the West they're called "snow flies" in the winter, for they can be seen buzzing around and crawling on iced-over riverbanks, and continue to bring both whitefish and trout to the surface.

I used to think it was just overcast days that brought up the best midge hatches. But I've seen many overcast yet arid days with little to no midge hatch, and sunny yet humid days with good ones. Overcast *and* humid days tend to be the best of all, especially when they are windless. Considering how dry most of the Rocky Mountain West is, such conditions are *not* everyday occurrences.

Overview of Hatch Periods Through the Season

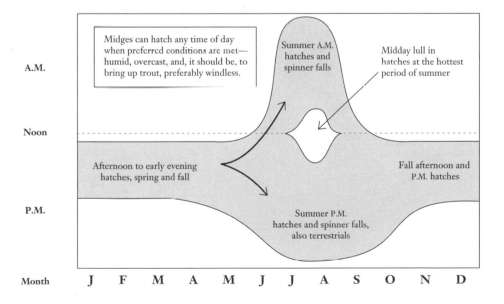

Many aquatic insects and trout shun bright light. This is particularly true in springtime, when trout have been used to low winter light levels and spend less time rising.

I've often seen spring trout and flies (*Baetis* and midges) rise and hatch like mad while clouds block the sun. The moment a sunbeam hits the water, all activity instantly ceases—till the next cloud! In continuously sunny weather, flies and fish grow somewhat used to the sun. They can't wait forever to hatch and eat. The next heavily overcast day with drizzle or light snow can bring on a bonanza of fly and surface action, though. (It is the midsummer Trico hatch that really gets trout used to rising in the bright midday sun.)

Yes, if it's calm and humid, good midge hatches can be anticipated morning, afternoon, or evening—spring, summer, fall, and winter. (Although midges hatch in the wind, too, the trout won't always rise to them on a ruffled surface.) This shows anglers more rising fish hours and days than any other insect group. Take note. Although other aquatic insects tend to have well-defined hours of emergence during the day and season, not so the eternal midge!

As summer wanes and temperatures cool, hatches again become afternoon affairs, with the possible exception of additional morning midges. The spring and autumn hatch-matcher has no great hurry to be on the river at those times of year. If it's overcast, calm, and humid, though, take the day off from work!

Perhaps the next most important trend of interest to the angler is that of the hatch's duration and availability to the trout. Look at the hatch chart below and see why small flies can be of such importance.

As a rule, large insect species tend to hatch for brief periods, and often in less than desirable conditions. As previously mentioned, this latter aspect is likely an evolutionary step to help hide the flies' noticeable bulk from winged and finned predators. Emergences of the largest stoneflies and mayflies can last for as little as a week in a given stretch of river. Triggered in part by warming water temperatures, these hatches progress up a river from low altitude to high. Anglers follow the hatch, which is often a disappointment, trying to hit the right place at just the right time. These hatches cause excitement and bring crowds but usually result in inconsistent fishing. But when hit right, the thrill of hatch-crazed big fish is indeed memorable and worth pursuing. The other 75 percent of the time the fishing can be slow—very slow. One hears stories of glutted fish, fizzled hatches, high muddy rivers, and bumper boat crowds. That is the legacy of big-fly hatches in many cases.

Insect Size, Condition, Duration Comparison

Insect Species	Hatch Conditions	Size	Hook Size	Hatch Duration	Fishing Notes
Salmon fly *Pteronarcys californica*	high water	50 mm (2 in.)	#4	2–7 days	Hatches at highest water levels; boom or bust situations common
Golden stonefly *Hesperoperla pacifica*	high to receding water	35 mm (1-1/2 in.)	#6–#8	14± days	Can provide better fishing than salmon flies some years in lower clearing waters
Western green drake *Drunella grandis*	high to receding water and controlled flows	14–18 mm (3/4 in.)	#10–#12	4–14 days	Most famous in controlled-flow situations like the Henry's Fork; hatches at high water levels
Pink lady *Epeorus albertae*	receding and clear water, swift freestone streams	8–14 mm (1/4–3/4 in.)	#12–#15	2–4+ weeks	Sporadic hatches in swift rivers, but very common; emergers and wet flies can be best
Pale morning dun *Ephemerella infrequens* and *E. inermis*	high, clearing, low and controlled flows	5–10 mm (1/4 in.)	#16–#22	1–2+ months	Dominant summer hatch in spring creeks, tailwaters, and freestone rivers late June into August
Trico mayflies *Tricorythodes minutus*	low, clear water	3–6 mm (1/8–1/4 in.)	#20–#26	2 months	Brings up the steadiest-rising fish you're likely to see at midsummer's low-water levels
Baetis mayflies numerous *Baetis* species	low, clear, and rising water in spring; low, clear water in fall	4–10 mm (1/8–1/4 in.)	#16–#24	3–4+ months	Top spring and fall hatches for steady-rising trout and clear-water conditions; often mixed with midges
Midges Chironomidae	all types, but best in clear, slow water	1–6 mm (1/8 in. or less)	#18–#28	12 months	Brings up steady risers in low, clear waters, especially important in fall, winter, and spring

Note the duration and hatch conditions of the smaller insect hatches compared to the larger, more famous ones. The duration of each hatch is an approximation for a relatively short, specific length of river.

The great differences in altitude throughout the Rockies does allow the big-fly devotee extended opportunities to ply his sport. Salmon fly hatches begin as early as mid-May on some rivers and finish up in mid-July at the highest elevations. And there are medium-large stonefly hatches before the salmon flies kick in. Anyone following "the hatch" this long is assured of some banner days. By commuting from stretch to stretch, river to river, and even state to state, big fly hatches can be pursued and drawn out to last the entire season. One could go from salmon flies to golden stones, to green and brown drakes, right into hoppers and attractors, on to October caddis, and ply Woolly Buggers at any impasse. This would entail racking up some mileage, for the right kind of river, water level, dates, and temperatures would have to be aligned. Big-dry-fly timing can be critical. Opportunities come and go quickly with the season's changes.

Small flies, on the other hand, tend to hatch for long periods under ideal fishing scenarios. One doesn't have to travel far to find the challenges. Waters are low, clear, and easily waded. The trout *must* rise repeatedly to fill up on small flies, often sipping for hours at a time. Whereas salmon flies might only hatch for a week on a given stretch of river, *Baetis* mayflies can hatch spring and fall, totaling up to four months. Midges can hatch year-round—assorted caddis up to eight months, Tricos two months, PMDs a month or more—in the same stretch of river. One can begin to see a pattern here, a good pattern!

Many of the largest insects hatch under poor conditions, for short periods, and in some cases only at last light and into darkness. High-water situations are common. Fishing opportunities here are noticeably limited in time but do portend exciting results for those willing to travel and put up with the higher risk of failure. Perhaps the most famous big-fly hatch that doesn't fit into the high-risk mold has long been the green drake hatch on the Henry's Fork and similar waters. There, the big flies hatch at civilized hours in controlled water flows with a historic population of big fish. Such a scenario does provide at least one sure thing—crowds. There is a big-fly, big-fish draw here that is oh so compelling to human nature.

Small-fly hatches in general offer the opposite when compared to most of the larger aquatic species. Most hatch in midday for long periods, affording anglers optimal fishing opportunities. For many decades fishermen shunned small flies, leaving rivers in peace for the "experts." Midges can hatch at any time of day; *Baetis* from 1:00 to 6:00 P.M.; Trico duns and spinners bring up fish from 7:00 A.M. till early afternoon; PMDs vary a bit, with late-morning and early-evening hatches; *Pseudocloeon* pop from 3:00 to 6:00 P.M. on local waters. All these great hatches, with the most steadily rising fish you'll ever see, occur in "civilized" hours, and under perfect fishing conditions. Certainly in extreme heat rising-fish opportunities will slow a bit and push more toward dawn and dusk, but where I live, rising trout can and are found all day long. Small flies encourage the most, the longest, and the best rising-fish encounters an angler will experience.

Another topic of interest is that of insect coloration. This has little to do with size but is important to anglers, especially if one is unfamiliar with a particular water's hatches and is thus shooting from the hip. If you will remember our brief discussion of dehydration and think of the color spectrum in its relation to qualities of heat absorption, then the evolutionary trends in color become clearer.

In springtime's colder flows and low daytime temperatures, aquatic insects are dark—blacks and dark browns. These are colors that absorb heat rapidly.

As the globe tilts us more directly at the sun, prompting the runoff, water and air temperatures climb and insect colors moderate. *Baetis* mayflies are generally gray. *Rhithrogena* mayflies, caddis, and March-to-June stoneflies all come in medium dark, heat-absorbing tones. Other species follow the trend.

Come mid- to late July, when waters have receded and cleared, insects lighten. It's the hottest time of year, when the brightest-colored insects are seen. The bright little yellow and green stoneflies liven up streamside foliage. PMDs epitomize the typical summer coloration. Light tan caddis are abundant. There are even lime green midges. The river is full of life. One exception here is the Tricos. Their darker-olive-to-black coloration perhaps reflects their ultrashort existence as winged adults. When combined with their small sizes—down to #24—and rapid molt, dehydration may not cause much of a problem. Indeed, the males hatch at nightfall the evening before the females hatch and molt in the morning coolness. It's their massive smokelike spinner falls that glisten in the sunlight so conspicuously as the day begins to heat up.

As fall crisply commences, the insects again darken. The gray-olive *Baetis* repeat their emergence. Gray drakes (*Siphlonurus occidentalis*) and darker *Paraleptophlebia* and *Epeorus* species hatch. Insect size goes up, too, for dehydration is no longer quite the problem it was. When winter closes in, it is only the black-gray midges that remain to animate eddies and ice floes.

These are but some of nature's trends that the angler witnesses. Surely there are some still to be perceived by the observant, and that perhaps go against the flow of human reason. There is still something intriguing and

General Trend of Aquatic Insect Color as It Relates to Seasonal Temperature Fluctuations

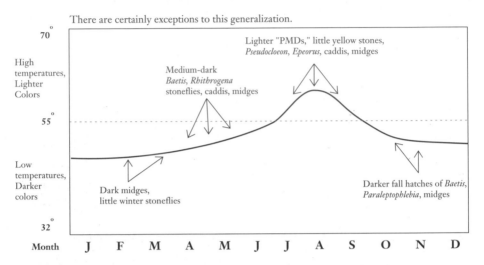

There are certainly exceptions to this generalization.

70°

High temperatures, Lighter Colors

Lighter "PMDs," little yellow stones, *Pseudocloeon, Epeorus*, caddis, midges

Medium-dark *Baetis, Rhithrogena* stoneflies, caddis, midges

55°

Low temperatures, Darker colors

Dark midges, little winter stoneflies

Darker fall hatches of *Baetis, Paraleptophlebia*, midges

32°

Month   J   F   M   A   M   J   J   A   S   O   N   D

PMDs epitomize the mid- to late-summer light colors of aquatic insects. PMDs hatch from June into August or even September.

This Epeorus *dun shows the typical darker color of fall-hatching mayflies.*

compelling about the unknown, and no fisherman lives long enough to piece together the entire puzzle. Indeed, ancient puzzles are disappearing faster than they can be solved—a result of human "progress." For the thinking fisherman, though, and when it comes to the duration of optimal rising-fish opportunities, there is a decided benefit in thinking small.

The Hatches: Seasons of Small-Fly Adventures

Not all rivers fish the same. Seasons and hatches too can vary a bit from year to year. Some high-altitude streams remain frozen over into spring and "blow out" with a rush of high water. Low-altitude rivers may be ice-free early on, with longer periods of good prerunoff fishing. Then there are the tailwaters, those "anytime" battlefields where fishing pressure favors an ongoing evolution of small match-the-hatch patterns. This is one arena where the small-fly challenge never fades.

No two anglers' perceptions of a river are quite the same, either. One may have had youthful successes with streamers and still have a wet-fly bent. Another may have had early dry-fly experiences and have concentrated on that realm ever since. Yet another will have realized that well-fished nymphs will outfish any other method, day in and day out, and will routinely start along those lines. Each experience is built around individual successes and failures. These imprint themselves on one's memory of the river—the same piece of water each angler sees differently.

Trout behavior varies from river to river too. A swift freestone river, over-loaded in springtime with succulent fast-water nymphs, is likely to show fewer risers than is a slow, meandering one dominated by midges. An angler's own backyard will likely shape his methodology and even his likes and dislikes. When one becomes accustomed to a particular style, he is somewhat more likely to pursue distant waters of the same nature.

Those not accustomed to small-fly work are usually doubtful about using a #24 hook when seeing the thing perched on their fingertip. It seems too small to fish, too small to hold, too small to land big fish on. That is not the case, though, and midging trout over ten pounds have been landed on #28 hooks. Small flies set easily and hold well when proper pressure is maintained throughout the battle.

What makes the small fly seem more practical is the sight of rising fish. When you have a known target, a known food source, and faith in your pattern, the battle is half won.

The step beyond that, casting small flies to *unseen* fish, those swimming merely in the imagination, takes greater faith. Ultimately, this faith comes from knowing what the fish most often eat, and where they lie. For even in huge rivers like the Missouri, Big Horn, and San Juan, studious anglers resolutely fish midge pupae blind with convincing results. Experience is the key here, tempered with knowledge. When fish are located (and once they settle in, they rarely move until the next spawning urge), you merely fish their most commonly ingested food source in their faces. On the big tailwaters this can be dismaying initially. But by watching others—and there *will* be others—you will figure out the trout's holding positions and succeed.

Knowing where they hold (experience) and what they eat (knowledge) adds up to successful outings. The experience end of the business is up to you and can be hastened by hiring a guide for a day, even in your own backyard. That learning process is part of the fun, especially if your personality doesn't demand instant gratification. The following might help in the knowledge department.

Western Small-Fly Hatches of Note

If you will recall, our definition of "small" includes flies from #16 down to #28. This allows us to include all of the small-fly superhatches of the West. Covering every hatch is beyond the scope of this book. The following hatches, however, are the most commonplace, widespread, numerous, long-lasting, and dependable to be found on a variety of western waters.

Importance of Smaller-Fly Hatches on a Generalized Seasonal Basis

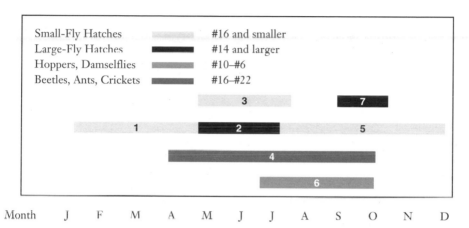

Small-Fly Hatches		#16 and smaller
Large-Fly Hatches		#14 and larger
Hoppers, Damselflies		#10–#6
Beetles, Ants, Crickets		#16–#22

Month   J   F   M   A   M   J   J   A   S   O   N   D

Note the overall duration of small-fly hatches as compared to large-fly hatches.

1. Long prerunoff period, midges dominate. Little winter stoneflies possible January to April. *Baetis* mayflies gain importance from March to June.

2. The "big" hatches occur, mostly at higher river levels. These include salmon flies, golden stones, western march browns, and green and brown drakes. Caddis hatches begin just before high water commences. This is largely a freestone-river scenario.

3. Small-fly hatches continue to be important on spring creeks and tailwaters. This includes midges, *Baetis*, the beginning of pale morning duns, caddis, beetles, and ants.

4. Small terrestrial insects are taken by fish from spring through fall, though most anglers consider them mid- to late-summer specialties.

5. Small-fly hatches dominate on most rivers from midsummer to winter, including PMD mayflies, *Tricorythodes* mayflies (Tricos), *Pseudocloeon* mayflies (Pseudos), caddis, *Baetis* mayflies, midges, and small terrestrials. Waters are low and clear.

6. The presence of large hoppers, crane flies, and damselflies are the exception to the midsummer small-fly rule.

7. Some fall hatches of larger aquatic insects occur, including October caddis, gray drakes, and mahogany duns. Generally these are sparse, localized hatches. The smaller *Baetis* and midges tend to dominate the trout's attention on many waters.

Dominant Western Small-Fly Hatches in Their Common Seasonal Order

1. Midges #18-#28

2. Little winter stoneflies #16-#18

3. *Baetis* mayflies #16-#22

4. "PMD" mayflies #16-#22

5. "Micro caddis" #16-#24

6. *Troicorythodes* mayflies #20-#24

7. *Pseudocloeon* mayflies #24-26

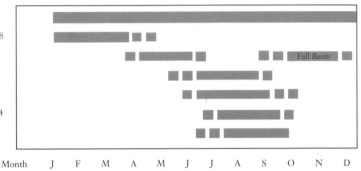

Month   J   F   M   A   M   J   J   A   S   O   N   D

Notes:
- Important caddis hatches of sizes #14–#16 occur from April into November.
- Note that varying location, altitude, and water type can produce varying hatch-date boundaries. There is no substitute for local knowledge!
- Through this book you'll find me using both the proper Latin names for insects and various popular names. This is not so much because I'm dull-witted but because this is what you're going to hear on the river. I thought it best to familiarize you with the various names so you'll be more likely to know what anglers in different parts of the West are talking about when referring to specific hatches. I rotate the different names to help you remember them better. Here are the insect names we'll be looking at the most, with their true Latin names italicized. The list below corresponds numerically to the one above.

1. Chironomidae. Common name: Midges.
2. *Nemoura, Leuctra,* and *Capnia* species. Common names: Little winter stoneflies, little black and brown stones, needle flies.
3. *Baetis* mayflies. Common names: Olives, little blue-winged olives, BWOs, *Baetis.*
4. *Ephemerella infrequens, E. inermis,* and *E. lacustris.* Common names: Pale morning duns, PMDs.
5. *Glossosoma, Helicopsyche, Lepidostoma, Oecetis, Micrasema, Mystacides,* and *Cheumatopsyche* species. Common name: Microcaddis.
6. *Tricorythodes minutus.* Common names: Trico, trike, tiny white-winged black. (The spinner or spentwing is the most important phase of this tiny mayfly.)
7. *Pseudocloeon edmundsi.* Common names: Pseudo, tiny blue-winged olive, little son of a b . . . you get the idea. Often lumped together with *Baetis* mayflies and called BWOs or little blue-winged olives.

Hours of Daily Small-Fly Hatches

Note that most small-fly hatches occur in the "civilized" hours of 8 A.M. to 8 P.M. Some hatches and spinner falls trickle into darkness, producing the common "evening rise."

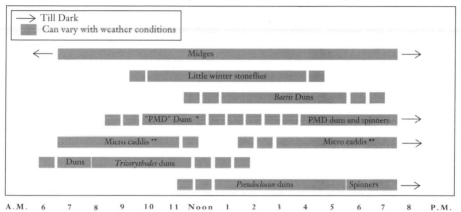

*PMDs hatch at a variety of hours. On many rivers, late-morning hatches of one to three hours' duration are the norm. Elsewhere, early-evening hatches from 5:00 to 8:00 P.M. take place. Spinners can fall A.M. or P.M. Clouds and rainstorms can bring on hatches at various hours.

**Both emergence and egg-laying can take place within these hours.

Midges

Midges, midges, midges—the angler's friend! There are so many of them, and so many kinds, that it boggles the imagination. They hatch by the millions all over the globe, year-round. Trout eat more of them in many waters than of anything else. Where in past generations and centuries midges were seen as the angler's curse, today's equipment allows easy imitation. There are midges that are just *too* small to imitate, but there are plenty of others that anglers look forward to imitating, so dependably do they bring rising trout to the surface.

With most anglers a seasonal progression of midge hatches and species isn't worked out—they're all just midges. I, too, fit into this category but certainly have noted some seasonal and general trends. There are good-sized river midges approaching #18, and others much smaller than #28. They come in black, gray, tan, and even bright lime green. The larvae are generally olive to black but can vary from that. Emerging pupae show more variation, even into the red end of the spectrum.

Midges

Order: Diptera
Family: Chironomidae
Species: Over 1,500 species in North America
Common name: Midge
Important fishing stages:

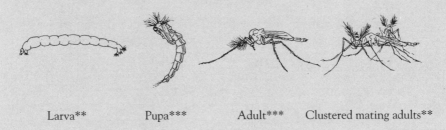

Larva**   Pupa***   Adult***   Clustered mating adults**

Color: Black, olive gray, tan, amber, red; bright green in larvae, pupae, and adults
Matching hook sizes: #18–#28 in rivers; #10–#24 on lakes
Water types: All, but best midge-fishing conditions are found in slower-paced edge waters, eddies, flats, and wherever trout can feed on them without fighting too much current.
Hours of emergence: Any hour possible. Calm (wind-free), humid conditions are best.
Popular fly patterns: Larva, various colors. Pupa, various colors, Serendipity. Adult, Griffith's Gnat dry, traditional Black Gnat dry; Palomino Midge dry, small Adams dry.

Special notes: Early-spring and late-fall hatches are most important to anglers because there are few or no other hatches available to trout. They continue to be important throughout the summer but can be overshadowed by larger insects, especially in the angler's mind!

*somewhat important
**important
***most important

With over fifteen hundred species of midges or aquatic dipterans (chironomids) in North America, one cannot even begin to hope to fully comprehend this group of important insects. A basic understanding of their lifestyles and relations with trout will be sufficient to catch fish.

There are five stages of the midge's monumental development that deserve the angler's attention. These correspond with its emergence into a promiscuous mating adult.

The midge larvae, which can be seen attached to rocks and bottom debris, are cute little wormlike creatures matched with #16 to #24 hooks. A downsizing trend has been noted in the midge life cycle, where the larva is actually bigger than the pupa, and the pupa bigger than the adult. In other words, a #18 larva ends up as a #22 adult. In any case, these little guys graze the streambed, eating algae. Trout will graze on them when pickings are slim, and in between hatches. They show up in trout stomach samples, especially in winter and early spring, when food choices are limited.

Larva patterns are fished deep near the bottom with added weight and indicators. They are dead-drifted through known or imagined trout holding positions. It is here that a good degree of faith is needed. Determination guides your fly into a fish's mouth. A popular way of fishing midge larva and pupa patterns is as droppers off San Juan Worms or other large "attractor" nymphs, such as a Beadhead. In many cases, the trout opt for the smaller larvae, especially on heavily fished waters. Extra weight is added to the leader, and one or more strike indicators above that. While this sort of rig looks clumsy and wouldn't be the first choice of style for most fly fishers, its effectiveness can't be denied.

One finds that he can get away with slightly heavier tippets beneath the surface than he can on top, where contorted surface shadows predominate. Tippets of 6X and even 5X will work for sunken-larva imitations, and we've used 4X successfully with a wind chop on the water. Simple and inexpensive ties are all that are needed for success. Controlled dead-drift presentations and mending skills should be honed for the best effect. The longer and more controlled the dead drift the better, for trout are used to seeing larvae right on the bottom. When wading, this is usually an upstream presentation to likely water. From a boat, slack-line drifts at current speed are drifted through known trout hangouts—often weed bed areas and troughs of moderate depth. This is not an exciting drift-boat fishing style but is the most productive at times.

On small waters, the task is easier to discern. Trout holding spots are more evident and familiar. The swifter the stream becomes, though, the

Midge larvae cling tenuously to the streambed in all types of water. Trout pick them off rocks and inhale free-drifting ones.

higher the percentage of larger nymphs showing up in the trouts' diet. Springtime rivers find the highest nymph loads, including the largest varieties. Some winter over as mature nymphs, too, and the larger stonefly species take several years to mature. Thus, in swift-water streams, larger nymphs are more available to trout most of the year and can make midge larvae less important a food item than in slow water, tailwater, and spring creeks. Stream trout still eat midge larvae, though, and lots of them, so prevalent are their numbers. Anywhere in the world you fish, midge larvae, pupae, and adults will be major food sources, and especially so where currents slow to a near standstill.

More important to anglers is the next phase of the midge's emergence. Emerging midge pupae drift toward the surface at a slow pace before actually reaching the surface. Many are nipped off by trout. These are easy targets and are taken by the dozens. As the pupae reach the surface to hatch, trout can be seen rising to adults *and* taking pupae just under the surface. This presents a most excellent scenario, for trout must eat many a midge to fill up, and they can rise for hours on end. Pattern choice can be critical here, and I often use a two-fly setup with an adult midge dry and pupa dropper. If trout are favoring the dry, I clip off the pupa. If the pupa is being taken a fair percentage of the time and the trout are choosy, I'll stick with the two-fly rig, experimenting with different drys and pupae simultaneously. This saves a bit of time while testing various patterns. One thing you might notice under these circumstances is that trout will move a little farther for the pupa than they will for the dry. They can see it better, and it's a surer target than an adult, which could buzz off at any second.

This is the classic midge scenario, the "curse" of old, where trout that were apparently rising were in fact taking subsurface pupae. Many an angler spent his day tossing traditional and oversized dry-fly favorites at such trout, then shrugging off his lack of success. Today's materials and interest in capitalizing on every angle of the trout's diet have made fooling midging trout a looked-forward-to event.

Quite a few emerging midges have trouble escaping their pupal shucks and struggle a bit at the surface, dragging the shucks around. A small traditional Adams pattern doesn't do a bad job of imitating this, with the tail passing for the shuck. Newer ties, including Palomino Midges and Z-lon-shuck

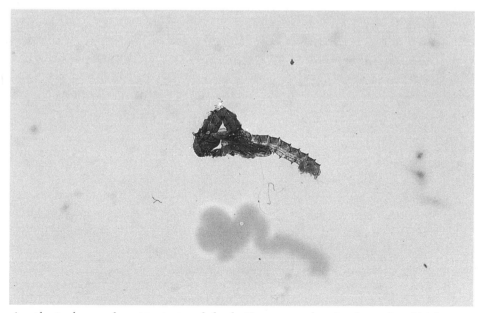

A midge in the act of escaping its pupal shuck. Trout target them just beneath and in the surface film.

models, try to imitate this occurrence more closely. Some do and some don't. Other patterns incorporate a ball of foam at the head, with the idea that the fly will float vertically, as emerging midges are wont to do. I have noticed that river midges are often swept up into horizontal positions when emerging because the current just below the surface film is swifter than the film itself. This variance in current has a tendency to push emerging midges up into the horizontal. This is only of interest because every other published account of emerging midges insists that they hang vertically. In moving-water situations this isn't always true.

Midges stuck and struggling in their shucks look twice as big as the adult or pupa by itself, as you might imagine. I've seen trout targeting these as they twirl tantalizingly on a surface eddy. Some days there will be a lot of these, and trout will then go for slightly oversized and twitched patterns. Other days they'll be less agreeable, requiring the smallest of patterns. Fortunately, one can stash a hundred midge variations in the smallest of boxes and will have spent a minimum in tying materials on them. With this little box one can dupe hundreds of fish.

The midge adult is the fourth stage of importance, and the Griffith's Gnat seems as popular today as Royal Wulffs were to another breed of fly fisherman. Traditional midge drys, which are little more than midget versions of traditional ties, still catch fish, too. These include Black Gnats, Adamses, tiny Renegades, and even micro Royal Wulffs. I often use #20 to #24 Elkhair Caddis as midges, since they're a bit easier to see than some darker drys (depending on your lighting situation). Seeing is a big part of successful midge fishing, something we'll look at more closely down the road.

Often, size is most critical, and exact coloration and form quite secondary. If one lives by this rule, he'll generally catch more fish. Of course it's better to imitate size, form, and color, and as one plays with more midge-feeding trout, he begins to stockpile imitations and fill in gaps in his arsenal. Having midge drys down to at least #24 in black, gray, olive, and tan will cover most situations. There are distinctly green midges too, and some with reddish body tones. One can add a few "attractor" midges in white, chartreuse, and orange—colors he can see in different lighting situations and when in the mood to experiment with the trout's psyche.

Unlike some dry-fly patterns, midges can produce as well or better at times with a little drag in the presentation. A little twitch or even a full-bore skid can single out your fly from the dozens of naturals on the surface. Motion seems to attract a certain percentage of midging trout. They are used to seeing midges skitter across the surface, and this movement merely imitates that natural behavior.

As previously mentioned, it takes many midges to satiate an adult trout. From a rising-fish viewpoint, this is ideal. To me, the more steadily a trout rises, the more desirous it is. And it is the small and numerous flies that bring trout to the surface for the longest periods—often for hours on end at a steady sipping gait. Midges hatch best in windless situations, where trout move into quiet edgewaters to feed on them. This presents ideal casting situations and is the real draw of small-fly fishing.

When midging, trout move into slow water to feed. They can't afford to fight much current and still get ahead in the nutrition game when it comes to small flies. Likely spots include quiet edge waters and eddies off to the side of the main currents. Anywhere currents slow and food collects is worth a long look, even if no cover in the traditional sense is present. Often such water is shallow, and can be *very* shallow. The novice might initially consider these places the least likely looking, until he starts depending on his eyes for information and not some preconceived notion of where trout "should" be.

The trout will fin just under the surface, grazing on midge pupae and adults. When holding just under the surface like this, their field of vision is quite restricted. What they can see on the surface is limited to perhaps a one-foot-diameter circle. They can see pupae just beneath the surface a bit farther away and are more likely to swerve a little farther to get one if there isn't much current to fight. A skidding midge dry can be seen from farther away, too (not much farther, though), because the disruption of the underside of the surface film is then more noticeable. Thus, trout will weave a bit farther for pupae and drys fished with movement. Of course, this doesn't describe all fish, and trout do have individual feeding habits and fishing tolerances.

Dead-drifted midge drys will need to be close to the mark. Fortunately, midging trout must keep rising to fill up, and their limited view of the outer world allows careful anglers to move into close proximity and ideal casting positions. In many cases there won't be much current to fight, and slight motion in the fly isn't usually fatal. Many such rising trout will allow many casts before spooking but nevertheless can be very selective. The overall benefit of this midge game is consistent rising trout, and often large ones, in ideal casting scenarios.

The last stage of the midge's life cycle that interests anglers is the mating clusters. Here, groups of midges huddle together, buzzing across the surface in tight formation. Anglers can get away with using slightly larger fly patterns that imitate multiple midges. Usually this just translates into fishing a one-size-up Griffith's Gnat, one that the angler can see better yet that will still catch fish. Some days this effect is more productive than others, and there are always some ultratough leader-shy trout to be reckoned with. Some such fish are "time wasters." The odd angler gets obsessed with fooling these resident trout, while others would rather spend more time *catching* fish. Since most trout are settled-in residents by midsummer, one can get to know individual and schools of trout, toying with them throughout the season with a fanciful array of fly patterns. As the hatches change and fishing pressure affects their behavior, such games will be necessary for routine success.

Little Winter Stoneflies

Little winter stoneflies, also known as little black and brown stones and needle flies, are not in the same league as the rest of the superhatches discussed in this chapter. But they are worth a paragraph or two just for the pleasure of knowing they are there. Their hatches aren't profuse or marked by the steady surge of rising trout. What makes them of interest is the time of year they're about.

Little winter stoneflies can be found on rivers from January to April, times when no other aquatic insects, save the midges, are out. As is true of cold-weather hatches in general, the naturals are dark, and as is true of many low clear-water hatches, their size is small, down to #18. There are a surprising number of species, and they are quite abundant in a scattered sort of way. You see them here and there—skittering across the stream, sitting on a snowbank, and occasionally making themselves available to ice-water trout. They hatch from most clean, cool-water rivers but are most commonly associated with freestone streams. I see plenty of them along the Missouri, which is a big, slow, and relatively low-altitude tailwater river.

One doesn't expect to see clouds of them or to have real big-time hatch experiences. But for those with a decided entomological bent, they are there to be imitated in the earliest season of all, and trout do take nymphs and adults.

Unlike most larger stoneflies, the nymphs of most little winter stones crawl out of the river during the afternoon, scrambling up streamside rocks, bridge abutments, and naked vegetation to make their final molt. Trout grab the nymphs as they awkwardly stumble over the streambed toward emergence sites. The adults are poor flyers and do more walking and scrambling. I often see them walking across the river's surface in a hurried sort of way, presumably after egg-laying, heading back for shore. All this is rather sporadic, and trout

Little Winter Stoneflies

Order: Plecoptera
Genus: *Nemoura, Leuctra, Capnia*
Species: Over 100 species of varied genera
Common names: Little winter stoneflies, little black and brown stones, needle flies
Important fishing stages:

Nymph**   Adult/Egg layer*

Color: Black, dark brown
Matching hook sizes: #16–#18
Water types: Swift higher-altitude streams in general. Some species like decaying logs and leaves for habitat. Others prefer rocky streambeds.
Hours of emergence: Midafternoon in winter and early spring
Popular fly patterns: None

Special notes: Little winter stoneflies are only locally important and can be overshadowed by the more numerous midges. Measuring about one-quarter to one-half inch in length, they are often of passing interest to intrepid winter anglers on snowclad winter streams. These hardy little stoneflies are the only aquatic insect anglers will meet on-stream, beside midges, when a fit of cabin fever ensues. It's nice to see them and fool a fish or two with a small black stonefly nymph or dry. I've seen trout single them out from a swarm of midges, and if nothing else, fishing them keeps your mind active. Tie them up yourself, for commercial hatch-matching ties are uncommon or unavailable.

*somewhat important **important ***most important

will be more used to feeding on midge larvae, pupae, and adults. I have seen trout single out skittering winter stoneflies from eddies of buzzing midges, and it all goes toward making a winter day on-stream more interesting. Tie a few patterns and take them along.

We couldn't leave the multitudinous stonefly families completely out of this volume, but since few of them fit into the #16 and smaller realm, this will be our last mention of them. One might make a case for the little yellow

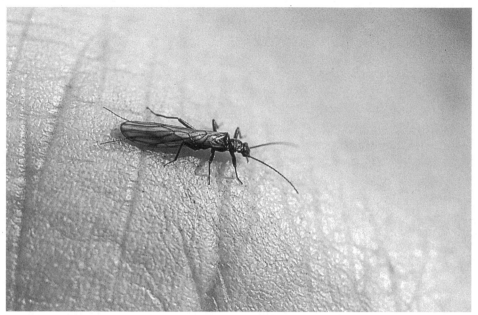

Little winter stoneflies are common February through April on many streams and rivers. They can be just numerous enough to entice trout to rise, especially when mixed with midges.

and green stones of midsummer, which fit into our light-colored-for-the-heat-of-summer category, and small for midsummer's low, clear levels, but they're really pushing the #16 dividing line on the #14 side. Be aware of summer's brightly colored little stoneflies though, which are widespread and more numerous than the little stoneflies of winter. Their activity and gay apparel match summer's carefree mood. I seldom if ever find trout selective to them, perhaps because there are other hatches, terrestrials, and nymphs to dote over. But one does hear stories of trout focusing on summer's yellow sallies, as they're sometimes known. I understand that they are a considerable hatch on the Big Horn. It never hurts to have some small, all-purpose, yellow-bodied Humpies on hand anyway, which suggest a variety of freestone meals.

When it comes to little winter stonefly drys, one can get by with a small, sleek, and dark caddis pattern in #16 to #18. Little black nymphs like the A. P. Black should be suggestive enough for that stage, though creative fly tyers with tons of winter downtime on hand will no doubt come up with more realistic ties. Don't slip on the ice!

Baetis

Baetis mayflies are the next insect group of great interest on a seasonal timescale, in duration and for overall numbers. One could go so far as to say that this is the preeminent mayfly hatch of the West. These blue-winged olives produce multiple generations in a year and are so widespread and important as to be the lingua franca of fly anglers around the country. They are the first mayfly on the scene in spring, have the longest overall seasonal duration, and are the last mayfly to be seen come late fall and early winter. They can be on the water, sailing in droves, for over four months of the year. This is generally in two shifts: spring (April to June) and fall (late September to November). They pop up in midsummer, too, usually during inclement weather and buffeting cold rainstorms. Anglers love these little grayish mayflies for their voluminous hatches and ability to bring up dozens of steadily rising trout at times of year when other hatches (except midges and some stoneflies) are still incubating. To the fly man, *Baetis* and returning swallows are harbingers of springtime and a new season on-stream.

In my neighborhood, *Baetis* make their first showing in mid- to late April. I understand that on some spring creeks and in warmer regions this date can be advanced by a month. Their gray coloration matches the mood of spring waters before streamside foliage has greened up. Overcast, humid days prove best for them. Snow and rain prompt massive hatches. No winds can daunt them. That such a small fly should come up against the fiercest of weather only heightens one's respect for them. Such weather can chase halfhearted fishermen off the river before the best hatches you've ever seen ensue. Afternoons provide sessions of exciting hatch-matching, especially on tailwaters and spring creeks. This can be as good as it ever gets.

In spring one often sees the phenomenon of *Baetis* hatching and fish rising whenever a cloud drapes the sun, all action ceasing when sunbeams pierce the water's surface. You can almost feel them flinch and huddle when the overbright spring sun glares across the riffles. But the next cloud will bring them up again! It seems as though spring trout, having endured a deep, dark winter, are sun-shy. During the fall *Baetis* hatch, this occurrence is less pronounced, though dark, humid, and even snowy days usually offer the best chances for success. Autumn trout are used to rising in bright sunlight, especially after the Trico feast.

Baetis hatches can be found on the water from about 1:00 to 5:00 p.m., sputtering here, booming there, and sometimes piling up in amazing numbers.

Baetis Mayflies

Order: Ephemeroptera
Family: Baetidae
Genus: *Baetis* (and hence the common name, *Baetis*)
Species: Over fifteen western species, most quite similar-looking
Common names: *Baetis*, little blue-winged olive, olive
Important fishing stages:

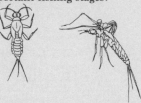

Nymph***   Emerger***   Dun***   Spinner*

Color: Nymph, amber to dark brown, olive-brown; three tails. Dun, olive, olive-gray, olive-brown; medium gray wings; two tails. Spinner, rusty brown; clear wings; two tails.
Matching hook sizes: #16–#22
Water types: Most rivers and streams, especially riffles and weed-bed flats. Very numerous in spring creeks and tailwater rivers.
Hours of emergence: Generally 1:00 to 5:00 P.M. Can be earlier on rainy days.
Popular fly patterns: *Nymph*, Pheasant Tail nymph, Beadhead Pheasant Tail. *Emerger*, RS-2, CDC Pheasant Tail. *Dun*, Adams, Parachute Adams, Blue Dun, olive and gray Comparaduns and Sparkle Duns, Olive Thorax. *Spinner*, Rusty Spinner.

Special Notes: This is *the* big spring and fall mayfly hatch, especially on spring creeks and tailwater rivers. Can hatch in tremendous numbers on overcast, rainy, and snowy days. When the multigeneration hatches are tallied for the season, *Baetis* mayflies provide the longest overall hatch duration of any mayfly group, with up to four-plus months of presence on some waters. Some of the spinners crawl underwater to lay eggs and are not as important to anglers as one would expect them to be.

Similar Mayflies that Could Be Confused with *Baetis*

Paraleptophlebia species: Some of these are darker gray in body and wing, #16, and hatch in April to May. I see these on Montana's Smith River in good numbers during that period. They have a more discernible leaf-shaped hind wing than does a *Baetis*. *Baetis* hind wings are mere stubs, and have to be looked for.

 Baetis remnant hind wing   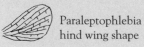 Paraleptophlebia
                                                                      hind wing shape

Attenella (was *Ephemerella*) *margarita:* This is a fall-hatching olive matched on a #18 hook. Its body and wing shape are similar to the pale morning dun and other *Ephemerellas*, but this species has an olive body, medium gray wings, and three tails. Again, the hind-wing shape is one of the easiest ways to tell it from a *Baetis* mayfly, which it generally resembles.

Serratella (was *Ephemerella*) *tibialis:* This is a close relative to *A. margarita,* above, but is slightly larger and darker, as is common with the season's late-hatching mayflies. Its body is more of a brownish olive and the wings a darker gray. Again, the hind wing is more developed than that of a *Baetis,* and it has three tails compared to two on most *Baetis.* It is matched on a #16 hook and is widespread.

All of these *Baetis*like mayflies tend to hatch from late morning to midafternoon, as do the *Baetis* themselves. This is common of most spring- and fall-hatching aquatic insect species.

Costal angulation
Ephemerella hind wing shape

*somewhat important **important ***most important

Their raked-back wings and tendency to float a long while on the currents before taking off can make the surface look like a staging area for a miniature regatta. Porpoising trout attack like oversized submarines.

Baetis are olive-gray in body and medium gray of wing. Authors have noted how the Adams gray-colored imitation often outproduces attempts at closer color-matching attempts at the vise. *Baetis* are matched on #16 to #22 hooks, depending on the hook manufacturer, river, and time of year. Baetis, like many aquatic insects, do show some variation in size as the season progresses. There are seventeen western species, all quite similar, whose variations are of small concern to anglers. As mentioned in the second chapter, cool-temperature hatches tend to be a bit larger and darker than midsummer hot-weather hatches, even of the same species. Some will start their seasonal emergence as, say, #16 to #18 and end up toward summer as #18 to #20.

A variety of basic gray and olive-gray dry-fly patterns fool a high percentage of trout. Successes with *Baetis* hatches might also be helped along by the fact that they emerge in periods that traditionally have seen less fishing pressure and when other hatch choices for the trout are at a minimum. Adamses and Parachute Adamses continue to fool thousands of fish. Comparaduns, Sparkle

Baetis mayflies are dominant spring and fall hatches, with the duns emerging afternoons and early evening. They are matched by #16–#22 imitations.

Duns, and other no-hackles tempt thousands more. General size and color-tone matches combined with exacting, repeated casts will produce in most cases.

Sometimes emergers will do better, though in my experience dun imitations are usually preferred because the naturals ride the surface so long. Popular emerger patterns include unweighted Pheasant Tail nymphs, the RS-2, and Parachute patterns—since the bodies sit in and often under the surface. Parachutes are indeed handy and can pass for any stage of a mayfly's hatch cycle at times, including emerger, stillborn, dun, and spinner. The Parachute Adams is perhaps my most-used dry-fly pattern and continuously proves to be an ideal tying style. I also use Parachute Pheasant Tail dry flies. They have the right coloration for several emerging nymphs, brownish duns, and rusty-colored spinners. Both here and abroad they have proved their value.

The P.T. (Pheasant Tail nymph), a British pattern, is the classic *Baetis* nymph imitation. (There are *Baetis* over there, too.) That general coloration and body shape convince many trout. The now popular Beadhead P.T. is often an even better producer, for it plummets down and catches the trout's eye with its gleaming bead. Black beads can also be used, which imitate the darker wing pads *Baetis* (and other) nymphs sport just before hatching.

Since many *Baetis* females crawl under water to lay their eggs, spinner falls are not that important on some waters. What's interesting here is that when the female crawls under water, preferably down a log (and also some-times your waders), she wraps her wings over her back, trapping a glimmering sheath of air. Whether she breathes from this or uses the air to buoy her back to the surface after egg-laying, I'm not sure. In any case this trapped air is very visible and glistens brightly. Here one could say that the shine of a Beadhead is imitating the glistening trapped air of a *Baetis* egglayer that's been washed out from her hold. It sounds good on paper and softens the judgment of those who see Beadheads as kin to spin fishing.

For in-the-know anglers, the *Baetis* hatch is the big early-season prerunoff hatch draw and is usually well mixed with midges. Some trout may be prefer-ring midges, others targeting *Baetis*. Most will take both or concentrate on whatever is the most numerous. Hatch densities will vary from day to day de-pending on weather conditions. Midges might be hatching from morning on if conditions warrant, with *Baetis* kicking in after lunch. Dry-fly action can con-tinue right up till dark, though the *Baetis* usually fade by then. These can make spectacular fishing days, spring and fall, as good as any to be found. Small-fly anglers look forward to the *Baetis* as much as others long for the salmon-fly

Baetis *nymphs are the inspiration for the Pheasant Tail nymphs. Note the lighter colors in the first and fifth abdomen segments. This is typical in the naturals but is rarely, if ever, imitated by fly tyers.*

hatch. The *Baetis* are more dependable, though, and last much longer. In fact, the salmon flies kick in just about the time the season's first generation of *Baetis* is dwindling—mid-June to early July. The mobile angler fishes them all! In the small-fly, clear-water, rising-fish arena, though, other prolonged hatches pop up to fill the void come the end of spring's *Baetis* hatch.

Pale Morning Duns

PMDs, or pale morning duns, denote a mayfly group that has entered the light-colored summer phase. The term pale morning dun can be a little misleading, for these insects can hatch better in late afternoon and evening on some rivers. In many other locations, mid- to late-morning hatches are the rule.

These #16 to #22 mayflies are widespread, numerous, long-lasting, and often found hatching in ideal fishing scenarios, as is true of most smaller flies. Hatching from late June into August, they are regarded as another of the prime hatches of the West. Two species, *Ephemerella inermis* and *E. infrequens*, are lumped together under this heading. *Heptagenia* and *Epeorus* species are often confused under this heading too. The latter are often referred to as pale evening duns.

PMDs hatch from most water types, including freestone rivers, spring creeks, and tailwaters. On the freestoners, they often start hatching as high-water runoff is receding but still murky. They can be overshadowed here by larger stoneflies and mayflies, and by the abundant fast-water nymphs that fill the streambeds in spring and early summer. As waters clear and drop, PMDs begin getting the trouts' attention. Still, the numerous and varied shortlived hatches of a freestone river can mean that the trout won't be overchoosy and will take a yellow-bodied Humpy as well as or better than a perfect match-the-hatch dun. Be prepared for both, though, for all freestone trout aren't pushovers, and fishing pressure is making them shrewder. Look to the tailouts, eddies, and quiet edge waters for steady-rising and selective freestone trout.

In spring creeks and tailwaters, PMDs and selectivity go hand in hand. Here pressured trout rise to well-presented and exacting imitations. I find that early on in the PMDs' seasonal emergence—which can last over a month—the trout take duns more freely than they do later on. Some of the largest steadily rising browns of the year are taken in late June and early July. As summer progresses, fishing pressure mounts, and mid-July rolls around, more and more trout begin focusing on the PMD emergers rather than the duns. Now there can be hell to pay!

The yellow veinlike patterns in the wings and the pale green body are trademarks of the pale morning dun. This generalized name applies to three Ephemerella *species.*

PMD emergers are the nemesis of many western anglers. I know anglers who have worked steadily for over ten years to find a cure for this shortcoming, and know of no one who can routinely, day in and day out, fool our trout when focusing on PMD emergers. The trout rush and boil all around you and rarely touch a fly. One day you'll catch a few and think you've found the answer. The next day you'll be shot down again as hundreds of trout surge all around. The flies that do work seem to do best on a swing, twitch, or drag. But nothing works all the time. This is perhaps the most perplexing hatch puzzle on western waters.

One dodge I use on the Missouri, where I guide, is simply to move out of the PMD emergence areas on a "bad day," dropping downstream a bit to where only duns and cripples are available to trout. The PMDs emerge out of riffles and weed-bed flats. Trout move into these areas and boil all around. When the trout here are cooperative, it's most exciting. When they're making fools of you, it's most exasperating! By dropping (or floating) downstream to deeper eddy-line areas, trout of a different temperament can often be found. Drifting duns and cripples can be mixed with other insects, too, say

Pale Morning Duns

Order: Ephemeroptera
Family: Ephemerellidae
Genus: *Ephemerella*
Species: *inermis, infrequens*
Common names: Pale morning dun, PMD
Important fishing stages:

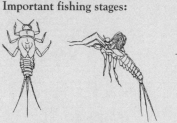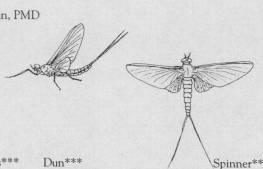

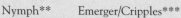

Nymph**   Emerger/Cripples***   Dun***   Spinner**

Color: Nymph, varied olives and browns; three tails. Dun, body is pale yellow with an olive cast; wings are pale gray with yellow vein up leading edge; three tails. Spinner, male has rusty brown body and larger eyes, female is light olive. Both have clear wings and three tails.
Matching hook sizes: #16–#22
Water types: Most rivers and streams. Numerous and prolonged hatches on spring creeks and tailwater rivers, where they hatch from riffle areas and weed-bed flats.
Hours of emergence: Can vary from 9:00 A.M. to 8:00 P.M. Many rivers have the standard late-morning hatch while others have better late-afternoon-to-early-evening hatches. Weather can affect hatch times, as is true with most aquatic insects.
Popular fly patterns: *Nymph*, Pheasant Tail. *Emerger*, CDC (Cul de Canard), PMD emerger, Soft-Hackle. *Dun*, Traditional hackled, Parachute, Comparadun and Sparkle Dun, Thorax. *Spinner*, Rusty and light olive spentwings

Special notes: PMDs are one of the dominant mayfly hatches of the West. Trout can be very selective when feeding on them, especially when focusing on the emergers. Bring lots of optional fly patterns! PMDs are widespread and numerous throughout the West.

Similar Mayflies That Could Be Confused With PMDs
        These include some light, cream-colored *Heptagenia* and *Epeorus* mayfly species. These are generally found in swifter freestone streams and are #16–#14. *Epeorus* and *Heptagenia* mayflies have two sturdy tails, which are about as long as the body. This helps distinguish them from pale morning duns, which have three relatively short and curly tails. The cream-colored *Epeorus* and *Heptagenia* are sometimes called pale evening duns

and are widespread mayfly genera. It is interesting to note here that some species of both these genera leave the bottom of the river to emerge as winged adults. Most mayflies emerge from their nymphal shucks at the surface, rather than at the streambed. Some *Epeorus* and *Heptagenia* species leave their shucks at or near the bottom and swim to the surface with their wings trailing over their backs. These can be successfully imitated with Soft-Hackle Beadheads or traditional wet flies. These, too, could be enhanced with a bead head for weight and visibility, for these naturals are supposedly buoyed to the surface by a bubble of gas trapped beneath their backswept wings.

*somewhat important
**important
***most important

caddis, Tricos, and midges, and the fish feeding on them can be easier to fool. This could be looked at as a guide cop-out, but most people prefer to *catch* fish, not watch them boil around their flies.

PMD nymphs are similar to *Baetis* nymphs but just a little thicker in the body, and are imitated on #16 to #22 hooks. They show quite a variation in color as both nymphs and adults. Nymphs vary from pale to dark olive, and reddish to dark brown. The duns are yellowish at first glance, with subtle tones of pale green, orange, or even pink mixed in. This variance of subtle coloration is thought to be one of the problems of hatch-matching. I feel that there could also be a behavioral motion as the emerging nymph hatches into a dun that is hard to imitate. To me, this would explain the boiling, surging riseforms that are often seen to PMD emergers. The nymphs are not fast emergers and wouldn't seem to warrant such rushed takes. I think the trout could be looking for a particular moment of vulnerability in the emergence process to capitalize on, one that brings them rushing to the fly at the last apparent second.

There are many PMD dry-fly patterns available in various ties, including traditional hackled, Parachute, Comparadun and Sparkle Dun, No-Hackle, and Cul de Canard. If you are planning to meet this hatch, I'd recommend buying every PMD emerger pattern you've ever seen in your travels, in sizes #16 to #22.

PMD spinners can be important in the eyes of trout on some waters. In my neighborhood they are so overshadowed by Trico spinners as to be irrelevant. I seem to see them mostly in the late morning, but others report afternoon spinner falls. The male and female spinners are different colors, the male being pinkish to rusty-colored and the female pale olive. Such variations between the sexes only serves to make understanding hatches all the more complicated. By the way, male mayflies have larger eyes than do the females, sometimes in the extreme. This can help in identifying sexes and species.

Mayfly spinners of various species do exhibit similarities in shape and coloration. One can standardize a couple of basic spentwing ties in various colors and sizes to match many hatches around the world. Colors that are prominent include reddish to dark brown (and even pink), pale to medium olive, pale yellow to amber, and tan or gray. Add small black ones for Tricos and you're set for most situations. Have spentwing generics on hand in sizes #14 to #24. Many additional fish can be fooled in a variety of river settings morning, noon, and night. Here is when those perfect dead-drift, slack-line, and well-mended presentations become essential. Mayfly spinner falls can come and go rather quickly, so the angler must constantly watch the surface to note any changes in the game.

PMDs hatch the same time other insects are proliferating at summer highs. In high-altitude freestone rivers, salmon flies are still around. Stoneflies, caddis, and fast-water mayflies are abundant in that "medium size" range. These provide some of the best attractor-pattern fishing of the year on appropriate streams. The aquatic insects are at their most numerous and diverse in the late-June-to-late-July period. Wulffs, Humpies, Stimulators, and Trudes dance and twirl down riffles and rush by waiting fish. This classic western fishing experience is relaxing and fun. It hones your casting skills but perhaps lacks the addicting anxiety of seeing large-shouldered trout repeatedly rise around your #18 PMD in some quiet swirling edge water. It is the spring creeks and tailwaters that give the longest and best sessions with steadily rising trout.

On these water types, smaller insects often mix with PMDs, giving those mixed-hatch experiences with choosy fish. Caddis, microcaddis, and midges can be present; the odd *Baetis* or *Pseudocloeon* mayfly might be seen. But the most amazing and abundant hatch of all now begins to distract knowledgeable anglers around the country—the ultimate in small-fly hatches.

PMD nymphs are a little more robust than Baetis *nymphs, and they are usually olive or reddish brown.*

Tricos

Tricos (*Tricorythodes minutus*) are among the smallest of mayflies but hatch most predictably for two months. The male duns hatch at the onset of darkness, and the females the next morning. Trout rise well to the morning hatch of female duns, generally around 7:00 to 8:00 A.M., but it is the spinner fall that captures both the trout's and angler's imaginations. From about mid-July to mid-September (there is some variance in hatch dates across the West; for instance, the cold-water temperature lag on the dam-controlled Big Horn sees Tricos hatching into October) the greatest exhibition of "herd instinct" and wanton excess awes streamside visitors and commands their attention! Morning mating swarms of Trico spinners build into columns paralleling the river banks. In what can only be described as clouds, these mating swarms sparkle in the morning sunshine and from a distance look like fog or smoke over the river, so numerous are their multitudes. They line up along roads and bridges near the stream, too, for any long ribbon of concrete with its parallel curbs looks like a river to Tricos. But let's back up a step and look at the Trico hatch a little closer.

The two rivers I guide on, Montana's Smith and Missouri, both have incredible Trico hatches. The Smith is a freestone river, though it's heavily spring-fed, and the Missouri is a giant tailwater. Let's look at the Smith first.

This is a classic case of a freestoner that has dropped and cleared after the high-water runoff period. The salmon fly and golden stone hatches have quickly passed and were fished with mixed results. The river has bottomed out now; it's running clear and is ideal for wading.

When the female duns hatch here in the rippling waters and flat pools, only a few trout are seen feeding on them, and rarely any big ones. The duns hatch in a less orchestrated and more sporadic fashion when compared to the spinner fall. In fact, the number of duns seen on the water in no way prepares you for what's about to happen. The female duns quickly make their final molt after they hatch, and many are seen flying with their molted skin still trailing from them. All of a sudden hundreds, then thousands, of spinners appear in clouds along the banks. The individual spinner dances up and down as all mayfly spinners do, but when mixed together it looks like so much swirling smoke. All of a sudden the spinners begin egg-laying and dying on the water. Soon the surface is littered with countless tiny spentwings. Their pale-olive-to-black bodies, clear wings, and long tails are easily imitated by fly tyers. It is the #20 to #24 size, competition with thousands of naturals, and mandatory perfect dead-drift presentation that erodes many an angler's confidence. Spinners hit the water from about 8:30 to 10:00 A.M., and a little later as the hatch progresses into the cooler mornings of September and on overcast days. Indeed, this is one of the few mayfly hatches that doesn't mind bright sunshine and hot days. Those conditions only serve to concentrate the hatch into more compressed and awe-inspiring spinner falls. On cloudy and cool days, the hatch will often spread itself a bit thinner over a longer number of hours, even carrying on into afternoon toward the tail end of the seasonal emergence.

On the swifter waters of the Smith, the spinner fall is soon washed downstream and disperses there after the main spinner fall ends. There will only be a couple of hours when the trout and whitefish rise gluttonously. Not many of the larger trout seem to rise to this hatch here, and they are more likely to be

Trico Mayflies

Order: Ephemeroptera
Family: Caenidae
Genus: *Tricorythodes*
Species: *minutus*
Common names: Trico, Trike, tiny white-winged black
Important fishing stages:

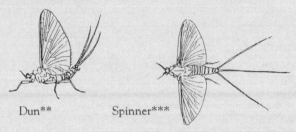

Dun**   Spinner***

Color: *Dun*, olive and gray body; light gray wings, three tails. *Spinner*, olive and black; clear wings; three very long tails.
Matching hook sizes: #20–#24
Water types: Varied river and lake waters. Widespread across West. The most fishable hatches occur on slower, slicker waters, where trout can dine steadily on the small but incredibly numerous spent insects without fighting too much current.
Hours of emergence: Male duns at nightfall. Female duns from 6:00 to 9:00 A.M. Spinner falls, which are the real highlight here, occur from 8:00 to 11:00 A.M., with spentwings lingering on the water for hours afterward, so great are their numbers.
Popular fly patterns: *Dun*, Parachute Trico, Comparadun. *Spinner*, black and olive Trico Spentwings, Parachute Trico

Special notes: Tricos have an incredibly dense spinner fall, which goes on daily for two months. Many consider this the ultimate fly-rod challenge. The spinner fall is likely to bring up the most, and most consistently rising, fish you'll ever see on calmer stretches of freestone rivers, spring creeks, tailwater rivers, and even lakes. The trout will be picky and exacting, so repeated casts are a must. It might take twenty-five perfect casts to intercept a trout during his morning Trico-feeding rise rhythm.

*somewhat important
**important
***most important

Trico spinners feature very long tails, olive to black bodies, and clear wings. They are matched by #20–#26 imitations.

taken on bigger fly patterns. This is a freestone phenomenon, due to the presence and abundance of larger insect types. One can catch the biggest browns here on a Humpy during the Trico hatch! Mounting fishing pressure will likely change this behavior, though. Another part of the angler's challenge is telling whitefish rises from those of trout, and the rises of larger trout from those of smaller ones. On the whole, splashy rises tend to be whitefish or juvenile trout, while quiet risers are generally mature trout. Many Trico-eating trout do "head rises," sticking the tops of their heads up out of the water. Consequently, their size can be determined and the largest trout targeted.

On the Missouri, a tailwater version of the same hatch amplifies the dry-fly possibilities. Currents here are slow and slick. At dawn trout are already rising halfheartedly to midges, and begin taking Trico duns when they appear, too. Another oddity here is what I presume to be spent aquatic moths. These whitish #14 morsels are scattered thinly among the Tricos but do get some of the trouts' attention. I'll often have guests with poor eyesight use a #14 to #16 Elkhair Caddis for a strike indicator, trailing a Trico dropper. The fish take both.

Trico spinners become so dense over riverbanks as to look like smoke or fog from a distance. When they die and hit the water, trout rise like mad.

When the Trico spinner fall hits the water here, hundreds of big trout graze the surface in their rhythmic, quick-gulping Trico way. Columns of spinners whirl in the air, and millions soon cover the water. The slow-paced current, giant eddies, and weed-laced flats find trout rising to spent Tricos right up till the evening hatches commence—not everywhere, mind you, but in places known to regulars. There are *that* many flies!

In the slicks of the Missouri, many trout soon become leader-shy and dodge imitations while continuing to feed. Other trout just go down but soon come back, so plentiful is the feeding potential. And of course large trout have to eat many a Trico to fill up, which is typical of the small-fly scenario.

Tricos are numerous, widespread across the country, and long-lasting. They hatch under ideal fishing conditions. It is certainly a challenge to imitate such small naturals that can virtually cover the river's surface. Casts must be repeatedly perfect. It might take ten, twenty-five, or fifty casts to intercept a steadily gulping Trico-eater, but nowhere else will you see such numbers of rising fish during banker's hours on a midsummer day. From eight till noon daily, for two months straight, this perfect small-fly challenge presents itself and is often regarded as the ultimate trout-fishing contest.

Pseudocloeon

Pseudocloeon mayflies are next on the seasonal list of small-fly hatches in my neighborhood. This is a very small mayfly, too, commonly called the tiny blue-winged olive or Pseudo. Closely related to *Baetis*, it is a smaller mid- to late-summer version and has no hind wing at all. *Baetis* have a remnant hind wing, which upon close inspection can be used to tell the two apart.

Pseudos are tiny indeed, no bigger than Tricos and matched on #24 hooks. Their bodies vary in color from tan to olive to a brighter medium green. Their wings are light to medium gray. Comparaduns and Sparkle Duns, No-Hackles, and tiny Parachutes are among the most commonly used dry-fly patterns. Size is often the most critical element in success.

Pseudos, like *Baetis*, are multibrooded, with hatches occurring from late June through early October. They hatch from riffles and weed-bed flats from afternoon into evening. They are most important locally when the Tricos begin to fade in mid-September, at which time Pseudos become *the* big daily hatch. Before that time they are usually overshadowed by other hatches, but this will vary from river to river. Overcast, humid, and rainy days will see more pronounced hatches, which will begin earlier in the afternoon. I've seen good hatches on the Smith during September snowfalls. The duns ride the surface a long time, making excellent trout fodder. The trout rise steadily in order to fill up on the little things.

Pseudo spinner falls can occur mornings or evenings. The morning falls are usually diluted in Tricos, but evening spinner falls can bring up good numbers

Pseudo Mayflies

Order: Ephemeroptera
Family: Baetidae
Genus: *Pseudocloeon*
Species: *edmundsi*
Common names: Pseudo, tiny blue-winged olive
Important fishing stages:

Dun***   Spinner**

Color: *Dun*, pale olive to bright green; light gray wings; two tails. *Spinner*, light olive with brown and orange hues possible; clear wings; two tails.
Matching hook size: #24
Water types: Riffles and weed-bed flats on most rivers and streams
Hours of emergence: Duns from noon to 5:00 P.M.; spinner fall morning or evening. In my experience, evening spinner falls provide the best fishing possibilities, for morning spinner falls can be overshadowed by Tricos and only add to that massive event.
Popular fly patterns: *Dun*, Compara- and Sparkle Duns, traditional hackle Little Olives, Parachute Olive, Swisher-Richards No-Hackles, Thorax ties. *Spinner*, light olive and rusty spinners.

Special notes: Pseudos are a very important hatch on many rivers. Don't be deceived into neglecting them because of their size. The trout don't, and they can be very size conscious. In John Juracek and Craig Mathews's book *Fishing Yellowstone Hatches,* they state that this hatch is one of only three mayfly hatches of the year that are important to fishermen on the Madison and Firehole Rivers in Yellowstone. The other two are *Baetis tricaudatus* and the pale morning duns. In my experiences on the Missouri, Pseudos become *the* hatch as the Tricos wane in mid September. They fill a seasonal gap between the Tricos and PMDs of July-September and the larger *Baetis* of October-November. *Pseudocloeon* mayflies have no hind wing, which helps in telling them apart from smaller *Baetis* species.

*somewhat important **important ***most important

of rising fish. This situation is often overlooked, for anglers are thinking caddis, PMD, and midge. Never stop watching the river's surface throughout the day, because localized occurrences can change quickly. Pseudo spinners vary in color from light olive to brighter green. Some are splotched with hints of orange and brown. Here again, a generic light olive or tan spinner pattern in #22 to #24 will do the trick when tied on to a fine tippet and well-presented cast!

Microcaddis

Microcaddis are the smallest of the widespread caddis clan and are encountered midsummer on a variety of waters. They, too, are tiny, almost approaching midge size, and are generally medium to dark gray or brown in color.

Pseudocloeon *mayflies, commonly known as tiny blue-winged olives, or Pseudos, are the smallest western mayflies that produce significant hatches. They are matched by #24 or even #26 imitations.*

I have certainly seen trout feeding on them during an emergence, and some seem to ride and skitter across the currents more than many larger species do. Their hatches are harder to define, though, and I've seen them midday and evening, usually from late July into September. They don't seem to have that long, drawn out, and predictable emergence that the small mayflies do and are more in the way of hit-and-miss occurrences. I would certainly keep a few microcaddis emergers and drys on hand for chance encounters, and for when picky fish just want something small. Extra-small caddis patterns can also pass for midges or even beetles. You can find plenty of generic uses for these minute down-wings. It is a size and shape that trout are used to eating.

Baetis have another brood in autumn and provide some of the best dry-fly fishing of the year then. The Pseudos usually fade at the end of September, and *Baetis* begin to hatch thickly just in time to take their place. The fall *Baetis* hatch continues afternoons from October into December, providing two more months of predictable dry-fly and nymph fishing on many waters. In the cool weather of fall, as back in spring, *Baetis* duns seem to ride the currents forever, giving trout easy targets. It seems as though you seldom see them fly off. This fishing generally occurs between 1:00 and 5:00 P.M. Overcast and humid days are best, including times of rain and snow. *Baetis* do hatch on sunny days in the fall, especially during continuous good weather. They can't wait forever. The trout, used to rising all summer, feed heavily on them because hatch choices are few and dwindling. They are not so sunshy as in spring. There still remain a few caddis, plus wholesale midges, but the *Baetis* duns are the darlings of the trout's eye. Here again, #16 to #20 gray-olive dry-fly patterns work well. I rely heavily on Parachute Adamses. Pheasant Tail nymphs and especially Beadhead Pheasant Tails can really nab fish before, during, and after the afternoon hatch. Have plenty of Griffith's Gnats and midge pupae on hand, too, because late fall and winter is decidedly a time for midges. They can hatch any time favorable conditions—calm and humid—are encountered.

I usually mix up fall days a bit, throwing streamers mornings, doing some nymphing toward afternoon, and expecting dry-fly action from one or two in the afternoon till dark. Some days midge hatches bring up risers all day. There are also areas where trout tend to rise all day, and one can spend his time targeting such spots. Fall is certainly one of my favorite dry-fly seasons, right into December. Many people are surprised by how late mayflies actually hatch in the northern Rockies, and there's no end to good midging. I draw the line

Microcaddis

Order: Trichoptera
Genus: *Glossosoma, Helicopsyche, Lepidostoma, Oecetis, Micrasema, Mystacides, Cheumatopsyche*
Species: A confusing array!
Common name: Microcaddis
Important fishing stages:

Larva**   Pupa (emergers)***   Adult-Egg layer***

Color: *Larva and pupa,* bright green to olive, tan to amber to brown. *Adult,* body green to olive, tan to amber to brown and gray; wings tan to mottled browns, grays, and black
Matching hook sizes: #16–#24
Water types: Most moving waters. Some of the smallest caddis egg layers have been noted to be most abundant along banks, where they come out of streamside grasses to hit the water and lay eggs. Some float on the currents a long time. This is the same location many small terrestrials are found, too. Bank-hugging trout are used to seeing and eating a broader array of food types than are fish out in a midriver weed-bed. Small caddis drys make excellent midday searching patterns and often work when cast to occasional risers or opportunistic bank-feeders.
Hours of emergence: Morning till night, though many microcaddis emerge most heavily toward late evening. I see caddis emerging sporadically throughout the day in select locations on the Missouri.
Popular fly patterns: *Larva,* Green Caddis Worm, Casual Dress, Cased Caddis. *Pupa,* Antron Sparkle Pupa, Soft-Hackles, traditional wet flies such as the Coachman. *Adult,* Elkhair Caddis, feather-winged caddis, Goddard Caddis.

Special notes: There are a confusing array of caddis species, many of which don't hatch with the routine predictability of the mayfly superhatches. As an example, a study was done on Montana's Gallatin River that found fifty-eight species of mayfly, sixty-seven species of stonefly, and ninety-seven species of caddis! Many of these different species are quite similar-looking and only serve to overload the angler with excess mental baggage! One has no reason to, or would ever hope to, imitate all these hatches. Instead, a system of tying styles, colors, sizes, and shapes will go a long way toward fooling most fish. With caddis, emerger patterns often outproduce drys. These are fished wet, either dead-drift or on a swing. Takes tend to be solid and even vicious. Anglers should carry at least a small assortment of caddis emergers as well as drys, in sizes #24–#14. The most common colors include greens, tans, grays, and browns.

*somewhat important **important ***most important

Very small caddis, or microcaddis, are common in midsummer. Having some tiny patterns on hand, down to #24, can be the key to angling success.

when my rod's guides continually ice up. After late summer's wary, overfished trout, fall fish get easier to fool, too. Catch rates go up and fishing pressure goes down. These are magic moments on-stream.

There are a few other smallish-fly hatches one might encounter that can be important locally, including species of *Ephemerella*, *Heptagenia*, *Paraleptophlebia*, *Rhithrogena*, *Epeorus*, and *Callibaetis*. Mass falls of flying ants happen, too, usually in midsummer or fall. The midges, *Baetis*, PMDs, Tricos, and *Pseudocloeon* are the most widespread and prevalent, though. Patterns of these should certainly be on hand. Add a variety of small caddis, beetles, ants, and a few "miniattractor" patterns in #16 to #22 and you're in business for most stream encounters. Tiny Royal Wulffs and foam beetles in #18 to #22 are great midday attractor patterns for modern trout. One does have to match his pattern selection to the waters actually fished. Gushing high-country streams will see less need for small flies and will have more scope for various stonefly patterns, attractors, and fuzzy nymphs in #10 to #14. Hoppers can fool fish on all rivers when the naturals are prevalent. But even on swift streams there are

Callibaetis mayflies are best known for their lake hatches, but these hatches can also occur in rich, slower-flowing rivers and spring creeks. They range in size from #18 to #14.

times when fly-shy trout will respond favorably to cased caddis, small mayfly nymphs, and midge larvae imitations.

On bigger, slower rivers, tailwaters, and spring creeks, small-fly hatches can dominate the season's action. Trout can rise year-round to flies that are primarily under #16 in size. Being mentally and physically prepared for them, knowing a bit about the hatches, and having the right gear will enhance your catch rate substantially. One soon comes to see that the angling calendar favors small flies overall, and that they are not to fear but to capitalize on and look forward to.

The Trout's Riseforms

Not fishing can be just as productive as fishing at times, and often more educational. Nonstop casting and fishing the water can detract you from what's happening on stream, though it does polish your casting skills. One should make a habit of approaching pools slowly, from a concealed position, and staying back to scan for risers and cruisers. Trout can be found rising in unexpectedly shallow flats, inside bends, and edge waters. These are just the places overeager and inexperienced fishermen wade through while jamming casts into deeper runs, dropoffs, and cut banks.

Large steady-rising trout prefer slow and often shallow water when rising to small-fly hatches, especially if they haven't been harassed by a parade of anglers. Such fish can't afford to fight much current. Shallow-holding trout can nymph or rise easily from the same holding position, too, with little wasted effort. Unless the stream is overrun with foot traffic, stay back and watch for a while before wading in to cast. Observing trout that are steadily rising in a quiet edge water is almost as much fun as is catching them. Observation will teach you more about trout behavior than nonstop casting will. And it's the trout's behavior—its riseforms, positioning, and wanderings— that can tell an angler what's being fed on. That information is often there for the deciphering for those who stop and look.

Sips

Sips are usually seen when trout are feeding occasionally or steadily on smaller food items that are unlikely to escape. This includes midges, little blue-winged olives (which ride the currents a long time before flying off), small terrestrials, and spentwings.

Trout do show some behavioral differences and individual preferences in feeding, though. A "sipper" on one river might be a "head riser" on another, or a "head-and-tailer" yet elsewhere. Small trout and whitefish can make splashy rises at what mature trout sip in with portly and quiet confidence. I have also seen trout sip much larger food items, including large mayfly duns, damselfly adults, and even hoppers. On the whole, though, steady sippers are taking easy targets, and usually small ones.

Keep an insect net handy to sieve the surface. Some tiny emergers, midges, and spentwings can be hard to spot by just bending over and gazing down, especially in rippled areas. These riseforms are often made by choosy trout that are focused on one food type.

It helps to have good eyesight when analyzing riseforms, for all of them create rings. The aftermath of a sip, head rise, or bulge (where trout are taking emergers just under the surface) can all look the same. It is visually capturing the exact moment of the rise that counts, the making of a mental picture like the stop-image of a camera. Naturally, this is only likely to happen when one is observing a steadily rising trout (which is what small flies bring up), or if one just happens to be staring at the right place when an out-of-the-blue rise comes.

One can watch a steady riser and often, upon closer inspection, see the trout's nose or entire head above the water during each rise. Regardless of a surface-feeding trout's riseform, he will usually leave a bubble of air behind as he goes back down. He takes in a bit of air along with the fly and vents it out his gills as he submerges again. This may seem like a small point, but it can help in telling whether fish are taking flies off the surface or taking emergers from just underneath. Trout can be very focused and single-minded about what they're eating. For very selective fish, all of these details are important to observe.

One can also tell the size of the fish by his riseform in most cases, though I have seen some large trout rise and make the slightest of rings. I have read of rivers where the trout make an art of this. It occurs to me that there have been many times when a blind-fished dry fly just "disappeared," and it usually was firmly implanted in a big brown trout's nose. Such fish seem to suck the fly under with very little surface disturbance or body movement. These surprises are always a delight! In general, though, big fish displace more water when they move and rise. The resulting wakes and rings tend to be bigger yet slower, for mature trout aren't rushing about when making the sipping riseform.

Head Rises

To me, this is the most exciting riseform, for the trout's size can usually be perceived. He doesn't just stick his nose in the air but the entire top of his head, as well. Many trout rise with their eyes completely out of the water, too, a curious performance that makes me wonder if the trout is just having a look around. Occasionally you find a big trout that rises with its whole head out of water, both the upper and lower jaws. I have seen this with flies as small as Tricos as well as to larger attractor patterns and hoppers. It's a trademark of larger brown trout and is commonly seen on New Zealand trout rivers.

The steadiest head risers I see are among Trico-feeding trout. You'd think they'd just sip Trico spinners, expending as little energy as possible. Perhaps the trout do on some rivers. Those I'm most familiar with stick the entire tops of their heads out of the water in a capturing motion. The upper jaw comes up and over the fly and a little "pop" is heard as that jaw hits the surface and descends. Trico-feeding trout set up a rapid head-rising rhythm, and those little pops are amusing to hear. Find a school of such head risers and they'll break the morning silence with their gluttonous slurping while their rings spread across the glowing gravel streambed like circles on the Olympic flag.

The best thing about head risers is that you can tell the fish's size. When it goes up and down with its head protruding, its body pushes a pulsing wake. The larger the trout, the bigger, slower, and more widely spaced the individual waves of the wake are. Between the observance of its head and wake, a trout's bulk can be ascertained. On big rivers with high trout populations this gives the advantage of hunting larger fish among the numerous steady risers. In many cases, during a profuse hatch or spinner fall, the largest trout will be rising in the slowest, shallowest water. Smaller trout are often found farther out, bucking the current. Big trout will hold in such shallow and calm edge waters that fishermen unaccustomed to this behavior will likely wade through and scare them off. One wants to depend on his eyes when locating rising trout, and hunt down the big ones.

Look closely and you can see that not only the top of this trout's head is out of the water, but its eyes, as well.

Head risers go even one step further in giving anglers a thrill. When you add a heavy Trico spinner fall to the scene you often come up with the next and ultimate riseform.

Gulpers

"Gulper" has become a universal term for a trout that is rapidly head-rising to blanket hatches of a small fly. In most cases this is to Trico spinners but can also be to profuse hatches of *Baetis* and *Pseudocloeon* mayflies, midges, or any fly that becomes numerous enough. Most often it is to the small and prominent hatches discussed in this book. In many cases it's the prevailing western winds that pile duns into one bank or another, exaggerating their density still further and getting gulpers to set up shop.

Gulpers are excited feeders, and in the case of Tricos are used to this morning feast for a solid two months straight in the midsummer season. It takes a lot of small flies to fill up one trout, and the getting's good while the spinner fall lasts. This all takes place at the most civilized hours—from 8:00

How Wind Can Intensify a Hatch in Wind-Free Slicks

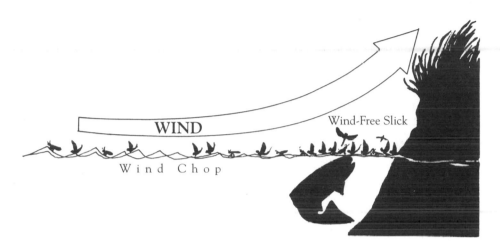

Wind can pile mayflies and midges into banks yet still leave wind-free slicks in which trout prefer to rise. This is a common scenario on breezy western rivers, and one to capitalize on during a hatch or spinner fall.

to 11:00 A.M. Spinners can linger much longer on slow-paced rivers, lasting well into the afternoon. Tricos bring up the most steadily rising fish you're ever likely to see.

Wanting to consume so many of them, the trout sets up an efficient and often excited rising gait. After making a number of rapid rises, it will go down for a moment and pause before renewing the gulping pace. I've watched them from concealment, and such trout often go down to work the Trico spinners from the insides of their mouths and teeth down their gullet. This is achieved by an exaggerated opening and closing of the mouth in the currents. It's rather amusing to watch. It's only a matter of seconds, though, till they come up to rise again.

Steady gulpers rise every one to three seconds, as unlikely as that may sound. They might rise five to ten times in a row, pause for a few seconds, and commence rising again. This can go on for hours. I know of fish that will head-rise virtually all day, unless the wind beats on them too hard. Gulpers don't seem to like rising in the wind, even though the spentwings are still there. Perhaps the acrid winds blowing across the tops of their exposed heads causes discomfort. The bugs are still there, and surely they can still see them. Trout will, in such cases, purposely move into wind-free slicks to continue feeding. These can often be found tight to the banks and to the lee of hills and trees. On many a western day the key to dry-fly success is finding wind-free water with rising fish. Bear that in mind as you wade or float, and keep your eyes working to scan subtle riseforms wherever they may be.

Porpoising Trout

Porpoising trout are synonymous with selectivity. Most are taking subsurface midge pupae or small mayfly emergers. Their targets are easily captured nymphs just prior to surface emergence. Some porpoising trout take both emergers and duns. You might see one head rise one moment and porpoise the next. This is like the classic head-and-tail rise, where head, back, dorsal fin, and tail slowly sail by in a slow and tantalizing parade of anatomy which tends to exaggerate the size of the fish and excite anglers. If the fish is porpoising for subsurface food items, the head may not be seen. If it's occasionally taking duns or midge adults, you should be able to see the nose in the air at times and the bubble that is left behind. Your most likely fly choice here will be the subsurface offering, be it a midge pupa or small mayfly nymph or emerger.

In such cases I'll often fish a two-fly rig, with a visible dry fly and suitable subsurface dropper. The dry fly acts as a strike indicator and is taken occasionally by the trout. The fly pattern chosen for this is one that corresponds to current hatches, or a very small attractor pattern like a #18-to-#20 H & L Variant, Royal Wulff, or Humpy. A small caddis is always a fair choice, too. The angler's eyesight and lighting conditions may dictate how small an indicator dry he uses. If a *Baetis* or PMD hatch is in evidence, mixed with midges, I would likely use a realistic *Baetis* or PMD dun as a strike indicator, and a midge-pupa dropper. Patterns can be changed until, it is hoped, a successful combination is found, ideally with both patterns fooling some fish.

Since porpoising trout are usually focused on particular stages of an emergence, these can be some of the most selective trout of all. The big fish will set up a slow-waking pace, scarcely gliding forward, dorsal fin and tail showing. This is exciting stuff. The prospects seem so good and alluring, but the trout's narrow-mindedness can be exasperating if you don't have the right fly! Be sure to carry at least a few midge pupae, small mayfly nymphs, and mayfly and caddis emergers for these trout. Most of the naturals they'll be targeting

Porpoising trout show the angler their backs, dorsal fins, and tails. They are often focused on subsurface emergers.

will be on the small end of the spectrum—from #16 all the way down to #28. Sizes #20 to #22 would perhaps be the most useful generic sizes. Larger emerging aquatic insects usually draw more energetic takes, as we're about to see.

Bulges

Bulges occur when trout take subsurface emerging insects, but without showing their fins. The flies are being intercepted a little deeper rather than just under the surface, as was the case with porpoising trout. Many of the targets are slightly larger insect hatches, including PMDs and caddis, but can still be to *Baetis*, Pseudos, and midges.

When the trout moves to intercept the emerger (or even sunk terrestrial or spentwing), it displaces water that shows on the surface. At first glance, the aftereffects might be erroneously considered a rise. If the trout is feeding steadily, though, and the angler pauses to observe, the reality of the situation should become clear.

True rising trout almost always leave a bubble behind, as previously discussed. Often you see a nose or the top of a head as well. Bulgers show neither bubble nor nose. This is the time to tie on a nymph, emerger, or two-fly rig. It may take some experimenting to come up with a successful pattern. If trout are bulging to midge or mayfly emergers, some adults will usually be on the water to aid in your diagnosis. Many caddis species leave the water so quickly that few adults will ever be seen floating idly downstream. If you see bulges (and boils) but no flies at all, suspect caddis emergers.

There are a few other cases where bulgers might be seen that aren't directly related to emergers. Trout in rich rivers and lakes intercept damselfly nymphs as they migrate, often in numbers, toward shore, where they climb out for their final molt. Baitfish, too, can be targeted. Trout that are semideep and chasing such food items can show a similar bulge to that made by shallower fish taking emergers, but it is not likely to be steady. Indeed, a one-time bulge is a good candidate for a Woolly Bugger!

When bulges become more violent and energetic, anglers know them as "boils."

Boils

Boils are made by trout rushing about to intercept emerging insects or baitfish. Some insect species, and especially caddis, emerge quickly, and the trout must take quickly or miss. The trout also seem to find certain moments of an emerger's ascent most vulnerable and rush to grab it at just that juncture. I see this when the PMDs emerge. This behavior seems strange because PMD nymphs are, on the whole, slow swimmers.

It is evident here that what gets the trout's attention is motion combined with a realistic fly pattern. The choice of PMD emergers can be ultracritical, and sometimes nothing works. Down-and-across presentations are often the key, with the fly taken most often on the swing. This makes sense, for emerging insects usually swim upstream against the current while seeking the sky. Trout take emergers fished this way hard, and can pop light tippets. Success sometimes depends on getting the nymph deep enough on a dead drift, and then lifting it or beginning the swing just before it comes to the known position of a bulging or boiling trout. Caddis emergers will be your most likely patterns here, unless untouched mayfly duns are seen riding the currents. Trout will often ignore duns or the winged adults in favor of the subsurface emergers. Multihatch situations are common, too, where mayflies, caddis, and

Caddis emergers commonly elicit boiling-type riseforms from trout.

midges are all hatching in force. Have at least a modest variation of pattern types on hand, and experiment till a solution is found. It's always wise to look up some local talent for updates prior to hitting the stream, be that a fly shop or some fishaholic friend. Keep some small weights on hand to add to your leader when situations call for deeper drifts and upswings. Increase your tippet strength a notch, too, for boiling fish seem less leader-shy (though they can still be highly selective) and can take boldly. If you were using 6X to 7X for dry flies, you'd want to go up to 4X to 5X for fishing emergers on the swing. Solid hits on tight lines have lost many a fly. This is fun fishing when your pattern is right!

Boils are also seen as fish chase larger food items, including baitfish, crayfish, and damselfly nymphs. This could be a onetime attack, or you might see a fish repeatedly attack and miss his prey. This tale is told through surface disturbance, even if the fish itself can't be seen. I see these kinds of attacks quite often when I'm guiding on the Missouri. One day we had stopped to have lunch adjacent to a shallow flats, when one big boil occurred within easy casting range. I quickly tied a crayfish pattern on a guest's fly line, and one cast later he was into an aggressive brown!

Flying Trout

When one sees trout in the air, as if they've been shot out of cannons, it's usually caddis emergers they're chasing. I've seen very amusing examples of this morning, midday, and evening. The last time I witnessed it was on Montana's Smith River during August's ultralow water. It was midafternoon and trout were shooting out of the water in every riffle up and down the river. Almost no insects were to be seen, and such behavior points toward the emergence of microcaddis.

Swinging appropriate caddis emergers down and across usually brings good results. One can also cast emergers up and over trout, which will take them on the dead drift. The current usually imparts more movement to the fly than you imagine.

The one other flying-trout scenario I see most often is when midsummer, midday trout try to take damselfly adults out of the air. These larger flies hang around exposed weed beds, on which they rest and submerge to lay eggs. Scores of damselflies will hover just over the weed beds and river, where the odd and energetic trout jumps in pursuance. While out of the small-fly realm, the takes to damselfly drys in such cases are about as smashing as you can get. It's great fun when you can find it.

Tails in the Air

This last feeding exhibition is perhaps the least common overall but is seen on rich spring creeks and lakes. These trout are securing nymphs and freshwater shrimp from weed beds, and swim nose down, tail up. At times their tails will actually wave slowly in the air. Trout have been known to rummage through weed beds to shake free their prey, then to turn around and swim through the area looking for evacuees. One would have to hang around the right kind of water to see this interesting behavior. I have only seen it once, and that was on a small spring-fed stream in New Zealand—the Hamilton Burn.

Tailing trout call for having some small but heavily weighted nymphs, shrimp, and cressbug patterns on hand, with additional weight and strike indicators as accessories. The trout will be nose-down and it won't see any imitation that's not down in its face. Freshwater shrimp and cressbugs are generally tan to pale olive or gray in color. *Baetis* nymphs and midge larvae are other likely candidates. Having a few of these patterns on hand in sizes

#16 to #22 (with some weight built in) will put you at the ready for such a chance occurrence. These patterns are excellent general nymphing patterns to have on hand anyway, and will catch trout most anywhere in the world.

While tailing trout are somewhat rare, sight-fishing to visible nymphing trout is quite common. In low clear-water conditions the trout hunter can sneak along many rivers, streams, and lakes and see trout lying out or cruising in shallow water. Unharried trout prefer the shallows, where food in various forms is most abundant and available. The fisherman with good eyes and patience can fool many of these fish with small weighted nymphs. The trout and its response to the presentation are all visible. The fish can usually be seen to take the fly, and the hook is set when the trout appears to take it, not by feel. If you wait to feel such trout, they'll often blow the nymph back out upon realizing its fraudulence. This is very exciting and addictive fishing, though a good many fishermen never seem to think about stalking trout, even when conditions are ideal. During midday midsummer outings, when brilliant sunlight makes the cobbled streambed radiant, nymphing trout will be there for the stalking. If no hatch is apparent and risers are not forthcoming, depend on your eyes to find the deeper action. Stalk first, blind-fish later.

If the angler pauses more often to inspect rivers for rising activity, he will find that he learns more about trout. Like watching any other form of wildlife, this can be a pleasure in itself. Dress drably, move slowly, and cultivate patience. These can pay off in some exciting sight-fishing challenges that you might otherwise have walked by.

Finding the Fish

Attractor patterns didn't gain that generalization for nothing. The whole idea is to cast large, fanciful, look-like-anything fly patterns upon trouty waters and have the fish move up and over to take them. Gung-ho fish of an innocent and rambunctious nature (as in *hungry*) are the targets here. This can be a regional or seasonal occurrence, and an experience that's diminishing in many quarters with the increase in fishing pressure. I still love this kind of fishing—when I can get it.

When fishing small flies, you have to put the fly in the fish's face. The trout are unlikely to go out of their way to get it, but are *more* likely on the whole to inhale it if it passes within a nose's reach. It is your job to put it there.

Although the real thrills of small-fly work come with sighted and rising fish, there are certainly many times and places where few or no risers will be seen. This is when your basic stream and trout knowledge come to play, when how you fish the water dictates success.

The trout has few concerns. Among them are eating, staying out of the full force of the current, and evading predators. When focusing on small flies, staying out of the current is of even greater concern. The fish can't feed on tiny flies, fight much current, and still win at the nutrition game. The trout are apt to slide off to the sides of the current—to the edge waters, eddies, riffle dropoffs, and tailouts—where they can dine at leisure for long hours. They also hug the bottom of deeper, swifter freestone runs, especially in the heat of

71

midsummer. The angler who is fishing the water blind must concentrate on these most likely places in order to increase his catch rate.

On swifter freestone streams, holding water is more familiar and easily defined. There will be more medium-to-large natural nymphs about, and thus smaller imitations might be unnecessary much of the time, especially in the May-to-early-July runoff period. As midsummer progresses, though, the average size of the prevalent nymphs goes down. The largest species include salmon flies and golden stones, green and brown drakes, and hatch by mid-July. There are big stonefly nymphs remaining, because they take several years to mature, but these big guys tend to bury themselves in the streambed come midsummer. They're not just under rocks, they're beneath the streambed, buried in the gravel. By midsummer on a freestone river the remaining available nymphs tend to be in the medium-to-small size range. If there has been a lot of fishing pressure, the trout can start avoiding the most commonly used and larger fly patterns. They will have their gung-ho moments, but these can be offset by longer periods of seeming inactivity and selectiveness.

Some small freestone rivers I'm familiar with not only heat up in the summer but change temperature daily as much as ten or more degrees. Consequently, the trout show well-defined on-off feeding periods that correspond with the most comfortable water temperatures and hatches. The trout *don't* feed all the time here (as they seem to do on some dam and temperature-controlled tailwaters), and vary in response to your fly from "dead" to "hot."

Among the most likely general-nymphs patterns on swifter streams are Hare's Ear and peacock herl variations, and cased caddis. Swift-water mayfly nymphs tend to be wider and squatter than slow-water nymphs, with more pronounced gill structures. The scruffy Hare's Ear is the classic imitation—both in color and configuration—for many swift-stream summer nymphs. A big exception here are the multitudinous midge larvae and cased caddis. Sunken ants and beetles add to the flotsam. A productive technique is to use two nymphs, one medium-size and one small. A Beadhead Hare's Ear or Prince Nymph is a good generic choice for the medium nymph. Below this can be fished a smaller mayfly nymph such as a Pheasant Tail, a cased caddis, midge larva, or wet ant. The trout can take either one, and some days they'll show a decided preference for the smaller offering.

It is not the first half of a freestone season that necessitates small flies, but the second. (Although the prerunoff early-spring period can have low and clear water conditions, midging trout, *Baetis*, and little winter stoneflies.) In late summer, waters become ultralow and warm. The big-fly hatches are

Freestone River Locations for Feeding Trout

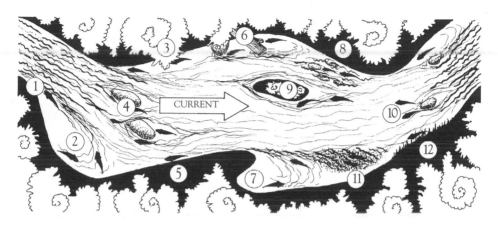

1. Any current line that borders a slower water zone, for instance an eddy.
2. The "eye of the pool," or the big slack-water eddy that's often found to the side(s) of the heavy current, where it drops into the head or beginning of the pool.
3. Shade cast by riverside foliage or hills. Can be particularly important in the heat of midsummer.
4. In front of, alongside of, and behind boulders in swift midstream runs. Especially important in hot weather and low flows.
5. Trout will move into very shallow edge waters to feed on insects that drift a long time on the currents, including mayfly spinners, some duns, midges, and small terrestrials.
6. Upstream and downstream of any bank obstructions such as logs, rocks, and clumps of eroded turf. Many hungry trout prefer the upstream feeding location, where they see the food coming sooner.
7. In bank eddies, especially where foam and cover are present.
8. In pocket water, where rocks make numerous holding eddies and ripple the surface, which camouflages trout.
9. In converging currents at ends of islands and gravel bars.
10. Free roaming in shallow tailouts and upstream of isolated rocks.
11. In depressions in the streambed, the result of shifting gravel, erosion, and ice-gouging in early spring (when the ice blows out).
12. Along grass banks of any depth. It only takes three to four inches of water to cover a trout's back. Here both terrestrials and aquatic insects are found.

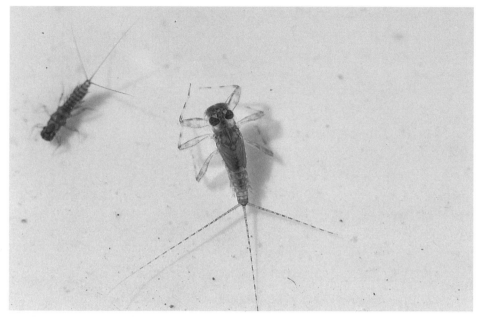

Swift-water mayfly nymphs tend to be wider than the slow-water models, with more prominent gill structures and gripping legs. The classic Hare's Ear nymph is a good general imitation.

largely over. Tricos swarm on beautiful summer mornings. Insects hum and crackle in streamside meadows. Terrestrials and even snails begin to make up a fair percentage of the trouts' diet. Morning and evening rises become the rule, with additional fish tricked during the day by blind casting and stalking.

One of the highlights of mid- to late summer is the possibility of stalking visible trout. It is likely at this time that trout will be used to eating smaller nymphs, duns, spinners, emergers, and terrestrials. They often supplement the diminished summer hatches by picking off cased caddis and snails. One can move slowly, sneaking up on likely riffles, dropoffs, pools, and eddies, spending a little "Polaroid time," and looking for fish before doing any blind casting. The gravel glows under the midday sun. The shapes and movement of trout reward the patient. Much can be learned of trout behavior by dividing time between watching and blind casting.

The heads of swift runs and the bellies of pools contain summer trout escaping the heat of midday. These fish can be harder to see if you can't get an elevated position. It is here that deep nymphing will prove most worthwhile.

Foam-covered eddies, cut banks, and spring seepages will all house trout. One should not be in a hurry here. Sneak slowly along and stop often. The reward of discovering a trout's probing nose and casting to fish that can be seen is worth the effort. It builds trout savvy.

If trout cannot be seen, fish the water blind, quickly and efficiently, before moving on. Those who effectively cover the most water usually catch the most fish. A small Humpy with a Hare's Ear dropper would be a good generic blind-fishing rig. When trout are spotted, try the same rig on them. If you are refused, try going smaller. Simply scaling down versions of the same patterns is often enough. Where trout boldly took #12 Royal Wulffs a generation ago, they look now with suspicion at most offerings so large. A size #16 to #20 of that same pattern often brings the desired results today, even on heavily fished waters. Other trout will be pickier.

Nymph, or two-fly, rigs take fish from swift midsummer runs, where trout find comfort and cover in the low, clear water. Work runs systematically before moving on.

I like small black crickets as drys to fish I can see, and A. P. Black Nymphs underneath. Mini-Wulffs, Trudes, Humpies, and Stimulators are great attractor drys for freestoners. Parachute Adamses are excellent, too. Precision casts to the slow-water slicks, eddies, and pocket water are what connect you with the fish.

I remember a lunchtime incident on Montana's South Fork of the Flathead River, where the big native westslope cutthroat are often reputed to be pushovers. We sat up on a low cliff eating lunch and watched a row of cutts feeding below, along the edge of a deep sloping pool. They fed at a lazy but steady gait, taking something underneath that was too small for us to see. I cast the usual Humpy over them from my elevated perch to no avail. On many days these cutts will greedily take most any fly. Next I tried a #14 Hare's Ear. No interest. All casts were within easy view of angler and trout. Finally, I hung a #20 midge pupa from the Hare's Ear. The biggest and leading cutthroat leaned over to suck it in on the first drift, just as it had been doing with the naturals. It was a beautiful fish of nineteen inches and typical of these waters. On this same trip we found cutts focused on flying ants that refused larger imitations.

Now, this was on one of the most remote fisheries in the lower forty-eight, where cutts are supposed to be dumb as nails. It is always detrimental to an angler's success when he goes about depending on such generalities and doesn't prepare himself for streamside realities. All trout focus on small flies at times, especially when waters are low and clear. It only takes a couple compartments of your fly box to carry a handful of midge pupae, small mayfly and caddis nymphs, emergers, duns, and spinners. Add some miniattractors, a beetle or two, ants, and Griffith's Gnats, and these add up to good on-stream insurance wherever you go.

I have mentioned cased caddis larvae a few times and have had just enough sight-fishing experiences with them to value their worth. I took an afternoon stroll one hot August day up a little swift and spring-fed stream in my area. Large trout move up this creek to spawn, and many end up getting stuck there through the endless beaver activity. By midsummer the creek is very low and clear but runs with pure spring water, keeping the trout in good shape. Where I was fishing, the trout, many in the fourteen- to twenty-inch range, were highly visible and edgy in the shallow water. I snuck through the willows, trying the usual upstream presentations, which spooked most of the intended targets. Only then did I sit down and watch, as I should have done in the first place. Soon it became obvious that the trout that were feeding

A big native westslope cutthroat that wouldn't take anything larger than a midge pupa. Such encounters can be expected once rivers drop to summer lows.

were picking off cased caddis, which covered the bottom in the riffle areas. I had tied up some simple but effective patterns and tried one on the fish from directly upstream. Casting down to the fish I had sighted, I dropped the fly with a big tuck cast and fed out a bunch of slack. Since the trout were occasionally swinging widely from side to side, I ran my fly off to the midstream side of one of them by two feet, fished with a long 5X leader. The first drift of the tumbling cased caddis brought an immediate response. The brown leaned over, flashed its amber flanks, and inhaled the nymph. Downstream he ran, with me following, but he was duly landed in the colorful graveled and weed-laced streambed.

Another time found me in New Zealand on a midsummer farm-country river of repute—the Mataura. On many occasions I had seen these plump browns nose down and tail up, vacuuming the bottom of nymphs. It was cased caddis they were after. Noted Kiwi angling writer Norman Marsh relates a story in one of his books of taking stomach samples of Mataura trout, one of which had over eight hundred cased caddis naturals in it. Yankee trout love them, too. Since many New Zealand rivers are ultraclear, and trout can

Cased caddis cover the streambed in many places. Trout love them, picking them off rocks when hatches are scarce.

usually be seen, lessons in trout behavior present themselves to observant anglers every day, and painfully at times!

I have found that trout focused on the bottom and cased caddis often lose sight of everything else going on around them. Once I was on a bridge and easily visible to any wary trout, casting to a cased-caddis snuffler just below. He never saw me, so intent was his nose-down posture, and he ended up rushing over to inhale my fly. Downstream a bit, I again found myself on a height, where any conscientious trout would have seen me and fled. Here again were three trout, nose-down and hunting cased caddis. They'd move out into the current, then back over a gravel bar and into a deep, slow backwater near my bank. Back and forth they travel all day, feeding on nymph or hatch as conditions warrant, all visible to the watchful angler. I caught two of these on cased-caddis patterns, reinforcing their worthiness in my mind. Since most streams have more caddis than either mayflies or stoneflies, this is a good addition to your arsenal.

Nymph, emerger, dun, and spentwing; mayfly, caddis, stonefly, beetle, ant, and midge—all come in the smallest varieties come the low-water seasons of a freestone stream. The angler thus prepared will have his most memorable encounters with fish he can see. This is the real reward of small-fly fishing, when all the cards are on the table.

The big tailwater rivers are a little tougher to decipher at first, but the same principles hold true. The trout will be staying out of the main force of the current, where a good food supply is delivered. The best areas include inside bends, riffle and eddy lines, gravel-bar dropoffs, tailouts (especially at the heads of island systems), edge waters, troughs, big eddies, and all around islands. Fish will gang up in ideal holds, with dozens of them living in close proximity. Tailwater fish will nibble all day long on small naturals, which are the mainstays in these steady dam-controlled waters. There will be less of that on-off behavior that you often see in freestoners, though hatches will certainly bring up many additional risers. During nonhatch periods, though, most trout here will continue to feed, as they must to maintain a healthy condition on the steady supply of small fare. And what they'll be eating most is from the multitudinous biomass of small aquatic insects, crustaceans, and aquatic worms.

Here on the large tailwaters, the breadth and volume of the river can be initially dismaying to small-stream anglers. It would seem foolish to fish tiny flies blind in so much water. What the angler must do here is cut the river down to size. You're not going to fish all of it, just the most likely zones. You

Trout Holding Zones in Larger Tailwater Rivers

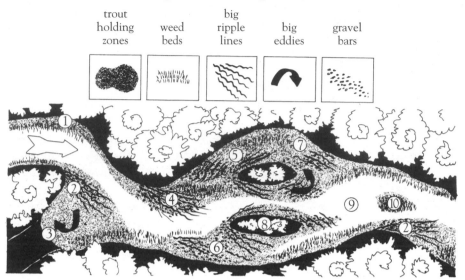

1. Any slow-paced edge water can hold trout. If it has weed beds, eddies, ripple lines, or overhead cover, so much the better.
2. Major ripple lines peeling off points or inside bends can house good populations of tailwater trout.
3. Big eddies and sloughs (usually the mouths of high-water channels) can hold cruising trout. They will feed at the current's edge or follow big foam lanes, where floating insects amass.
4. Some major ripple lines tail out into expansive and wadable flats of gravel and weed beds. Many trout are scattered through such areas and make for good stalking during a hatch.
5. Gravel bars are often part of island systems. Trout hold in their dropoffs and wherever depressions in the streambed give trout cover from the current. Midriver gravel bars without islands are common, too.
6. Upstream from many islands is an expansive tailout flat. Trout favor these slowing and shallow currents when rising to a hatch or spinner fall.
7. Big-river trout like the intimacy of smaller side channels, where currents are reduced and habitats are favorable.
8. The water all around islands holds the promise of trout, including the tailout above, ripple lines down both sides, and converging currents below.
9. The converging currents at the ends of islands feature gravel-bar dropoffs, troughs, and big eddies. Varying populations of trout can be found here, both rising and deep-nymphing.
10. A variety of troughs and midriver pockets hold schools of trout. These might not be visible and take a great deal of experience to come to know. Many guides capitalize on such hidden hot spots when drifting, using deep-nymph, strike-indicator rigs.

can always sweep a Woolly Bugger and catch some fish, but more are likely to be taken in the right places on small stuff. Since at this point we're still talk-ing about fishing blind, it's the nymphs that offer the greatest potential here. Blind-casting small drys might bring up the occasional fish, especially in well-defined holding positions like grass banks and narrow ripple lines. But on the whole, small nymphs or two-fly systems produce best.

As on a swift freestone river, trout here must also stay out of the main force of the current. Since most tailwater rivers have few large insect types and infinitesimal numbers of small ones, it is especially important for these trout to hold in slower water to feed efficiently. They dine virtually all day, which is not always true on freestoners, and the trick is to put drag-free, deep, and likely offerings right before their noses on a fine tippet. This is helped along somewhat by the high population of fish and their being spread over wide zones of slower water. But there are areas of higher trout-holding poten-tial, and these hinge upon reduced water flows and food abundance.

Broad tailwater rivers are a little intimidating at first glance. Cut the water down to size and concentrate on the margins, where the main currents are diminished and trout can hold with ease. Slow, shallow zones can show many rising fish.

Anywhere the water slows on a tailwater is a likely fish-holding zone. Edge waters all hold some fish, and often a good number. They don't need any cover in the traditional sense, either. Inside bends and especially where points of land transmit expansive ripple lines are prime locations. The trout will be in the ripple or eddy line, and on the bank side of it in slower, shallower water. If a good hatch or spinner fall is on, many rising fish are likely to be seen in these quarters. Nymphing such ripple lines and just to the bank side of them is a very likely tailwater choice.

Anytime a broad gravel bar is encountered, trout are likely to be found both upstream and downstream of it. The downstream location will generally have the most fish and prove to be the best nymphing site. This should be fished very systematically—cover all the water a bit at a time. Often schools of trout are located, and they can be tightly bunched. There is enough food on these rivers that trout tend to have reduced territorial aspirations and will huddle closely. Trout will rise well here too during a hatch, but can be tricky to see in the rippling water. Stare hard and scan widely. More on this in a moment.

Note the riffle line out toward midstream—it's peeling off an inside bend or point. Trout focused on plentiful hatches or spinner falls will move into the slow shallow-water zone nearer the bank. This is just the kind of shallow area beginners have a tendency to wade through while making casts to midstream. If trout are feeding on quick emergers such as caddis, they'll stay out in the riffle line itself.

Upstream of gravel bars or islands is a broad and shallowing tailout. This can be a very expansive and wadeable flat. Here trout will be more thinly spaced but widespread. It is a good location during a hatch in which to pick off steady risers but a bit more work to nymph when compared to the downstream gravel-bar dropoff position, which is more concentrated and well defined.

Island systems draw fish and fishermen to their varied water types. The tailout above them (upstream), the ripples emanating from their heads, and converging currents below all house trout. Extensive gravel-bar systems are often associated with islands, and trout will be found in dropoffs, depressions, and anywhere the water velocity is reduced to ideal holding levels. Tailwater trout seem to like the confinement of small side channels, too, perhaps being desirous of small-stream intimacy.

At the tails of islands and along the true riverbanks are converging currents, troughs, and big eddies. Some can be quite deep, and all hold varying concentrations of trout.

Any quality bank cover and eddies will hold fish, as they do on any stream. But on tailwaters, even straight, shallow banks with no cover have some fish, for currents are reduced here, and food is delivered. These are the conditions tailwater trout need most. No water is too shallow for them if it can cover their backs!

Small weighted nymphs are best bets here in nonhatch periods, including such contemporary classics as Pheasant Tail Nymphs and Beadhead P.T.s (*Baetis*, PMD, and Pseudo nymph imitations); Brassies and midge pupae (midge larvae and pupae imitations); scuds and cressbugs (crustacean imitations); and San Juan Worms (aquatic worm imitations). San Juan Worms are fished in sizes #8 to #14, scuds and cressbugs in #12 to #18, Brassies and midge pupae in #18 to #28, and P.T.s and Beadhead P.T.s in #14 to #24. These are among the most consistent tailwater producers in nonhatch periods and are fished deep and dead-drift, often with extra weight and strike indicators added to long leaders. The average depths of holding trout are six inches to six feet. Other major pattern types include caddis worms and emergers in #14 to #22, and crayfish and baitfish (minnow and sculpin) imitations in sizes #8 to #4.

Blind-nymphing a tailwater calls for a degree of faith and patience at first. There seems just too much water to dally with. But if you cut the river down to size, concentrating on the most likely zones, success will follow. It certainly helps to talk to others, stop in at local fly shops, and watch successful anglers on-stream if you're a newcomer to the scene. Highly experienced tailwater nymphers catch a lot of fish, and in a seemingly effortless manner. It is their

Tailwater trout like slow, shallow edge waters to rise in. Food is delivered with little current to fight. Many of these spots have no cover in the traditional sense. Use your eyes to find the quarry.

understanding of aquatic life, trout-holding zones, and line control that allow them to do it.

Hang around a tailwater long enough and the picture will likely change. When the small-fly hatches begin, a different river world lays itself bare. Small flies plus numerous fish equal steady risers. This is where the true small-fly excitement really reigns. For there is nothing more alluring to fly men than the sight of steady-rising trout. And nothing gets them rising so resolutely, so consistently, and for so long as blanket hatches of small flies.

Now the angler no longer need prospect for fish. They give their positions away wholesale. These locations should be catalogued mentally for future use and reference, for tailwater trout tend to use the same unchanging stream locations year after year. These will no doubt make your next nymphing session more productive. Several outings teach you further trout holding positions, and once they set in for the summer, they seldom move far until the next spawning urge.

Trout do make some minor positioning adjustments when rising that center around food types and supply, and water flow. If the flies are widespread and well distributed, the trout will slide over to slower and often shallower water to feed on them, so that fighting the current is minimized. Prime examples here include:

- Trout in runs and pools dropping back to shallower, slower tailouts or sliding over to edge waters to rise.
- Trout moving from under ripple lines to the quieter bank-eddy side of them to rise.

If the bugs are concentrated in any way, trout can move over to capitalize on them. Typical scenarios include:

- Concentrated feeding lanes, often laced with foam and flotsam, that will draw trout to rise from nearby sanctuaries, whether such lanes are found along banks, in big eddies, or even right down the middle of a slow stretch of river.
- Windblown duns can pile up along the banks. Trout will prefer wind-free slicks in which to rise to them, if available, and the fish will move into such slicks.
- Little channels through gravel bars will siphon duns, spinners, or nymphs. Trout that may have been spread around the gravel bar dropoff in nonhatch periods will push up into such minichannels to capitalize on the current glut of flies.

The speed at which insects emerge and fly off will also affect the trouts' positioning. Insect adults and spentwings that float on the surface a long time allow trout the luxury of moving into slow, shallow edge waters to feed on them. Most conspicuous here are early- and late-season midges and *Baetis* duns, some PMDs, Trico spinners, and small terrestrials.

Flies that take off quickly, and especially caddis emergers, don't allow trout this luxury. Instead, trout must stay out in the swifter currents where these insects hatch, and rush about to intercept subsurface emergers rather than take floating adults. Trout concentrating on PMD emergers can do the same thing, especially on windy days, whereas trout focused on PMD duns can be found downstream of emergence sites in quieter edge waters, eddies, and tailouts.

In most of the above cases the trout don't move very far. If rising, they will remain fairly close-by in nonhatch periods for the nympher to capitalize on.

But this is a dry-fly session, and there are ways to increase your odds and expand your horizons. Not all rising fish are easy to see or find. Naturally, your timing on the river will affect what you see and don't see, both on a seasonal and daily basis. Showing up when the hatch is on can be inspirational. Hitting the same piece of water on a windy afternoon between hatches is a little dismaying. Of course, being on the water all the time is best, for something is always happening somewhere, even if it takes a lot of looking to find. But for most anglers, a little research and phone work will put them on the water at the most desirable hours, weeks, and months of the year. There are excellent fishing experiences to be lived from early spring to late, late fall. I know many anglers in my area who missed out on big-time dry-fly action for years because they just didn't know that some of the best mayfly hatches of the season go well into November and even December. Top rivers plus top hatches equal supreme angling experiences.

Perhaps the most important factor of fishing small-fly hatches is in the looking. An angler should shed that immediate fish-the-water impulse and start depending on his eyes to find fish. He should become the trout hunter and fish the water only as a secondary tactic if any trace of a hatch is on. He should cultivate patience and cover new ground. In the process he'll learn more of the trout's world. One begins to see things he was too busy casting to notice before, nuances of river life that affect trout behavior at every turn. For trout lie in unexpected places and feed randomly on the food sources at hand. I have often seen anglers out blind-fishing midriver runs while unbeknownst to them subtle risers were feeding steadily behind them, in shallow edge waters

Trout Feeding Positions in Big Tailwater Ripple Lines

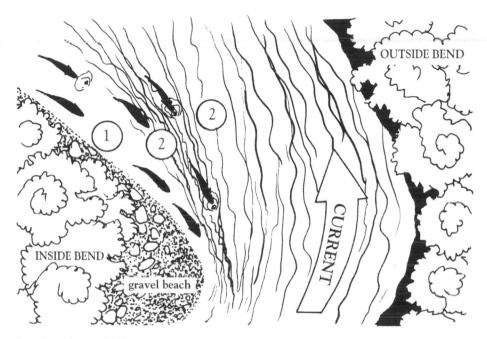

Broad ripple or eddy lines that peel off inside bends or points can be very productive, especially on tailwaters. These are shallow and devoid of overhead cover due to the floodplain nature of rivers. Trout take different holding positions to suit hatches and circumstances. Anglers should inspect calm edge waters for rising trout before wading in to fish the eddy line.

1. Some trout will move into very slow and shallow edge waters to feed on insects that drift a long time on the surface, including midges, some mayfly duns, spentwings, and small terrestrials. Surprisingly big trout will feed in the shallows, even under the midday sun.
2. Trout can hide under ripple lines and will move into them to feed on sparse hatches and hatches of quick-emerging insects, including caddis and some short-floating mayfly duns. Trout can be spread through the entire riffle area. Spooked trout will hide under the ripples or race for midriver.

and flats. Trout can be caught blind and trout can be stalked. It is often the angler's choice, depending on his awareness. Of the two, stalked visible trout generally offer the greatest thrills per cast.

There can be more to "looking" than first meets the eye. There are better and worse places, and lesser and more likely viewing conditions. Trout can be found where you expect them and where you don't. It's the latter that take more concentration.

Upon approaching the bank, it's always wise to stay back a bit and scan the immediate edge waters for subtle risers. Spend a good minute or so doing this before stepping out in plain view. Trout are wild animals after all, and respond as such to movement and human presence.

The next place to look is up and down the edge waters, those quiet waters within one to ten feet of shore. Large trout like rising in this slow-current zone but are easily scared out by footsteps or by the passing overhead of a bird or fly line. The idea that big trout will be down sulking in some hole at midday is something of a myth. Certainly there are some extra-large specimens lounging in hidden river rooms, but a good number of trout up to and over twenty inches will be finning in edge waters. It is just another place where both food and a break from the current are found. Trout are by nature shallow-water creatures. It is well for anglers to remember this.

As you look beyond the edge waters upstream, down, and across, you'll want to focus on areas where the trout can stay out of the full force of the current. Stop at this point to inspect the river's surface for insects, as well. As we mentioned earlier, a good hatch or spinner fall of a fly species that floats on the surface a long time will show more nice fish in the quietest water zones, where they can feed at a relaxed gait. On the other hand, a sporadic caddis hatch will show more fish out in the currents, boiling after the quick-rising emergers. A little bit of knowledge can go a long way in finding fish.

When it comes to spotting risers in the currents and eddy lines, I find that it's easier to distinguish them looking upstream rather than across or down. The way a river drops altitude, and the forward push of a rising fish make this so. The flat holding water and riseforms are more conspicuous when viewed from behind. Working upstream is also the classic "come from behind" trouting approach, which capitalizes on the trouts' blind spot, directly to their rear.

Trout rising in flat water are the easy ones to see. It's those making subtle rises in the ripples that call for more concentration, especially on the vast glariness of big open-prairie tailwater rivers. As ripple lines peel off points or

Some big trout haunt shallow edge waters, even under the midday sun. Fish holding tight to banks can be more adventurous in their feeding habits.

inside bends of the river, rippling eddy lines transmit out toward midriver. These locations are especially important on big tailwaters and rivers without pocket-water sanctuary. On flat-surfaced rivers, trout use such riffles as over-head cover from predators in lieu of overhanging foliage or other traditional small-forest-stream cover. Many western waters flow through grasslands or have flood plains that reduce stream-edge overhead cover to a minimum. The broken water of ripple lines fills this void, camouflaging trout well, even when only inches deep. And although some consider riffles as swift-water areas, this really isn't so. Riffles are where the main velocity of the river slows against bottom strata—be it cobbles, gravel, or rock. Here trout find shelter from the current, camouflage, and abundant food. Nymphs love the highly oxygenated riffles and trout know where to find them. They have little else to think about!

If a good hatch is on, you'll want to inspect riffle lines closely for the rings, noses, and heads of rising fish. When a hatch first starts, trout can move from the flats inside the eddy line out into the riffle, eager to take the first flies. If the hatch thickens and lasts, some of those same trout might drift over to the quieter eddies and edge waters to feed more leisurely. Trout in the ripple line can be hard to see. As many as twenty-five or more fish can be feeding in close proximity in tailwater eddy lines but can easily go unnoticed by those who don't look first and cast later. I have even seen schools of flat-water fish create an "artificial" riffle by rising vigorously to Trico spinners. Even this spectacle goes unnoticed by some fishermen, who can't imagine such a phenomenon is possible. These are situations you're really looking for, and several fish in a row then can often be taken by observant anglers.

Not only does viewing from behind make spotting risers a bit easier, but crouching down and viewing from a low angle can be even more advantageous. There are trout noses and heads to be seen, and every advantage you give yourself tends to increase your catch. Scan big riffle lines from beginning to end, from where they emanate from the bank (which can be a real hot spot) out toward midriver. On a broad tailwater river some eddy lines can be one hundred yards long. On freestoners, they're likely to be shorter and more compact, but equally important. Often it's the first twenty-five feet or so, where the riffle line begins, that shows the most fish, for trout tend to push forward, eager to feed. In other cases, trout will be spread up and down the eddy line and feeding to the bank side of it as well, in calmer, shallower water. When approaching such a situation from below, take time to view all the water before rushing in. One can pick off the lower fish first, which often have a tendency to rush for midriver when hooked, and on downstream in the currents. Be prepared for "hot" fish, too, especially on the tailwaters. Big trout hooked in the shallows can get you into your backing in a hurry. It is here that quality reels that can pay out line quickly and without breaking ultrafine tippets are prized tools of stalking anglers.

It could take several minutes to spot all the trout in an expansive ripple line. It's beneficial to know where they all are to help plan catching as many as possible without scaring off the rest. When food is very abundant, the trout aren't likely to stay down long after being scared by a bad cast or one of their party being caught. Sparser food supplies generally develop twitchier trout that are more alert to danger. Their defensive posture is up when not feeding or when feeding on sparse fare. It can be reduced to a minimum when they are chomping on profuse hatches. This works to the advantage of stalking anglers during the hatch.

Half the battle of spotting rising fish is looking in the right places at the right times. Edge waters, eddies, riffle lines, flats, and island systems all provide opportunities. Long-duration hatches of small flies will show the most consistent rising fish day in and day out. There are a few other conditions that can thwart success, but these can also be overcome. They include lighting, glare, and wind. Such conditions are common on expansive western waters and need to be addressed on a daily basis.

Lighting and glare are very important factors when one is trying to spot rising fish *and* see the small-fly offering. It can be a lot harder to see your #24 fly than the head of the trout you're casting to. Sky reflection and glare are problematic, even with a hat and polarized glasses. The need often arises to use your mobility to every advantage, not the least of which is gaining the best lighting situations possible to see fish and fly. Staring into bright sunlight is a great distraction and hard on your eyes.

In many cases you can shift your position sufficiently to achieve maximal viewing and casting potentials. At other times you just have to put up with glare and look all the harder. Since I use boats for most of my fishing, my position can be changed at whim by focusing on either side of the river. Big-river wade fishermen will have fewer options, but there are still ways to combat glare.

The most common glare situation is when you're fishing from the bank and look out across a broad river that reflects nothing but big western sky. The river is a sheet of glare, especially on gray or windy days, presenting acres of tough spotting water. Any time fishermen can position themselves to have a bank, hill, or forest as a backdrop, sky glare will be significantly reduced and spotting will improve. There are many cases on flats and shallow riffle areas where an angler can wade out into the river and look back to his own shore while targeting risers. He must wade very slowly and cautiously, of course, for trout can easily be scared by the waves you emit and the sound of gravel crunching under your feet. But the advantage gained in seeing both fish and fly can be worth the effort.

If one is on a big and straight stretch of river in a bad glare situation, he can move up into an island system, when one is available, where lighting backdrops are more adjustable. The holding water, too, is more intimate and varied. If you are starting at a bridge access, something as simple as choosing the side of the river that will give the best lighting situations will go a long way toward increasing your fish-spotting potential. If you are fishing in the evening, fish the side that allows you to look east rather than west, at the setting sun. Trout have a harder time seeing stalking anglers when they are staring into the bright sunshine at your back. All of this is of real importance to the small-fly hatch-matching trout hunter. Seeing is everything here, and fishing blind a decided second choice.

There is another angle of this lighting situation that deserves consideration, and that is the color of your fly pattern, and especially the wings. For example, I tie Parachute Adamses and thorax patterns with four general
wing-color variations to meet different lighting requirements. I find this very
important to do, particularly on wide-open tailwater rivers.

The first wing variation is with true match-the-hatch colored wings for
picky fish in ideal lighting and viewing scenarios. The rest of the fly's color in
all these cases is otherwise unchanged. The second variation is with the standard white Parachute Adams wing. This gives excellent spotting visibility in
most, but not all, cases. The third choice is a Hi-Vis, or high visibility, wing. I
find fluorescent chartreuse to be more visible than orange or red in a variety
of lighting situations. This can be helpful for those with poor eyesight, which
in my guiding experience includes about half the human race under forty, and
75 percent of it beyond that age.

Now for the fourth variation I find particularly helpful, especially on
the broad tailwaters where I spend much of my time. Here sky glare reigns
as the dominant background. There are many situations when this is hard
to eliminate. Gray, breezy days are the worst, and this is where black wings
can be so helpful. In many glare conditions match-the-hatch, white, and
even Hi-Vis wings can be hard to see. Black can stand out as a bold silhouette in the right lighting conditions to both the angler and trout. Nowhere
is this more important than when sky glare, gray days, and evening light
fuddle your vision. Black stands out like the proverbial sore thumb, and the
trout seem to like it. It is often alleged that the wing of a mayfly is what the
trout keys in on, for it appears first in his limited field of vision, and black is
very visible when viewed against the sky. I seem to use these most in spring
and fall, when dark-winged *Baetis* are on the water and light levels are low.
Baetis have medium-gray wings, but the trout focus well on the black ones,
which are surely quite visible from below. Indeed, trout like black, for there
are few things to be found in most streams that are black and *not* food
items. Think about it—beetles, ants, crickets, black caddis, stonefly
nymphs, and even some mayfly nymphs are black or very close to it. All are
relished by trout. Black beetle and ant patterns have long been considered
premium midday searching patterns. Little black crickets are great, too. Yes,
black is good.

Not only do black wings show up extremely well on gray-sky-glare water,
but also when evening light washes the river in subtle pastels, when
nighthawks swoop, bats whirl, and the noses of trout appear as stark silhouettes.

Here, too, black wings show up as beacons to fish and fisherman alike. I always have some on hand for just these everyday occasions on-stream.

The situations in which black doesn't show up well are when dark backgrounds like hills and trees are the dominant lighting backdrop. This is generally the case when one is float fishing and casting in toward the shore, or when on smaller waters where the sky is rarely reflected, particularly if the hillsides are steep. I don't use black wings all the time, just when the lighting conditions necessitate them. I find myself changing patterns through the day not only to meet hatches but also to battle lighting conditions and achieve fly-to-background contrast. At times this is quite often, for seeing your fly *and* the fish is a very important aspect of small-fly fishing.

Wind is another normality on western rivers. Learning to deal with it is a must. You not only must learn to cast in the wind but also learn firsthand how wind affects trout behavior. Most trout don't like rising in the wind, though they make exceptions for certain food items. There are hatches that are nullified by wind, and others that come off just the same, with the trout still taking them.

Perhaps the most noticeable food item taken in the wind—at least in the public eye—are hoppers. These are blown in and at times taken with relish. Small terrestrials are blown in, too, and most likely in greater numbers. Because of their small size, they are often overlooked by anglers, though not by trout. And trout can get jaded by being bombed with a parade of hopper patterns. This is another case where heavily fished trout often respond better to smaller fly patterns. Finding a wind-free slick along a grass-clad bank will often be identification enough as the likely location of beetle-eating, between-hatch trout.

There are hatches that don't seem to mind wind. *Baetis* and PMDs are notable examples here. Although many trout may turn their attentions from duns to emergers, there are still fish found taking winged adults—wind or no wind. Mayfly duns in these cases tend to blow and sail across the surface. A little twitch or even drag doesn't necessarily detract from your offering. But rather than continue to fish wind-chop reaches, it will generally be better to find some sheltered area where the duns and rising fish pile up. Trout hate to miss out on prime feeding opportunities, and these can actually be magnified by the wind in the right places. Great successes often occur through the simple maneuver of finding wind-free slicks. My most memorable encounters in this regard seem to center around spring and fall *Baetis* and midge hatches, and the Trico spinner fall. No weather is too foul for *Baetis*, and midges, although hatching better when it's calm, will hatch well in the wind and concentrate along lee and sheltered areas. If it's calm when the Trico spinner fall actually takes place and the wind comes up in early afternoon as usual, calm-water pockets of fish can still be found rising to the leftover spentwings. The river can be empty of risers except in these wind-free locales. Being mobile is the key to dry-fly success here, and even on the worst of days it is possible to find a handful of ideal fishing scenes. Stormy days that chase a good many fishermen off the stream can give brief but glorious moments of heavy hatches, wind lulls, and gung-ho rising fish. The lighting situations between thunderstorms can be inspirational. Rich earthy scents are never sweeter than just after a deluge. The drama of rampaging storms animates river valleys with moments ranging from the exciting and fearful to the sublime. The river can come to life with insects popping, fish rising, and swallows circling, as bursts of cool humid air give relief from summer heat or spring sunlight's brilliance. Wind and storms are to the atmosphere what mountains are to a landscape—something that gives it life, drama, and variation to keep the mind alert. Although many hate casting in the wind, and I certainly hate rowing in it, one cannot ignore the wind or the way it affects the fishing. If it gets too windy to fish, sit back and enjoy its power as it sweeps across those huge western landscapes.

Finding rising fish is a great part of the fun in fishing small flies. It takes concentration, determination, mobility, a good river, and a working knowledge of the hatches for the best results. Good eyesight helps, too. When all the elements are in place and those special fishing situations arise, one can expect the most sublime rising-fish moments in all of trout fishing. It's up to you to have the right equipment, flies, and techniques to dupe them. Ultimate challenges are there, while the trout keep rising.

Fishing Small Flies

The fishing of small flies generally requires a step up in skill level for those new to the art. Casts must be more accurate, more repetitive, and more controlled, because trout won't move far to take small flies. The flies are decidedly harder to see, and the trout are fussy about feeding on them. Just having the right pattern isn't a guarantee of success.

On the plus side, small naturals are overwhelmingly numerous and are what trout eat most. They need to feed on them constantly to fill up. The steadiest-rising trout, and thus the most alluring targets, will be surface grazing on small flies. And there are not that many hatches that need to be matched.

Perhaps the biggest difference between fishing small flies and larger ones is the need for repetitive casts. With large-fly patterns one generally fishes the water blind but also casts to visible fish. Just a few casts are generally worked over any single piece of water before the angler moves elsewhere. The trout are expected to be hungry and move to the highly visible fly. In my own experiences, I've seen clear-water trout move sideways ten feet to take an attractor dry, and chase one forty feet downstream to catch up with it! This is *not* the kind of trout behavior you'll solicit in the small-fly game.

When the trout are up and dining on small flies, they hold just under the surface. They see a parade of minutiae pass overhead and generally choose what they're most familiar with, or what are most numerous. When the food

95

supply is high enough, as it often is with dense and long-lasting hatches of small flies, the trout develop a rising rhythm. They might rise once every five seconds in a drift-up-take-drift-down glide, helped along more by the current than by their own swimming efforts. A simple tilting and posturing of the fins does it. This is the classic case of trout feeding efficiently, spending the least amount of energy while capturing as much fly as possible.

No matter how good the angler's fly imitation, it will never look just like the numerous naturals. The trout sees countless choices float overhead. He has a rise rhythm, a mealtime dance. He's tangoing to the beat of the current hatch. What the angler must do now is *intercept* the trout in its rise rhythm with his own rhythm of casting. It's a curious ballet featuring a stooped angler, flicking line, and hovering trout. In this situation the trout seldom rushes up to grab the angler's fly, though even here a big fly sometimes fools the odd specimen, bringing a lunging take. This is the exception to the rule. Instead, the angler must repeatedly put perfect casts down the trout's feeding lane. As the trout comes up to take another natural, his fly should be there. The trout's feeding inertia leads him to take the artificial if it's realistic enough. The trout doesn't want to break its timing and gulping pattern, despite the forty-foot line and angler attached to the impostor. It is thus fooled, or "intercepted" in midrise by the tireless and accurate caster.

To the uninitiated this might sound a little preposterous, but it is indeed an on-stream reality. What is necessitated is a series of repetitive, accurate, and well-controlled casts. It might take five, ten, twenty-five, or even fifty casts to fool a given fish, presuming you don't scare him with a bad cast in the course of this pursuit. Working on your side here is the trout's desire to capitalize on the hatch while it lasts. Some trout will take an endless procession of casts without spooking and will merely feed safely around your fly. Others will spook much more quickly. Line control and drag-free floats are keys to success.

If it takes twenty-five casts on average to fool picky fish (presuming you do have the right fly on), it becomes obvious that the faster you can run these twenty-five perfect casts over the trout, matching its rise tempo as closely as possible, the sooner you'll catch it. Speed in casting becomes a major tool. Downtime is to be minimized. Today's high-tech rods enable anglers to cast much faster, and we'll talk about this a little more down the road. Whereas in past generations (both of anglers and rods), fly casting was often a slow and graceful motion admired as much for style as effect, today's skilled small-fly caster is likely to be lightning-quick and mechanical. His fly is on the water much longer than in the air, where no fish dwell. Drop the fly four feet in

This angler has moved in closely on some trout that are piled up in a riffle line and rising repeatedly to a dense hatch of small flies. Rapid-fire, accurate casts are the most efficient way to intercept picky rising fish, though the landings must be delicate and on the money.

front of the fish, let it drift four feet below, snap out another quick two-to-three-second cast, and repeat the process until the fish is, we hope, intercepted. This speed-casting scenario is the name of the game, aided greatly by the graphite stick.

The angler here is likely to be hunched over, trying to see his small fly. Hook sets must be on a visual basis. To a passerby the scene looks somewhat comic. The knee-deep hunchback snaps out casts every five seconds, as if he's beating the water into submission. Not so noticeable is the delicacy with which these speed casts land, and the control born of repetition the angler is able to exert. His theoretical twenty-five casts have been run over the trout in short order. A tight line, bent rod, and more relaxed posture are soon to follow.

Speed and accuracy are cornerstones of small-fly success. This isn't to say that you want to rush into the water and start pounding away. Such repetition is carried out after finding and cautiously moving into an ideal position on a targeted fish. The leader is checked, fly chosen, currents pondered, and all manner of approach details thought out. The speed-casting finale is the last movement of the sight-fishing stalk. Of course, one doesn't have to cast fast. It isn't a race. But if you multiply the number of casts needed to fool the average picky trout by the time you spend making each one, it becomes obvious that the speed caster will catch more fish in a day and spend less time doing so. Because to most anglers the number of fish caught is the bottom line of their perceived success on-stream, speed casting will help achieve that goal. Modern fly rods allow anglers to cast lines traveling perhaps one hundred miles per hour. Utilizing the potential of the equipment helps in fooling more selective trout. If you've already paid for the latest-generation graphite rod, why not use it to its full capabilities? In the casting techniques to be discussed, remember that speed is an ally.

Before covering some small-fly casting styles, let's first look at what spooks many a trout. I spend much of my time guiding on the Missouri, where clear water, smooth currents, increased fishing pressure, and ample food adds up to spooky trout. These fish are at times as furtive as any you can find, sometimes going down on one perfect cast. There are fish that studiously avoid any fly connected to a leader. This helps one learn ways to avoid scaring trout while noting what spooks them.

The first thing that scares trout is quick movement. Even the passing of a sparrow can send them darting for cover. Trout have many overhead enemies, including eagles, osprey, kingfishers, cormorants, mergansers, blue herons, and pelicans. There are also otters and mink to dodge. Evading predators is an ongoing pastime, even during hearty feeding.

For the angler, this means keeping himself, his rod and fly line out of the trout's view so as not to startle it. The slower, deeper, and slicker the currents, the more important this is. Trout in a rushing freestoner will be less spooky than those in a flat-meadow spring creek. The vision of fast-water trout is somewhat obscured by surface chop. Trout in shallow riffles can't see as far as can those in deep pools.

In a fishing sense, this means don't false cast *over* your intended prey, one of the most common mistakes made on-stream. For it's not just the motion, line glare, and shadows that spook trout but the water droplets that fling off your line, as well. When you pick your line up off the water for another cast, quite a bit of water adheres to it. When you cast and false cast, this water sprays off your line and across the river. If you can get up on a bridge and watch someone cast on flat water, the effect, you'll see, is quite noticeable. False casting over flat-water fish can be like throwing a cup of water over them just before your fly lands. Many trout are scared by this, unbeknownst to anglers.

Speed casting has another advantage here—several, in fact. It dries your fly off more rapidly in one false cast. When you make upstream deliveries to trout, they have a harder time spotting fast, low casts going overhead as compared to those high, slow, and lazily unfurling ones. Those send many trout packing. If the trout upstream has a steady rising rhythm, you can make a low fast cast over his head just as he goes down from a rise. In this way, his own satisfaction and spreading rings tend to mask your delivery. Ideally, you'll lay just enough fine tippet above him to coincide with his next rise. When he tilts up again, the current will have carried your tippet and fly into a position just in front of his nose. This may sound fantastic on paper (in the true sense of the word) but is workable on-stream.

Aggressive wading scares many a fish as gravel is crunched underfoot and wakes are spread by your progress. Just standing in the current of a flat-water stretch pushes subtle wakes that are noticeable to ultrawary trout. Although there are decided benefits to being as close as possible to your fish (better sight of fish and fly, and shorter, more accurate, and less time-consuming deliveries), there are also times when it pays to stay as far away as you can comfortably cast. Often it is the fishes' behavior and lighting situations that will make this clear on-stream. Fish rising rapidly to a thick hatch might let you wade very close to them, especially in low-light situations, for instance at dusk. I've had plenty of midday experiences when rising trout wouldn't let me wade very close at all. They'd take off in fear when approached any closer than midcasting range. Perhaps it is the higher angle of the sun in this case, and the more obvious shadows cast by angler, line, leader, and wake. Perhaps trout just feel more vulnerable under bright light and keep an extra edge of watchfulness up. I know anglers who routinely get down on their knees and very slowly shuffle to within fifteen to twenty feet of their trout before casting. I tend to cast farther and remain standing. Each angler's personality, patience level, and casting skills will shape his approach. The trout will let you know when it's out of hand.

Edge-water trout are likely to see the angler himself if they are not approached with extreme stealth. Clothing to match the background should be worn, be that green for foliage, gray for rocks, or blue for sky. A dingy old sweatshirt is almost the ideal color on many rivers.

Fishermen would do well to imitate the blue heron. Movement should be deliberately slow and calculated. Your feet shouldn't outstep your eye's progress. If casting close-range to a fish, you might want to cast sidearm, so the trout doesn't see your rod in the air, which can happen. One can move

Using the Trout's Rings to Mask Your Delivery

If a trout is rising very steadily, you can use its rings on the surface to help mask your cast. A low, fast delivery with a long, light tippet should be made just when the trout goes down from his last rise. You are ready for this by continuously false-casting a shortened line off to the side of the fish. Shoot out the final delivery just as he takes another natural and begins to go down. Ideally, you will place just enough tippet over him to coincide with his next rise. When he rhythmically tilts up for the next natural, your fly should be there!

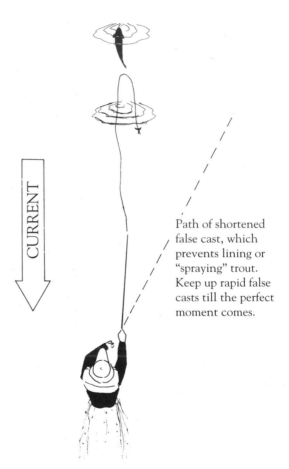

CURRENT

Path of shortened false cast, which prevents lining or "spraying" trout. Keep up rapid false casts till the perfect moment comes.

incredibly close to some bank-hugging trout if enough patience and slothlike motion is used. I have dapped or flicked only my leader to many a trout. It's quite amusing to view them from so close, especially if they are rising. Watching them take a fly pattern is decidedly the highlight of this game.

Let me relate a couple of other concerns New Zealand fishermen voice, not because you might fish there some day, but because their big clear-water trout can be so alert, which is a universal instinct. Many Kiwi anglers firmly believe that if you wade upstream of trout (in shorts and bare legs), crossing the river above them to gain a better stalking position, the trout will pick up the human scent and spook. Numerous incidents of this nature are reported, and the theory is considered a given. Obviously, if you kick up streambed silt, this can alert wild trout, notwithstanding the few places, like the San Juan, where they'll actually line up below you to feed on the food you've dislodged. Many of the New Zealand experiences are where anglers crossed quite far above their targeted clear-water fish while fishing partners watched as the fish disappeared from sight not long after the wading angler had crossed above. This kind of routine observation can only take place where visible fish dwell in ultraclear water, and when spotting partners are there to observe the trouts' behavior. New Zealand is a most educational trouting classroom in this respect.

Another thing some Kiwis swear against is fly floatant, for trout can perceive that, too. If nothing else, you can drop a freshly treated fly on the water and see oil slicks emanating from it. It's hard to imagine that ultra-alert trout could find this very appetizing! I still use floatant routinely in most cases, but I might hesitate to in one-shot big-fish situations where the trout seem edgy or overselective. Calm edge-water eddies would be a case in point, where not much current is moving through to dilute a fresh application of floatant. One could at least make a few casts away from a fish in hopes of washing away floatant residue before the moment-of-truth cast is made.

Such matters may seem trivial but can add up in the long run to the successful capture of larger visible trout. These are the most memorable stream encounters you're likely to have. It's worth taking the extra steps needed in stalking, positioning, leader repair, fly selection, and presentation in order to maximize these opportunities. It's a low-water game going on worldwide, and the small-fly natural is often the target.

The Basic Approaches

Trout feeding steadily on small flies in low clear water are apt to be edgy. Your basic approach to them can decide the outcome of the game. There are many trout around that will go down after a couple of casts from the wrong quarter. I know of many trout that don't take a liking to upstream presentations in bright daylight hours when feeding on Trico spinners, midges, and small terrestrials. Come twilight and the evening hatches, you can often cast up and over the same fish with abandon. Much of this has to do with lighting and water flow, surface smoothness versus ripple chop. On broad flat waters like the Henry's Fork, down-and-across slack-line presentations have long been favored. On swifter freestone streams and tailwater ripple lines, up-and-over presentations are just fine. Whenever possible, I like casting across and slightly downstream on slick-surfaced water. Each river encounter can call for case-by-case approach judgments, presuming the terrain and streambed allow you the mobility and choice.

Casting directly up and over trout gives the surest hooking angle. One can often move up very closely behind rising trout, too, taking advantage of the blind spot to position oneself at point-blank range. Stealth in wading is needed, of course, but anglers can work themselves within rod's reach at times, especially toward twilight and during dense hatches and spinner falls.

Problems with upstream presentations come on very smooth, slick currents during bright midday hours. Line and leader shadows scare many fish, for they are easily discerned when the sun is high, as are all the angler's mistakes. Trout seem twitchier now, too, and seem more aware of their well-lit vulnerability to predators. Yet many will haunt very slow and shallow water positions in midday hours, rising to leftover Trico spinners, PMD cripples, midges, and small terrestrials.

One trick to consider, as mentioned earlier, is that of casting low and fast when fishing upstream to flat-water rising trout. They have a more difficult time spotting your leader overhead when it's zipping at high speeds. The trick here is to cast low and fast but without slapping your fly on the water. Delicacy in the landing is a must. This takes practice, as do all the more demanding techniques. Some mistakes are always made along the way.

You also want to false cast well to the side of your target to keep him from seeing your line in the air, any shadows, or the spray your line throws off. The sun's position in relation to your line should be kept in mind, and the casting of shadows minimized as much as possible.

Extra long and light tippets are advisable. Ideally, nothing but the lightest end of the leader will be dropped over the fish's back. How far above the trout (which is usually visible) you drop the fly depends on how often he's rising. Trout rising every few seconds to a heavy hatch can have the fly dropped closer to their noses, especially in low-light situations—as close as six inches to one foot. The shorter the drift needed to cover the fish, the more rapid-fire and precise the presentations you can put over him in a shorter period of time. Brighter conditions and a slower feeding gait call for a little more lead in the presentation, with two to four feet being about right. And as mentioned above, I will try to time my cast to go up and over a trout's back just after he rises to a natural. In that way, the surface rings he makes when rising can help camouflage a low and snappy cast. The trick here is to put just enough leader and tippet out in front of the fish to try to match his rise rhythm. When he's coming up again for another fly, yours should be just floating into his view.

Because seeing small flies can be difficult, casting directly upstream can give superior viewing in most cases, for you can move in close on your quarry. Even if you can't see your fly momentarily, you can generally see the leader. If the fish rises and your leader twitches, tighten up smoothly but firmly with your rod. Don't yank it back. In this way trout won't spook, even if they haven't taken your fly. Controlling your nerves is a big part of such up-close and personal trouting encounters!

There are times when trout just won't take upstream presentations of any kind. If fish after fish flees from your initial offering, take the hint. There are other ways to fool them. Up-and-across presentations can be just as bad as direct overhead shots at trout, for your line is then on the perimeter of the trout's blind zone. If the trout is swinging widely from side to side in its eagerness to feed, you can try running your fly repeatedly along your edge of its rising parameters, timing casts with its rise rhythm as much as possible. In this way, you're much less likely to spook the fish on a cast. Here again, casting as the trout goes down will add another small edge of concealment to your low, quick cast. You might even want to cast sidearm, stopping the forward motion abruptly to throw a curve in toward the trout. This takes practice to put it on the money but helps in hiding your rod and line from watchful trout. Remember that we're talking about trout in slick currents, where they spook most easily. Fish in choppy water are good candidates for upstream or up-and-across presentations. But those are not the ones that will test your skills most!

Your next option, if the position is attainable, is to cast across the current, or slightly down and across. Obstructions to gaining this position include deep water and tall bankside foliage. Most places I fish allow anglers to wade around their quarry and take a casting position of choice, depending on currents, surface character, lighting, and wind direction.

I prefer the across and slightly downstream presentation, for it allows me to keep most of my line and leader out of the sight of the fish. It also allows both aerial and on-water manipulation of my line, leader, and fly just before they come into the trouts' view. This can be very important in fine-tuning a presentation. One can also obtain a "fly first" drift from the side and above. This is especially important when dueling with trout that won't take a fly if the tippet precedes it. Some trout get in the habit of ducking a presentation without spooking. Every time your leader with whatever fly concoction

Fishing the Outer Perimeter of a Trout's Feeding Pattern

If a trout is weaving from side to side in its eagerness to feed, work your side of its broad feeding lane to avoid lining and spooking it. This can take extra time and patience but will pay off in the long run.

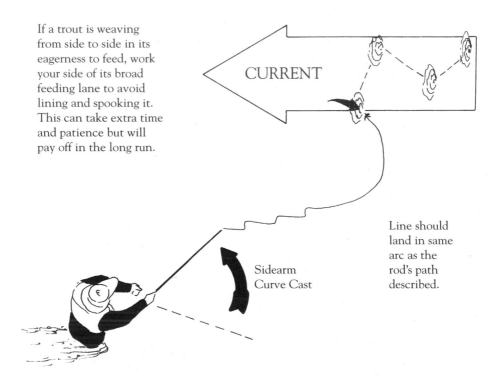

CURRENT

Sidearm
Curve Cast

Line should land in same arc as the rod's path described.

This angler is using a sidearm curve cast. By overpowering a sidearmed cast and stopping it abruptly, the line lands in a curve that continues beyond the rod tip's progress. This keeps the line and leader low and out of the sight of fish but is more difficult to execute with on-a-dime precision.

comes near, they just sink down a bit and wait for it to pass. As soon as it's gone by, up they come again, feeding as ravenously as ever. I have seen trout, however, that ducked flies continually while feeding for almost an hour but finally rose with confidence to flies they liked the look of. In one case it was a foam beetle at the end of a Trico spinner fall. This is part of the fascination of small-fly fishing. It's hard to leave visible and extra-steady-rising trout alone!

The most important aspects of the side approach are your positioning and the reach cast. I like to be slightly upstream of my fish, but well to the side of them. Obviously if you get too close the trout is likely to see you, though trout rising very steadily in shallow ripples can be approached closer than you might think. I prefer medium-range casts of, say, forty feet, including leader and using a rigid, fast rod. The importance of being slightly upstream of the fish is in making fly-before-leader presentations and effective reach casts. They only work well when cast from directly across to directly below. They don't work well at upstream angles yet still offer some advantage in keeping the leader away from the trout.

The mechanics of the reach cast are very simple. It will give you much longer drag-free drifts than a straight cast will. Indeed, a straight cast on moving water is the last thing in the world you want when fishing dry flies or dead-drift nymphs. If I was going to teach someone to fly cast on western rivers, this would be the first cast I'd show them, so valuable are its assets.

The Reach Cast

This is perhaps the simplest of any specialty cast, but by far the most useful. I use it for about seventy-five percent of my casts with drys, nymphs, and streamers. Here's how it works.

Wade into a position directly to the side of a rising fish, or slightly upstream of it. You'll be casting upstream from the trout far enough that he can't see the line in the air, a very important point on flat water. This should be six to eight feet upstream of your target. On riffly water it can be closer. You don't want to be angling your cast at too much of an upstream tilt, and this is why being slightly upstream of your fish helps the effect along.

Make your casts as you normally do, only insure that your final forward delivery is a straight overhead cast and not a sidearm one. Sidearm deliveries have a way of throwing curves into your presentation, which tend to work against you in the reach cast.

Now several things are about to happen. While making your final delivery, you will actually want to cast beyond your fish by several feet. Your forward

The Slack-Line Reach Cast

Landing position of fly line. Note that the fly was originally cast beyond the trout's feeding lane but has bounced and been pulled back into it, after having been fine-tuned during the reach.

After the reach, the line lands here. Now drop the rod tip down near the water. Follow the line downstream till you're reaching downstream. Mend when necessary.

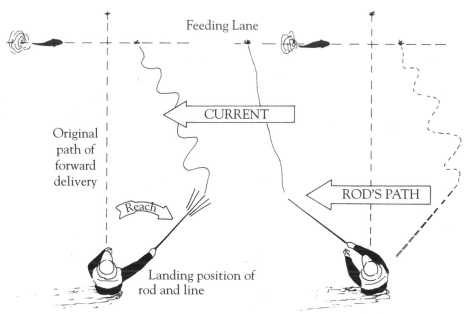

Feeding Lane

CURRENT

Original path of forward delivery

Reach

ROD'S PATH

Landing position of rod and line

The upstream reach is made smoothly, while the fly line is still in the air. Wiggling the rod tip up and down as you reach builds more slack into the final delivery.

The reach cast is used most when fishing across even-flowing flats and when fishing to banks from midstream. Casting from a bank eddy out into a fast current actually calls for a reverse, or downstream, reach.

cast also should be a little high, made with your casting arm held higher in the air than normal. This forward cast also should be overpowered. As the cast fully extends, it will bounce back a bit from the excessive force. This creates slack on the water when the line lands, which is necessary for longer drag-free drifts of your fly.

Just as your fly line shoots out in front of you and begins to turn over or fully extend, you want to begin "reaching" your rod and arm upstream as far as they can comfortably go. This should be a slow, smooth, and continuous motion, completed while the fly line is still in the air (which is why the extra altitude is needed and also why the cast needs to be well upstream of the fish).

The reach cast at this point has created a triangulation. The extra distance you casted beyond the trout is taken back in as you reach upstream. There is also a "bounce back" effect from the overpowered cast. It will take a little practice to actually have the fly land in the trout's feeding lane, but it's easier than it might sound on paper. There is another ploy that can be used at this point, which we'll look at in a minute.

At this point we find the angler reaching and even leaning upstream. His rod is held high, pointing upstream, with his fly line and fly angling downstream. Theoretically, his fly is in line to go over the trout, which is now about four to six feet downstream of his fly. The fly is preceding the leader and is the first thing the trout should see. If there are too many curls of slack line around the fly, a little upstream twitch of the fly rod should straighten them out.

Here the next phase of the presentation begins. The angler drops his rod tip close to the water, creating more slack, and begins following the line downstream with his rod tip to eliminate drag. If the current begins bellying his line, he makes a quick mend, as usual, but then continues to bring his rod tip on downstream at the current's pace, keeping up with the fly line and eliminating drag. In the final analysis he began by reaching upstream and ends reaching downstream. The tip of his rod may have covered twenty-five feet or more in doing this when you add upstream and downstream arm reach, body English, or lean, and rod length. The overall effect is a fly-first presentation with three times the attainable length of a drag-free float. This is often just what you need when making repeated casts to picky, hatch-oriented fish. The farther upstream you reach and lean, the longer the drag-free float you can achieve.

When you first practice this, you'll have a little trouble getting the fly to land where you want it to, but refinement usually comes quite quickly. What I actually do is cast well beyond the fish's feeding lane and fine-tune where it lands with my reach. In other words, as I reach upstream and even back, I am slowly pulling the still-airborne fly back toward the fish's feeding lane. When it gets over that point, drop the rod tip and you're there. Now follow the drift on downstream with your rod tip.

There are adjustments to this basic reach cast that come in handy. If it's windy and your line is blowing away just before it lands, execute the reach with a little more speed and snap. This accelerates line speed and forces the fly to turn over and hit the water a little more quickly. Even if it splats down hard, it should be far enough upstream not to spook the trout. There will likely be wind ripples on the water, too, masking rude presentations a bit more.

To get extralong drag-free drifts, one has to add more slack to his cast *and* after-cast presentation. The traditional way to build more slack into a cast was to wiggle the rod tip from side to side as line shot out on the forward delivery. This is known as a serpentine cast. I have found that serpentine casts often cause barely perceptible serpentine drag. The fly line lands in extensive side-to-side curves, where more, not less, current can exert force on it. Submerged weed beds cause many nuances in surface currents as they wave below. Each wave creates eddies and swirls that grab line, leader, and fly. Subtle drag is caused, taking flies from their intended course. This can never be wholly eliminated as long as a line is attached to a fly, but it can be reduced with extralight, long tippets and the proper presentations.

The serpentine cast can be improved upon simply by wiggling the rod tip up and down, rather than from side to side, as the final delivery shoots out. In this way the extra slack tends to be less spread out across the surface and more piled upon itself. It is also easier to place your fly where you want it when compared to the side-to-side wiggle. Overall drag is somewhat reduced. This up-and-down wiggle of your rod tip is performed while you reach upstream. Again, it's easier on-stream than it might sound on paper.

More slack yet can be added after the cast is made and your line is on the water. More line can be peeled off the reel and mended out in the same direction as your fly line. Repeated mends to add slack are known as "slack mends." When mends are done properly, they don't move the fly.

Most anglers I see can't mend without moving the fly. Often mending becomes a self-defeating process as the fly is whisked from its intended course, and often sunk, as well, in the shuffle. The trick is to mend both out toward your fly *and* upstream, releasing line from your hand at the same time. Mending without releasing some line can only move your fly. The rolled line has to come from somewhere, if not from your hand, then from your line, leader, and fly. Mending *before* drag actually sets in is also necessary. It should be an anticipatory maneuver and not a last resort. Mending before drag sets in and feeding out line during the mend will help keep your fly floating along nicely. With stack mends, however, the mends are not necessarily thrown upstream but are just as likely to be thrown in the direction of the fly, downstream and right at it. The currents will dictate where your mends should be thrown.

Fine-Tuning the Fly's Landing Position During the Reach

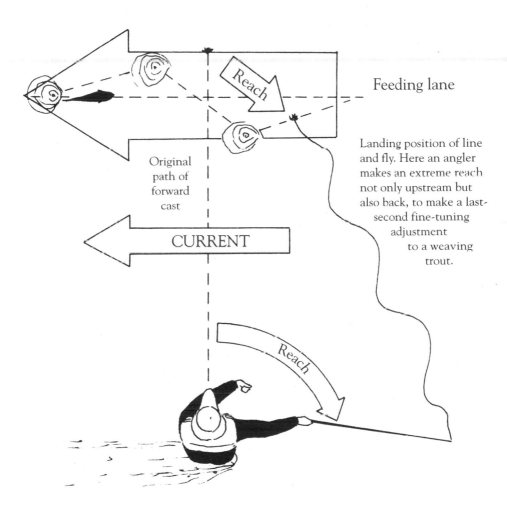

Reach

Feeding lane

Original
path of
forward
cast

CURRENT

Landing position of line
and fly. Here an angler
makes an extreme reach
not only upstream but
also back, to make a last-
second fine-tuning
adjustment
to a weaving
trout.

Reach

The extreme reach allows you to move your fly as far as ten feet at
the last second, just before it lands. This can eliminate the need
for any on-water mending while landing your fly right on the
feeding lane. It must be done far enough upstream so that the
trout doesn't see it in the air. The lower you can make it while
still keeping the line and fly airborne, the better.

Your first attempts at reach casts will likely be a little off the mark, and not exactly down the trout's feeding lane. If the cast is too short, let it go by. Too short is much better than too long! But if it is too long, a simple ploy can be of great help, especially for beginners. I use it all the time.

After the cast is on the water, and just before the fly reaches the trout's field of vision, say four to six feet upstream of it, lift the rod tip back upstream and skid the fly across the surface till it comes in line with the trout's feeding lane. As soon as it does, quickly drop the rod tip near the water, following the path of the line downstream with it, and let it pass over the trout. The higher you lift the rod tip during this maneuver, the more slack you'll get when you drop it to water level and end up reaching downstream. This simple dodge is extremely effective when fished at downstream angles. The skid works best with dry flies that won't sink during this performance. When fishing caddis patterns or other imitations of more active insects, this little skid just in front of trout can actually solicit takes. Other insects that skitter across the surface include midges, windblown mayfly duns, quick-emerging mayfly duns, and egg-laying caddis and stoneflies. Small terrestrials, too, struggle and kick. Doing the skid slowly with a nymph can imitate the emergence process, especially if the nymph has had a chance to sink before the lift is performed just upstream of the trout. Soft-hackle patterns, conventional nymphs, and even midge pupae are all taken with subtle, controlled drag at times.

The reach cast is not only a highly beneficial wade-fishing tool, it is a necessity when float fishing. When casting from a boat, anglers are usually out in the heaviest current casting in toward slower edge waters and pockets near the bank. Unless a good reach cast is used here, drag almost immediately sets in due to the variance in currents the line crosses. From a boat, reach casts should be made well downstream, with both anglers working at close to a forty-five-degree downstream angle. Mends will have to be made soon after the line hits the water, as well, for the quicker current near the boat grabs it immediately.

Wading anglers on big tailwaters often find themselves in the same position as float fishermen when wading out into a flats and casting back in to shallow bankside trout. Here again, the fisherman is standing out in the heavier current while the fish leisurely rise in calmer edge waters. And here again, reach casting a little farther downstream on a roughly forty-five-degree angle might be necessary to achieve a long-enough drag-free drift to fool the trout. Mends and stack mends might be needed too. Extreme reach and added body English will help in making these acute down-and-across presentations. This is far from the classic "cast with a book under your elbow" style. The modern

Stack Mends

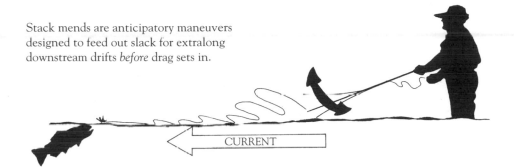

Stack mends are anticipatory maneuvers designed to feed out slack for extralong downstream drifts *before* drag sets in.

CURRENT

The reach cast is made and the rod tip lowered and pointed in the direction of the fly. Extra line is peeled off the reel and fed out by flipping the rod tip both up and down and out toward the fly. These extra loops of line can give amazingly long drag-free drifts. The extra slack built into your original reach cast allows you to make all the stack mends needed without moving your fly. The sooner you perform them after your fly lands, the better.

fly caster uses superior equipment and more athletic styles while meeting greater challenges worldwide. Distance, wind, and drag are all battled. Confidence and a full utilization of the equipment's potential are keys.

Downstream presentations, from a forty-five-degree angle to directly below, are the final approach. These are often performed where other options are limited since the hooking angle is less sure and it becomes harder to recast without alerting the fish. In extreme downstream cases they can become one- or two-shot deals. It soon becomes obvious that after you've fed out line directly downstream, you now have to do something with it if the trout doesn't take.

Compounding problems is the poor hooking angle, from which there is a tendency to pull the fly up and out of the trout's mouth. A good deal of nerve is required here, and proper timing, for the trout must be allowed to descend a bit before the hook is set. As a general rule, though, your hooking angle is best when casting directly upstream and becomes less and less ideal the farther downstream you cast. There are ways to overcome this, at least to a workable degree.

Downstream casts call for extreme reach casts and stack-mended line to achieve the best results. Most fishermen I see cast downstream just as if they were fishing upstream, and then try to add a lot of slack. Generally their presentation ends up being a continuance of drag, and with Murphy's Law prevailing, the fly usually drags the most just in front of the trout.

The old puddle cast, where an underpowered cast dumps a pile of slack helter-skelter on the surface, was often a case of wishful thinking. The belly of the line would land well before the fly and so start dragging all the sooner. The loose coils would undo, with the fly setting up a serpentine drag as it approached the fish. It can hardly be considered a precise casting option.

If one were going to "puddle" or drop a pile of slack line with any control, an extreme tuck cast would be more worthwhile, dropped on the water just upstream and out of the trout's aerial view about six to eight feet. Here the line is cast on a higher plane than normal, overpowered, and stopped very abruptly. Yanking back a bit with the line hand adds to the effect. The end product is a cast that turns over then under itself, with the fly landing well before the line. This only works with flies that don't have much air resistance, and works better yet with weighted nymphs, which build greater inertia. Now you have a little slack built in, enough only for a short drift. But if you can quickly add some downstream stack mends or just wiggle out some slack line before the fly starts to drag, a much longer drift can be attained. Feeding or mending out slack without moving your fly is critical with downstream presentations. If you can't quite pull it off, at least make the final adjustment before it's in the trout's view on the water, about two feet upstream if he's close to the surface. If you can get a good dead drift at that critical moment, it can all still come together. What the fly does upstream and out of the trout's view is of little consequence unless it sinks your dry fly. But come to think of it, I've caught many a trout on sunk dry flies too!

To me the most practical downstream presentation is an extreme reach cast. The important thing here is that when your fly line lands, your rod should be pointing directly upstream and *not* downstream at the fly. This is performed just like the previously discussed reach cast, but on a more dramatic scale. You cast downstream with a good aim on your fish. The cast is on a higher than average plane and overpowered a bit to get that bounce-back effect (though it's not so important here as it is on across-river casts). While the line is still extending out in front of you, reach upstream as far as you can reach, and lean. A good deal of body English will help in maximizing the length of your drift. In the downstream case we're talking about here, the rod will be shifted almost 180 degrees while the fly line is still in the air—from being cast directly downstream to pointing directly upstream. As the line extends you can also wiggle

The Downstream Reach Cast

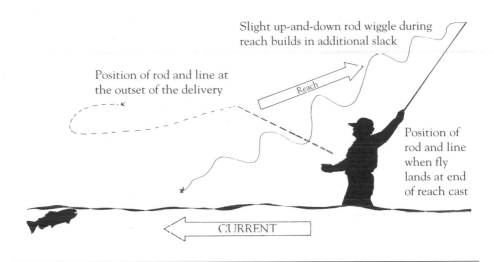

Slight up-and-down rod wiggle during
reach builds in additional slack

Position of rod and line at
the outset of the delivery

Reach

Position of
rod and line
when fly
lands at end
of reach cast

CURRENT

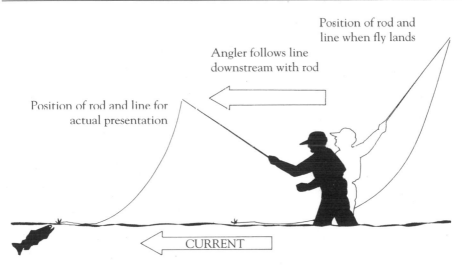

Position of rod and
line when fly lands

Angler follows line
downstream with rod

Position of rod and line for
actual presentation

CURRENT

The direct-downstream reach cast lands with the rod pointing upstream. The angler then follows the fly's downstream slack-line progress with his rod tip. Applying up-and-down wiggles of the rod tip and stack mends can prolong drifts. Long, light tippets are desirable here, for the fly must be cautiously led away from the fish if it's not taken.

your rod tip up and down to build in additional slack. Now when your line lands you can follow it from the upstream reaching-leaning position to a downstream leaning-reaching position. Stack mends can easily be made well before even a hint of drag sets in, allowing controlled drag-free drifts of in- credible lengths. This is the easiest way for most people to achieve precise and drag-free downstream casts.

If your aim is off the mark, this can be rectified on the water before the fly enters the trout's view. If you will recall the skid we discussed earlier, you'll find that it can be easily applied to the downstream presentation. When you perceive that your fly will be off to the side of its target, and while it's still four to six feet upstream of the fish, slowly pull your rod back to the up- stream-pointing position again, just as it was when your reach cast landed. At the same time pull it sideways till the fly skids into a line destined to float over the trout's nose. Now, quickly point the rod back downstream, dropping the tip low, and feed out any slack needed before drag sets in. This is almost like making the cast from scratch again without the aerial journey. If your fly sinks or is otherwise deemed unworthy of confronting the trout, pull it up and away before it enters the trout's field of vision. One could also make a big mend toward midriver at this point, which will slowly drag your fly out of the trout's feeding lane before you make another backcast.

Another downstream application of the reach cast is made with the idea of having the fly line float off to the side of the fish rather than right over it. The cast is made downstream, and a few feet to the heavier current side of the fish. An extreme sideways reach cast is then made toward the slower-water side of said trout (if that condition exists—other situations find the trout tight against a bank or out in even-flowing flats). The act of reaching sideways and upstream takes up that extra line that was cast beyond the trout's feeding lane and fine-tunes its landing point. Once the fly lands, the rod tip is lowered and slack is fed or mended downstream. If a little skid is needed to line up the drift with the trout, do it right away, and then feed slack. Now the fly will float over the trout, but only a little of the leader, and none of the line. It would be wise to run your fly just a bit outside of the trout on the first cast or two, rather than directly over it, to minimize the chance of lining. This can work well if the trout is swinging from side to side a little and showing some promiscuity in its feeding pattern. Your fly only has to be a few inches off to your line's side of the fish to add a margin of safety while still fooling risers.

Wading anglers fishing directly downstream also have to concern them- selves with kicking up mud and spooking trout. If a good fish is located and no other approach is possible, you'll want to use extreme patience and care moving into position. You might even have to wait for the trout to begin feeding again if it grows suspicious.

What you do with the leader and line after an untaken fly passes over the fish becomes your next great concern. You can't just rip it off the water without scaring the trout, as you can on upstream and across casts where the current carries it out of harm's way. It's best to use an extralong light tippet here,

Down and To-the-Side Reach Cast to Avoid Lining Fish

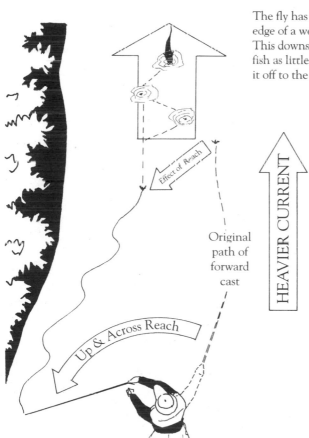

The fly has been placed on the near edge of a weaving trout's feeding lane. This downstream cast will show the fish as little leader as possible, keeping it off to the slow-water side of the trout.

The problem with direct downstream casts is in the retrieval of the fly and line if the trout doesn't take on the first drift. Long, light tippets are advisable, perhaps three or more feet of 6X. Once the fly passes the trout untaken, it must then be led or mended to the side of the fish before the heavier leader and line come in to its view. The sidearm curve cast is another option in such cases, but few anglers can place those with any accuracy.

measured in feet rather than inches. Three to four feet would be a good working length for special one-fish situations where extra stealth is called for.

After the fly goes over the fish you have few options. The farther your
line and leader are angled to the side in the first place, the easier your task
will be. The most common ploy is to slowly reach your rod and arm out to the
side as far as you can just after the fly passes over the trout. This will slowly
drag the fly off to the side while only the light tippet is in the playing field.
It's all risky, but the subtle drag of a fine leader doesn't always alarm fish, especially when they are feeding heartily. One can also mend the line out and
away from the trout in an attempt to insure that the act of mending doesn't
create any sudden and undue movement of the leader, which alarms trout.
Keep things as fluid and low-key as possible through the retrieval process,
taking as much time as necessary to do it right.

Now you can strip in line very slowly until it's well upstream of the trout
before making a backcast. Some fishermen like to give the line a short jerk to
sink a dry fly, because it makes less disturbance under the water than it does
skating across the top. Don't be in a hurry to rush any of these steps, for repeated casts directly downstream are chancy at best anyway. You might want
to pause a minute or two between each drift of your fly to make sure the
trout's confidence is still up. Whenever you can get slightly to the side of your
quarry, the ease of presentation and hook set improve.

There is one more approach, one that is quite exciting but little used. Its
possibilities are very limited, though one can look specifically for them in
many places with ease. What angle could be left beside upstream, across, and
downstream, you ask? Flies presented from above!

Dapping is an ancient respite and was often necessary in bygone reelless
eras when casting horizons were limited. The angler cautiously sneaks along
the banks, staying hidden, and lowers the fly to bankside fish. High-tech casting weapons are of small concern here. A limber rod might be better to take
the short line-thrashing shock. This point-blank-range approach is more exciting than you might think, often more difficult than a standard cast—and
thus more sporting. There is nothing quite so thrilling as finding yourself directly over a feeding trout that doesn't see you crouched behind the streamside foliage. You can see his every move, count his spots, see his eyes roll in
his head, and look down his throat as his fins spread and he drifts up to take a
surface morsel. This is exciting stuff!

You must move your rod into position over the fish oh-so-slowly, or risk de-
feat. The trout will be scrutinizing the flow, looking hard for his next meal on

the ever-moving, ever-providing surface. If an ant crawls down your neck, forget it! Stillness is your ally, camouflage your defense. Patience is the key to success. When you finally lower your fly and see the trout tilt up; when you see his forefins flare and his interest pique, you can only hope that his inquisition lasts not a second longer than your fly's brief drift. If his head protrudes and your fly disappears down that white gullet of greed, pray that your nerves are up to the task! Don't yank the fly out of his still-unclosed mouth. Wait till he sinks down in glowing satisfaction, then put the steel to the fish. Be prepared for the worst, though. Big fish on short lines spell disaster in such quarters. He may dash for midstream or roll under the bank. He might wrap around log or rock. When he sees your devilish grin above and skyward lunge of the rod, he'll no doubt be beside himself with disgust and wild fear. Such bank-edge adventures take time to cultivate but are indeed worth the effort. Few trout will be as memorable.

How you approach a rising-fish situation could depend on restrictive water depth and bank foliage. If mobility is unlimited, a final decision could hinge around the currents and eddies to be overcome, lighting and the best view of your fly, or wind direction. Because both controlled drifts and seeing your fly are so important in small-fly fishing, gaining a position that gives you both is ideal. You might be able to approach a rising trout from any angle you desire, given time and care in positioning yourself. The angle that gives you the best viewing position would be the top choice, all other considerations being equal. This goes for seeing submerged trout, too, those feeding only on nymphs. With the sun at your back, these can be quite easy to see and fish to. This often means lining up some bank, hill, or trees as a reflective backdrop, as opposed to glaring sky. The hooking angle is another consideration and is surest when you are fishing directly upstream. Trout can be well hooked from any angle, though, if you employ the proper technique, as we'll see in the next chapter.

If drag can easily be avoided from any angle, lighting and the visibility of my fly become my major concerns. If the trout in a particular river are very spooky about up-and-over-their-backs presentations, then I go right to the down-and-across delivery using the reach cast. Often this finds me out in some flats casting back toward shore or float fishing from a boat, and in both cases I get the reflections off the bank as good low-glare lighting. Seeing a #20 or smaller dry fly can be difficult when lighting is less than ideal. Using a wing color on your fly that contrasts well with your backdrop is another plus. Gain every advantage you can *before* you make the first cast.

I use a two-fly rig extensively when fishing small flies. The first fly is usually the smallest pattern that I can easily see in any light situation, often a #16 to #18 Parachute Adams. This acts as a strike indicator. The second fly, or dropper, is the tinier imitation, and the one that's really targeting the fish.

On a swifter freestone river I would increase the size of the indicator fly to a #14, #12, or even #10. On tailwaters and spring creeks I generally keep it small, though a little experimenting never hurts. There are trout around targeting larger surface-food items, including hoppers, crickets, cicadas, damselflies, crane flies, and moths.

Because most of the sighted trout I'm casting to are fish rising in shallow water (or trout holding just under the surface in deeper-water feeding lanes), I keep the tippet between the first and second fly fairly short, usually ten to eighteen inches. This allows me to keep closer tabs on the small fly and maximize its precise placement. Both flies can actually pass through the trout's field of vision, and fish can take either one. If the flies land coiled up around each other a bit, a little application of the skid usually separates them.

With the indicator fly there for easier viewing, it's often possible to find and see your smaller fly as well, even if your eyesight is less than perfect. It always helps to know where your smaller fly is, and whether or not it's actually floating where you think it is—over the nose of a rising fish. If I'm not using an indicator fly, I find it most important to see where my small fly lands. In this way it's easier to follow its progress downstream. If there are a lot of naturals on the water, it can be hard to find your fly again should you lose track of it. Instead, you'll have to watch your leader and tippet for unusual movement possibly indicating that a steady riser sucked it in. Seeing the take is very important in setting the hook properly. If you wait to feel the fish, a higher percentage of missed strikes will result.

When a trout takes the smaller fly on a two-fly rig, the indicator fly will jerk upstream and under. Set the hook immediately, for the fish has already had the small fly in its mouth for a second and may be in the act of shaking or blowing it free. One benefit of small flies in such situations is the hook's extreme sharpness and ease of setting. Some fish will even set the hook themselves with the forward pulse of their rises or the shakes of their astonished heads when they are trying to dislodge it. This is much less likely to happen with larger hooked flies in slower-water rising-fish situations.

Another benefit of the two-fly rig is that you can imitate two hatches at once, or two stages of one hatch. This can be important with ultrapicky fish

Four Common Methods of Tying Two-Fly Rigs

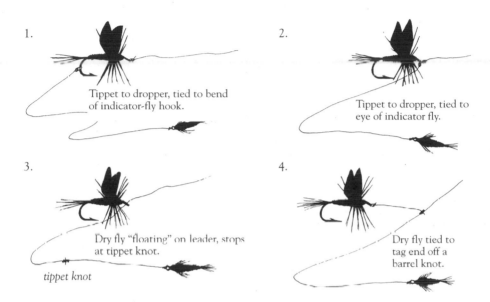

1. Tippet to dropper, tied to bend of indicator-fly hook.

2. Tippet to dropper, tied to eye of indicator fly.

3. Dry fly "floating" on leader, stops at tippet knot.

   tippet knot

4. Dry fly tied to tag end off a barrel knot.

and during multiple-hatch situations. In spring I find myself using a *Baetis* dun pattern as a strike indicator with a midge pupa or adult as the dropper. This rig has fooled hundreds of trout, and on both flies.

When the annual blitz of caddis begins, a caddis dry with a trailing emerger is a smashing combination. As summer progresses, PMD duns, caddis, Tricos, little BWOs (blue-winged olives), and small terrestrials vie for tandem positions, with the added options of emergers, soft-hackles, and the continuing use of midges. Most of these are fished shallow, in the top foot of the water column.

In nonhatch periods and when fishing blind by boat or foot, the tippet between the two flies is lengthened to match the depth of bottom-holding trout, usually by two to four feet. Slightly larger indicator patterns come into play here, with #14 to #16 dry flies holding up weighted nymphs. Beadhead and regular P.T.s in sizes #16 to #22; caddis emergers in #14 to #24; Brassies in #18 to #24; shrimp, cressbug, and sowbug imitations in #14 to #20; and San Juan Worms up to #8 are among the most commonly used droppers. Naturally, you'll want a dry fly with enough buoyancy to remain floating while toting a weighted nymph around, especially if a little additional weight is attached to the leader. Ultimately, you'll switch over to a regular strike indicator if the two-fly rig becomes more trouble than it's worth. As long as the dry indicator fly continues to catch the occasional fish, it's worth having on. Each river will have its own idiosyncrasies when it comes to fly pattern, fly size, weight requirements to get nymphs down, and required leader length and diameter. There are 4X fish, 6X fish, and trout that bring forth singular assemblages of profanity.

If the trout are rising well, routinely taking a preferred pattern, and visibility is good, I cut down to one fly. A dead-drifted midge pupa or small nymph would be an exception with which I would likely still use an indicator dry. If the lighting were perfect, I might just rely on using the leader and tippet as a strike indicator, watching it for telltale movement. The old practice of greasing the leader to within a foot or less of the subsurface nymph is still a common ploy. This keeps it floating high and visible on flat water, where large trout tilt, bulge, and rise to small fare. You might want to cast it in the water a couple of times away from the trout, so that the oily residue of a fresh floatant application can disperse a bit. If a nose or bulge is seen and the leader moves, an adrenalin rush is in order! For those with good eyesight, this remains a small-fly and shallow-nymphing choice, especially if you find your strike indicator causing drag or spooking the odd fish.

One problem I see fishermen having on our expansive tailwaters is with their depth of field perception. When they cast to rising fish on a one-hundred-yard-wide flats with no landmark to use as a positioning guide, their fly is sometimes off the mark. If the trout is rising very steadily, say every three to five seconds, this isn't such a problem, for it will continually give its position away. It's the slower-paced and occasional risers that are harder to pin down. Many anglers will cast too long, too short, below, and too far above their targets. There is so much glaring water and so little to mark the trout's position by.

On rivers with heaving weed beds (which describes many of the tailwater and quality small-fly playgrounds), the surface swirls that weed-bed movement throw off can give some surface definition. There are lanes and pockets in weed beds that trout hold in, and these can sometimes be perceived by surface distortion and coloration. These same swirls also cause the most criminal drag in your presentation at times, causing a percentage of refusals by fly-wise veteran trout. This is another setting where I prefer the fly-first presentation and control of the down-and-across slack-line reach cast.

Inexperienced fishermen seem to have a habit of constantly adding line to their casts when pursuing a rising fish. They start off short, eventually get their

This trout has taken the dry-fly half of a two-fly rig. Note the extra tippet section leading down to the nymph dropper. Trout do sometimes hit this tippet section with their heads when going for the dry fly, pushing the fly away and not getting hooked.

fly to the trout's feeding lane, but then keep adding more line, casting beyond the trout and lining it. This is one of many situations in fly fishing where human nature is somewhat predictable. Some guides will have their guests clamp down with the line hand when a cast gets a perfect drift over a feeding lane and will tell them not to let go of that hand position on the line while making repeated casts to the same fish. If this isn't done, the tendency to strip off another foot or two of line for the next cast seems compelling. Apparently this is the human response to an untaken fly, and it is universally predictable.

It takes practice to put your fly on a dime, the proper distance above and right down a trout's feeding lane on these big-river flats. If you cast it too far upstream of the trout, it drags just as it comes to the fish. If you drop it too close, it is likely that the trout will see your line in the air. There is an ideal lead distance to be found for each encounter. Achieving it is a skill that only experience can build.

I commonly use the pull-back of the reach cast to fine-tune where my fly lands. One can adjust his distance and the fly's landing position by as much as ten feet while the line is settling but still airborne. For me, this is a big plus and the most tangible benefit of the reach cast. Once landed, the "fly first" and extralong drifts come into play. It's hard to beat the reach cast for ease of operation, accuracy, and effectiveness.

The trout out in these extensive weed-bed flats are among the pickiest in the river. More than any other fish, they can be focused on one and only one stage of a hatch. There are multiple hatch times when they're less discerning, but also moments that cause sheer exasperation. There is a reason for this.

Trout lying out in flowing weed-bed flats see a predictable sequence of hatches plus a known variety of nymphs, crustaceans, and aquatic worms. Their focus is sharpened by these well-regimented emergences and more limited options.

A bank-oriented or eddy trout sees more. It receives the benefit of the hatches that a flats fish does, though a higher percentage of cripples and long-floating insect types tend to come its way. Edgewater fish can be less concerned with emergers (which can be harder to match at times) and quick-flight bugs like some caddis, focusing more on mayfly duns and spinners, midges, and whatever remains waterborne. Not only do edgewater and eddy fish have the hatches to play with, but they also have a broad array of small and large terrestrials added to the stew. Other dishes, including foliage-oriented caddis and stoneflies (in season), damselflies, houseflies, midges, and moths are taken. There are even floating snails to be relished. The edgewater trout's palate is decidedly more adventurous than is his weed-bed-flats-dwelling cousin.

Trout in big, swirling foam-ladened eddies have the added benefit of "leftovers." A hatch or spinner fall that may have ended hours ago out on the main river still shows a remnant population of crippled duns and spinners circulating in the catchall eddy. Such fish can rise all day, and they make for good between-hatch stalking. A big wind-protected eddy on your typical breezy western afternoon can provide bonus rising-fish adventures for the mobile. Some of these big-river eddies are as large as ponds. We typically see eddy trout still rising to Trico spinners in the late afternoon and early evening, even though the actual spinner fall ended before noon. Yes, different sections of a river can show decidedly different feeding patterns, and each fish has its own personality.

One can often adjust his position in the river to find the type of fishing he prefers. For anglers preferring dry-fly work, this can be important. One common scenario finds trout focusing on emergers in riffly and shallow flats, while trout downstream and in quiet edge waters and eddies concentrate more on the floating duns. If the trout are being extremely picky on PMD emergers, for example, you might have better luck and dry-fly opportunities by moving down and out of the actual emergence zone, to where only duns and cripples remain. There can even be trout focusing on PMD emergers on one side of the river while those on the other side take caddis and duns from beneath the cover of willows. There are usually more fishing opportunities about than an angler new to the scene is likely to perceive.

Finding the fish is a big part of the small-fly game, adding an exciting sight-fishing element that is lacking in other stream blind-fishing situations. The more one depends on his eyes to find fish, the more fish he tends to find. He may locate fish that he had been walking by for years, in places that seemed unlikely when his knowledge of the river and trout was less complete. For trout are shallow-water dwellers at heart, and subtle feeders of small flies. It is here that the most exciting challenges are found, the largest rising fish,

Let him run! Big tailwater trout hooked in the shallows can make long, bold runs for midriver sanctuary. Seeing your backing is not a novelty here. A high-quality reel is a great asset when fishing ultralight tippets.

and the wildest runs. A big trout fooled in a shallow edge water is explosive and swift. The safety of midriver beckons and can be more than a full fly line's length away. One sees his backing here, and smiles. Are your fighting skills and equipment up to the light-tackle small-fly challenge? There are major concerns when hooking, fighting, and landing big trout on fine tackle, and that's what we'll look at next.

Hooking, Playing, and Landing Fish on Small Flies

Duping a visible trout is half the battle and half the fun. Seeing that nose heave over your fly is the kicker. It is here that your nerves, skill, and tackle will be tested, for the next moment portends wild goings-on. The head-shake, wallowing recognition of duplicity, and supercharged run now animate the scene. The trout's self-satisfied rise has turned to bedlam, and the reel is screaming.

Hooking Trout on Small Flies

There are many considerations to hold in mind when we hook mature trout on tiny flies, and thresholds of eagerness and overreaction to be subdued. The trout will have his own reactions, and how you react to *those* will be of immediate concern.

The first and perhaps most obvious difference between fishing small and fishing larger is that you can't set the hook with the authority that you would on a largemouth bass or tarpon. Your tippet is frail, your hook supersharp. All you need do is raise the rod tip smoothly and snug up on the trout, firmly but not dramatically. You don't need or want to yank back on the rod, as is required with large barbed hooks. There are 1X hook sets, 4X hook sets, and 7X hook sets. It takes practice to steel your nerves and use the appropriate amount of force in each case. You will break off big trout on the hook set with small flies and light (5X to 7X) tippets till you've mastered your own nerves and physical reactions to the take. Subdue your excitement and just tighten up on the trout. The latest and most rigid high-tech graphite rod can cause you more problems at this moment than a softer-tipped model will.

Not only do you have to scale back the severity with which you set the hook, but you also have to consider your angle of presentation and the trout's position in the water. Direct upstream presentations give the surest hooking angle and least concern for timing the hook set. As your fishing angle goes to across, down-and-across, and straight downstream, the timing of the hook set becomes more and more critical.

A trout fished to at an upstream angle can be hooked as soon as his head appears to take your fly. Waiting till he descends a bit can be surer still. The angle is optimal, though the odd fly will still be popped free from his mouth. If you wait too long, he'll feel the pull of the tippet and start shaking his head and flaring his gills in an attempt to blow out the fly. As sharp as small hooks are, though, the weight of the current on the line can be enough to set them, especially if the trout is pushing forward on the rise.

As you approach trout more from the side with across-stream presentations, you must become concerned with the trout's rise rhythm and position in the water when you set the hook. This is particularly true when fishing to larger trout rising steadily to profuse hatches of small flies.

Anglers used to attractor-pattern fishing and large flies often learn to set the hook quickly. Swift-water trout often rush up to these flies and grab them before the current carries them beyond reach. Larger attractor flies also tend to be taken in nonhatch periods, where the trout comes up off the bottom and lunges at them from a distance. In some cases, I think they try to sink the fly before turning to grab it underwater, where it's a sure target. I believe this is the reason for many flagrant misses on the trout's part when attacking hoppers, stonefly dries, and other large patterns. In any case, the freestone trout isn't as likely to have the slow and steady feeding gait that a slick-water fish does, and it can have that explosive take that is more suited to swift water. In such cases the hook should be set quickly, and if the fly is missed by the fish, it should be left in the water for him to grab again. Since the tippet used here is generally in the 3X-to-5X range, hook sets are made with more authority.

Now the trout feeding on big hatches of small flies is a different animal. He's likely to be found in calm water with a steady rise rhythm established. The bigger the trout and the smaller the insect, the slower that riseform will likely be. They are exciting to watch and stressful to cast to!

Timing the Hook Set on Across-and-Downstream Presentations

Mature trout feeding
on a profuse hatch of
small flies tend to
hover just under the
surface, setting up a
steady rise rhythm.

Large trout generally make
slow and graceful rises to
small flies. Setting the hook
when you first see them rise
to your fly can pull it free of
their still-unclosed mouths.

Waiting till big trout
begin to descend with
the fly gives the surest
hooking angle.

The timing of the hookset becomes especially important when casting across and
downstream to larger trout feeding on small flies. You must time presentations to match
their rise rhythms and set the hook when the trout descends with your fly. Striking too
quickly can pull it out of its still-unclosed mouth.

These fish tip up slowly, open their mouths languidly, and ease back
down, often with mouths still open. If you set the hook when the head first
comes out to your fly, you'll likely yank it away from the still-unclosed mouth.
You must wait for the fish to descend, till its head turns down and body just
begins to bury back into the deep. Now tighten up firmly but without undue
or jerky force. Be prepared for a strong reaction, though. Anticipate feeding
out a lot of line fast. A trout's head-shake alone can break fine tippets if you
hold too tight a line. And certainly *don't* try to hold a big trout on his initial
run if he's intent on going places! This is a critical moment requiring instant
decision-making and physical control—not the fish's—your own!

As one's angle of approach goes more to the downstream, this timing becomes even more critical. Here you can actually look down the trout's white
throat as he takes your fly. The tendency to yank it out of his unclosed mouth
is pronounced. Wait for his porpoising motion to arc back down. This can
seem like a long wait but really only takes a second. The more downstream
you're fishing, the more important this delay becomes. Learn to fish with your
mind and not your flinching nerves!

There is another kind of rising trout that can call for an even longer delay in striking. He's usually a large brown and most exciting to watch. You're not likely to see many of these unless you haunt big-fish waters a lot. New Zealand is where this riseform is most common, for the trout there can average twenty-two to twenty-six inches. Here one learns to adjust quickly. The old Kiwi saying is to recite "God Save the Queen" between the time the fish actually rises and when you should set the hook. The rise is that slow. You don't have to travel so far to see these head risers, though. I see them across Montana in rivers where surface meals are regularly taken. They are almost always larger specimens with big mouths and heads. It is the small trout and whitefish that splash and rise quickly. Mature fish feed on abundant fare with more grace and dignity.

These bigger head risers have a way of moving more up than forward as they take. They come from below with jaws protruding. Some drift downstream under their prey a bit before deciding to engulf it, and can then thrust their whole head in the air. It is a slow and lazy motion that can seem to take forever to end. At times the head seems to hang in the air so long that it must be drying up! If your fly is dangling in one of these trouts' mouths, for goodness sake don't set the hook yet! Take a breath and let him sink back down, tail-first, the same way he came up. When he straightens back into the current is the time to hit him, but not with too much force.

Large brown trout have many ways to break you, not least of which is the unintentional (perhaps) raking of their big, sharp teeth across your weakest link—the tippet—as they shake their heads wildly upon feeling the steel. I have broken off more than my share of big-toothed browns on the hook set, largely due to this head-thrashing maneuver and my overenthusiastic strike. The take itself is so exciting, though, that the aftermath is soon forgotten (*not!*). One has to set the hook and be prepared for the worst while hoping for the best. If the fish goes nuts, be very prepared to give him some line. Make sure your line is in control at all times and that any slack isn't tangled around your feet, in streamside brush, and so on. Feeding out line just after the hook set is one of the most common moments of loss. Any momentary tangle can end the game by a snapped tippet. Line control and a quality reel to feed further line out are important facets of small-fly fishing success. Once the trout's through his initial reaction and run and is hovering in midstream, your chances of a landing begin to go up.

There is a small-fly scenario, however, that illustrates human nature at its purest and that presents itself so often that it becomes rather comic. One

The Head Rise Made by Some Large Brown Trout

This type of riser is also seen between hatches scrutinizing surface morsels throughout the day. Bank huggers prove most common in this category. Some trout will drop downstream a bit, inspecting the fly before taking.

It is not unusual to see both jaws in the air, or even the entire head. Such fish tend to sink back down the way they came up. The angler should wait till they sink back down and face into the current before setting the hook.

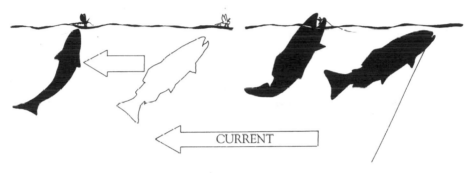

CURRENT

Big head-risers are most exciting to locate. Plan your approach thoughtfully and check the leader and tippet for frays. Such opportunities don't come along every day!

should anticipate this malady and, it is hoped, prevent it with controlled thought. It goes like this: The angler is matching a hatch of a small and populous fly. Big trout are rising steadily all around. Five, ten, twenty good casts are made. The trout isn't fooled yet. Nerves are getting tense, hands jumpy. The angler is hunched over in single-minded anticipation. More casts are made, and still more. The fisherman is anything but relaxed! Finally, a porpoising rise, an intercepted fly, and the angler explodes on the fish like an overwound catapult! Another fish lost on the power hook set! The longer he fishes without a take, the more predictably violent his rod-rearing reaction becomes. I see it all the time and still do it myself.

It takes practice, which means catching a lot of picky fish, to really get your mind to overcome your natural reactions. Constantly rethinking your proper plan of action certainly helps, especially as your tippet diameter goes down. One can take precautions with equipment as well, particularly if one's rod is very rigid. Long stretchy leaders and tippets and "bungee butts" help absorb unintentional line shock. Other techniques for setting the hook can be learned, too, but of course these take as much practice as getting your nerves under control does. Several light-tippet hook-setting techniques have been proffered over the years, though in actual practice good mind control (and thus rod control) is the ultimate end.

One technique calls for holding the line lightly under the index finger of the rod hand when setting the hook. As you come up with your rod on the strike, you also let line slip under your finger, thus moderating the impact.

Another idea uses mends rather than direct rod-to-fish pressure. I found that throwing a light downstream mend at the take would set the hook most of the time. It also puts the line downstream of fish, where the pressure of the current helps keep trout hooked. Additional slack line can also be quickly mended downstream with little actual rod pressure exerted on the fish, which amounts to actually fighting the line dragging downstream in the current and not the rod. You could then reel up excess line at leisure, until direct rod contact with the fish is made. This method of getting the fish on the reel would have obvious limitations if ultralight tippet were used across heavier currents. I use this technique on even flowing flats, where it works quite well.

Compare this relaxed hook set and putting line on the reel with the usual method. Man hooks fish, reaches and stumbles back with the rod held high, reeling madly to get excess line on the reel to best control the fish. While he's reeling in, adjusting his hands to spool the line properly (working the line from side to side while keeping a steady tension to avoid tangling loops), and also trying to keep a steady pressure on the fish, a time-proven moment of disaster can occur. Power surges by the trout at this juncture can pop the tippet, for most anglers are in less than total control when trying to get fish on the reel. It's the hand that is trying to feed line to the reel smoothly while keeping the proper tension on the fish that's to blame. If a trout lunges, it's hard to react in time with the line hand so occupied. Here you must be ready to let line slip through the fingers if the trout wants to go. Make a point of not clamping down on it, which is how these losses originate. All methods have their faults, though, and some fish always seem to be lost on their first wild dash.

Another proposed hook-setting technique calls for a quick up-and-down wiggle of the rod tip. This supposedly moves the small fly and ultrasharp hook enough to set it, but not enough to break the tippet. This is the same idea as the downstream mend, but on a vertical plane. Moderation of force is desired in both cases. With this latter technique, you'd obviously have to rein in slack quickly after the hook set and be in more of a scramble to tighten up on

Using a Downstream Mend to Set the Hook and Get Fish On the Reel

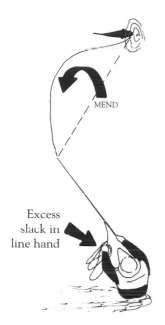

Excess slack in line hand

A quick but gentle downstream mend can set the hook without applying enough force to break the tippet. The leader that now trails downstream of the fish is kept taut by the current while maintaining a good hooking angle.

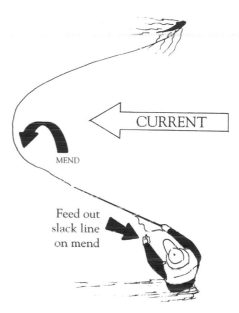

CURRENT

Feed out slack line on mend

Extra slack in the line hand can also be mended away downstream. Now the trout is effectively fighting the line dragging in the current rather than an uplifted rod. Keep the rod low and pointing downstream while reeling up the line remaining on the water till direct contact with the fish is made.

the fish. This is not a technique I have experience with, but I can see where it would work.

It's probably becoming obvious that if you have the control to perform these maneuvers at the hook set, then you can probably just moderate your traditional strike enough to avoid break-offs. Your strike should evolve from a yank to a lift. Small hooks are so sharp that they take little pressure to set, though timing can be critical.

Getting the trout on the reel is another important stage of light-tackle fights. Having just read about the possibilities of break-offs at this critical

Getting Line on the Reel While Playing a Fish

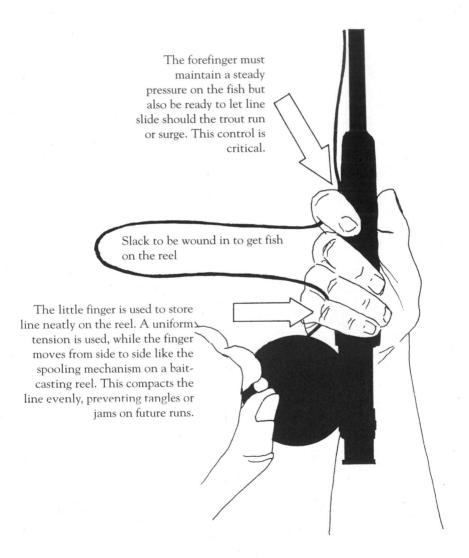

The forefinger must maintain a steady pressure on the fish but also be ready to let line slide should the trout run or surge. This control is critical.

Slack to be wound in to get fish on the reel

The little finger is used to store line neatly on the reel. A uniform tension is used, while the finger moves from side to side like the spooling mechanism on a bait-casting reel. This compacts the line evenly, preventing tangles or jams on future runs.

Getting fish on the reel can be a critical moment in a light-tackle fight. Trout can be broken if the forefinger presses down too hard on the line and the fish makes a sudden bolt or run.

moment, you might wonder why you should bother in the first place. The ideal situation is when a trout runs and ends up taking all the slack in your line hand before he stops. Now he's on the reel, which means you have direct trout-to-reel tension and not a mess of slack line dangling from your line hand. Those anglers who only fish where there are small trout in confined quarters may never have seen a need to play a fish from the reel. One can just strip them in, unhook them, and recast the same quantity of line back out again. In this situation, it might save time and effort.

The need to play fish from the reel comes with larger and faster fish, which have more room to run. Murphy's Law clearly states that if you have a bunch of slack draped around your feet, or across streamside rocks or brush, a tangle is likely to occur, and the worst tangles will happen with the biggest fish. Just accidentally standing on your fly line can spell disaster. Suppose you have just hooked a trout on two-pound test tippet and it plans to zoom a hundred feet out to midstream in just seconds. Any momentary stop of your exiting line's smooth flow is likely to break off such a fish. Any tangle, regardless of how minor, can end the fight. Line control here is often the most critical element of the entire game.

Once the trout is on the reel and all slack is removed, you want to fight the fish by reeling in line combined with proper rod attitude. Reel in smoothly and quickly, keeping a steady pressure on the fish. Jerky motions made with your rod and when reeling have a tendency to panic fish more. Smooth and steady pressure is what you want, and, ideally, pushing your equipment to near its limits. In most cases the rod should be pointed downstream and to the side, not up. You're not trying to lift the fish out of the water with your rod, just to tire him with a relentless down-and-across pressure. The rod can be used as a brake or drag system, too. The farther back and away from the fish you point it, the more friction is created on the line by the rod's guides or eyes. Now when a trout surges, you merely let go of the reel handle and swing the rod tip in the trout's direction. If he jumps, the old rule of thumb of bowing to the trout still holds true—reducing tension during his wild gyrations and if his weight should fall upon the tippet. When the trout eases up, you put more pressure back on, steadily reeling and applying pressure with the rod. By playing the trout off the reel, you greatly reduce the risk of having a tangle end your battle. The best overall control is exerted this way. Quality reels are a boon here, defined by the ability to feed out line quickly and smoothly, without overspooling. Fast and far-running trout on light tippet put trout reels to the ultimate test. It's not a drag to slow them down that's needed, it's the opposite effect that counts—a reel that can un-spool a hundred feet of line in seconds with little friction but also without overspooling, and without snapping the 6X tippet.

You don't need a fancy drag. Indeed, that can be a hindrance. These crit-ical moments when the trout explodes and your chances for failure are at their highest are *not* when you want to be diverting your attention by fum-bling around for your drag control. If by chance you set your drag too tight in a previous fight and forgot it till now, a lost fish is your likely outcome. Con-sider that as a trout runs out your line, the acting diameter of the reel drum decreases with the amount of stored line left. This creates its own drag, and at a time when you might not want it to. If you want to slow a fish down, all it takes is a finger's friction on the line or reel spool or a change in rod attitude to increase pressure on the fish. Dinking with a drag system at critical mo-ments guarantees disaster on ultralight tackle, particularly at the outset of the fight. A reel that can feed out line as fast as a trout wants to go on his initial run without overspooling is your ultimate trout weapon. After all, we're not talking about hour-long duels with hundred-pound tarpon here. An angler should be able to master twelve- to twenty-two-inch trout without the aid of a multihundred-dollar reel's high-tech drag system. The human hands are complex enough for this task.

Mastering the light-line hook set and getting the fish on the reel take practice to become automatic, and automatic is what you want them to be. With these tense moments out of the way, the odds of winning the fight may turn your way. These stages lead to the fight or tiring of the fish, and the landing. To win more battles, each phase of the fight should be considered as clear-cut stages, each to be mastered through experience. Though there is but one line connecting you to the fish, there are many ways it can be broken.

Fighting Trout on Light Tackle

Once hooked, the trout might take a variety of evasive actions. These usually reflect his position in the river and the immediate setting. Older trout often have sanctuaries that are a distance from some feeding stations. They'll head for them as fast as they can, intentionally running your leader through obstructions along the way in a habitual obstacle course. I've watched hooked trout do this in the ultraclear waters of New Zealand. Their speed and deter-mination are astounding, the lack of hesitation a key to their survival.

Trout feeding on small-fly hatches are likely to move over to calmer edge waters, eddies, and flats to feed, where fighting the current is minimized. These trout can be expected to make bolting runs for midriver when the hook is set. On big rivers, seeing your backing isn't a novelty. How you feed out excess slack gathered in your hands, around your feet, or in the bushes is now of paramount concern. Any tangle or knot that causes an abrupt stop in the outflow of your line is likely to break off medium to large trout on fine tippets. This is a common way anglers lose fish right from the start.

Once you get all your slack fed out safely, your reel comes into play, along with the angle and pressure you put on your rod. When the trout has completed his initial run, which can be quite long on broad western rivers, it's time to pressure it back in. What tires a trout most is a sideways and downstream pull, which makes it constantly force its head and body back into a position facing the current. Whenever the terrain allows, move yourself downstream of the fish with the rod pulling downstream and sideways, not up. It is a mistake to stand firm and try to pull a trout that has washed downstream back up to your steadfast position. Sure, you'll land *some* trout this way, but you're more likely to lose big ones. The more line you have out, the more pressure is exerted on it by the current. Every ounce of such added current weight effectively decreases your acting line strength by that amount. If a fish bolts, you now have his weight and his energy plus the weight of the current to contend with, all on an ultralight tippet. The fish could be dead and you'd still have a perceived fight on your hands! Staying close to your fish and just downstream of him reduces these factors to their minimums.

Trying to pull a fish back upstream also lengthens the duration of the fight, which increases the chances of the hook wearing a larger hole in the trout's mouth and pulling out. Consider that you are effectively pulling the fly in a direction that's up and out of his mouth. Hooks bent straight are another likely result here.

When fighting a trout from the down-and-across angle, you're pulling the hook back in to the corner of its mouth, the surest holding position. You'll wear it out in the shortest time, which translates into lessened chances of escape. It takes practice to know just how much pressure you can put on various strengths of tippet, but it is likely to be more than you'd think if you're a beginner. The leader can take quite a rod load if the pressure is smooth and steady.

It's the power surges and head-shakes that pose the greatest risks under heavy pressure, along with jumps. In these cases, pressure must be slackened instantaneously by letting go of the reel handle, pointing the rod toward the fish, and releasing finger-braking tension of line or reel. This is the real trick

Use of the Rod in a Light-Tackle Fight

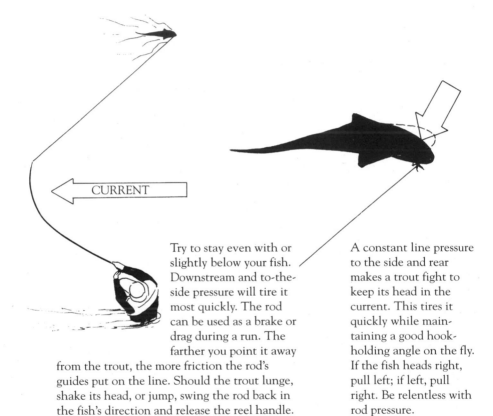

CURRENT

Try to stay even with or slightly below your fish. Downstream and to-the-side pressure will tire it most quickly. The rod can be used as a brake or drag during a run. The farther you point it away from the trout, the more friction the rod's guides put on the line. Should the trout lunge, shake its head, or jump, swing the rod back in the fish's direction and release the reel handle.

A constant line pressure to the side and rear makes a trout fight to keep its head in the current. This tires it quickly while maintaining a good hook-holding angle on the fly. If the fish heads right, pull left; if left, pull right. Be relentless with rod pressure.

of light-tackle fights—knowing when to let up pressure, and doing so instinctively. A second's hesitation can be too much. Until you've played many a fish, it's hard to master this "feel" of nerves and equipment. You can always play them easier and take longer doing so, but there is some deep and mysterious pleasure in knowing just how much pressure you can put on a fish and your tackle, and how far you can push the battle your way. This experience really comes in handy when extralarge specimens are hooked in settings fraught with disaster, such as logjams, rock gardens, rapids, and tangled banks. A trout on a steady glide allows you to put an amazing amount of "rod torque" on him, even with a very light tippet. One that throws his head from side to side and makes short, wild lunges is of much greater concern.

Throughout the battle the fish will likely change directions several times, which should bring a like reaction from you in positioning and rod angle. If the fish swims right, pull the rod sideways to the left. Should the trout dart left, swing the rod to the right. Keep a steady and unending pressure on him till he's led in.

Trout hooked along deep banks can have a different reaction. Instead of running, they might just wallow under the bank, rubbing the irritating fly against the bottom, as trout are wont to do. They might go straight for entanglement, which is perhaps the worst of light-tippet scenarios. There may come a time here when maximum pressure needs to be put on a fish to lead it away from cover. Smooth and steady power has been known to move them

Be prepared to let up on the pressure whenever the trout makes a powerful run or jump. This should become an instinctive part of your trout-playing skills.

better than erratic and vibrant force, which increases panic. At times it comes to parted company. Ultralight tippets can be no match for big fresh fish with an undeniable urge for tangling line. In other cases you'll just be able to pry them away once, twice, and yet again before they tire and are brought to net. The skill with which rod, reel, and line are manipulated, and thus the trout, is the deciding move in the chess match of light-tackle small-fly fishing. Successfully meeting those challenging situations when knowing how much pressure your light tippet can take are hallmarks of experience. Every open run and desperate surge needs the smooth-feeding line capabilities of a quality reel and quick reactions; every gliding lull the steady pressure and proper angle of the bent rod. The fight is like a boxing match with the opponents feeling each other out in the early rounds. Knockout victories go to the trout through early break-offs. Late-round decisions usually go to the angler, who wears his opponent down in a calculated fashion.

Fishermen will increase their odds by habitually checking their leaders for frayed spots and weaknesses, and also checking the sharpness of their hooks. Tippets should be changed often, for even long-term water saturation weakens them, not to mention the raking of the trout's teeth. Attention to the river's surface also pays dividends as hatches, "leftovers," and terrestrials are noted. These can vary in importance to individual trout, and with changes in time and location. Attention to detail is a must in the light-tackle arena.

Landing Trout on Light Tackle

Even when the trout seems subdued and can be led over the shallow gravel and weed beds, the battle is not yet won. Another danger point is near if the fisherman wants to hold his prize for a moment and admire its graceful spotted form. The trout can be expected to make a last stand and final rush, a testament to the resolve of wild things to keep their freedom. Once again, the odds can turn in favor of the fish, especially if it is big, strong, and healthy.

There are several elements that can work against anglers when landing fish. The reduced line and leader length beyond the rod tip means less stretch and give is possible. A surge by the fish now can break a fight-weakened tippet. In knotted leaders, which are preferred in small-fly work for their superior casting and fishing qualities, the knots can get temporarily snagged in the rod's eyes during last-minute rushes by the fish. Consider that the leader may be twelve to fifteen feet long, and the rod eight to nine feet. Those few extra feet of knotted leader traveling up your rod as a fish is being landed have been known to hang in the eyes or guides. If the trout makes a second run now, a break-off can be expected. One must be extra-ready to drop the rod tip and let the fish go, and maybe even wiggle the rod tip up and down a bit while pointing it at the trout to free knots from the rod's eyes. Expect a last-ditch attempt at escape as you lead the fish to the shallows, which will repre-sent extreme danger to the battle-weary trout. If it happens, you'll be ready for it; if not, you can lead him over the rim of the net.

When a trout is brought into extremely shallow water and sees the angler, panic is the natural reaction. Over the decades and centuries fishermen have found ways to avoid this panic factor, reducing the risk of last-second losses. Some early English anglers would stay hidden during the entire fight, crouched in streamside rushes. They'd never let the trout see them through-out the fight and landing, which reduced the fish's panic level sufficiently to land it on the fragile leaders of that day. Lee Wulff popularized tailing At-lantic salmon in thigh-deep water, again lessening the last-second panic fac-tor by not dragging the fish up into ultrashallow water.

Today's angler seldom hides from his fish but can reduce these panic losses by netting trout out in knee-deep water rather than at the bank. An-other old ploy is to kick some silt up as you bring the fish in. When it can't see well it will tend to be easier to subdue. You may have noticed that when trout are landed with weeds draped over their eyes, which effectively blinds them, they can cease fighting altogether. Bringing trout over the net in silted water sometimes has similar quieting effects.

Light-tackle landings are further jeopardized by the possibilities of frayed tippets and straightened hooks. Both tend to become more likely the longer the fight is drawn out. This is another reason for fighting your fish as effec-tively as possible right from the start. Trout have sharp teeth, and as they switch angles, shake their heads, and roll during a fight, their teeth can con-stantly rake the tippet. Small light-wire hooks can bend straight, too, if the fight goes on too long in heavy currents. Trout over ten pounds have been landed on #28 hooks, though, and holding abilities of small hooks are excel-lent. Skill in fighting and landing quickly maximize the light-tackle potential.

A net is almost compulsory in small-fly fishing because you can't drag a big fish in by the leader, as you can with small fish on heavier tippets. A vio-lent head-shake of a medium-size fish can break 5X tippet when you're hold-ing the leader firmly near the trout. Being out in a broad flats with no net is most troublesome. I always seem to break off fish and flies while scrambling to grab fish in such situations. Rolling them on their backs while they are still in the water is a good way to pacify them. Even when using a forceps release, you have to stabilize trout to get a grip on the fly. A net is a necessity here.

Trout should be led over the net head-first, not scooped up tail-first, which causes many losses. If you can get the fish sliding in, head up and on his side, and keep him coming under steady pressure, he's ready to be led over the rim of the stationary net. This is preferred to scooping wildly, which understandably increases a fish's panic. Once his head and the bulk of his body is over the rim of the net he can be safely scooped. Keep him in the water where he can breathe.

If you're without a net and have a big fish on, beaching will be the most promising way to land him. Pick a gently sloping beach if possible, one that will cause the least amount of damage to the fish. Half-submerged grass or weed beds are ideal. Smooth gravel and silt are okay, but jagged and abrasive rocks should only be used as a last resort. In the latter case, it would be better to break the fish off rather than land it, or reach down to undo it in the water, if possible. Gorges and steep areas of rapids can make no-net landings on light tackle very difficult.

Beaching a trout works well because trout are ineffective at swimming backwards or backing up. The trick here is to keep the fish coming head-first. In this way every move it makes merely pushes it farther up the beach until it is stranded. As long as you keep its head pointing up the shore, you're likely to capture it. Should the geography allow, you can just walk backward, leaving your entire leader and a bit of your fly line out the rod tip. This will allow for more shock absorption while the beaching is taking place. If the trout gets its head off to the side, it's bound to make toward midriver again. As soon as the fish is stranded, run up and get a gentle hold on it, placing it quickly back in the water. If you hold it upside down while it's in the water, you can usually get it unhooked with as little struggle as possible. Make efforts not to squeeze it or flop it around on the ground. This same upside-down method works well with netted trout, too, and you can keep the fish submerged through the whole operation, minimizing the chances of handling.

Many anglers using barbless hooks like to use forceps to remove the fly, and do not touch or lift the trout at all. This is the best route to go. Barbed hooks—even tiny ones—don't always come out so easily. Forceps can ruin a good dry fly that's troublesome coming out. I wish they made forceps with a lining of rubber teeth so it would be less damaging to flies.

Trout being released are held gently facing the current, until they take off on their own accord. Slower-paced edge waters are preferred over heavy currents.

Releasing Trout

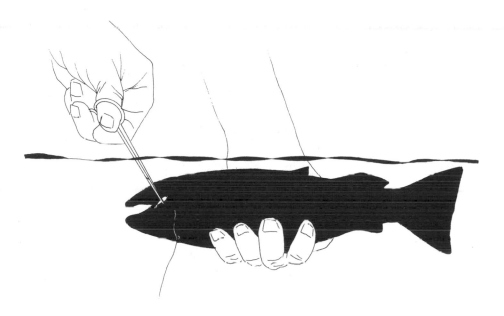

Rolling trout over on their backs tends to pacify them, easing the task of release. Barbless hooks and forceps make the unhooking process easier yet. Keep the trout in the water as much as possible, if not all the time.

One thing I've noticed here is a different reaction after release by different species of trout. Browns are apt to sit right where you release them, or very near, especially if they are exhausted. They often remain motionless but upright on the bottom for up to half an hour. If left alone, such a fish will just rest there, heaving its gills. If you touch it, it will then take off and rest elsewhere.

Most rainbows, on the other hand, tend to swim away, far and fast, getting as much distance between you and them as possible. This is just one more little behavioral trait that shows evolutionary differences between rainbows and browns. Browns seem much more likely to depend on their camouflage, while rainbows generally prefer flight. Browns are even known to bury themselves partially in stream- and lake beds, enough to stay hidden from probing eyes.

Landing trout on the finest tackle is a moment of truth. To many anglers the visible take is the real thrill. For me, admiring the trout's coloration and spotting before the release is an important ritual, especially with brown trout. Perhaps this is why I've never been overly interested in night fishing or fishing in light so low that the fish's color can't be fully appreciated. What's the point? Sometimes I'm content not to fish at all but just to watch the river and its fish, appreciating that there are still places of such beauty left in a world that's rapidly being overrun with human habitation. Trout are perfectly adapted to and formed by their world and are as beautiful as anything in nature. So, too, are the mayflies they feed on and the swallows soaring overhead.

On other days I like to feel the flex of graphite and oars, to feel the pull of the current and cast dry flies to steady-feeding fish. It is the equipment we'll look at next, and even though it's only as efficient as the caster wielding it, there is no doubt that today's fly gear is superior in every regard to the rods of my youth. Nowhere are the modern advances in line, leader, hook, and rod technology more pertinent than to the fishing of small flies.

Equipment for Fishing Small

S mall-fly fishing in the West can place conflicting demands on tackle when it comes to delivery, presentation, and the fighting of trout. The birthplaces of the small-fly sport—England and the spring creeks of Pennsylvania—have their own idiosyncracies. They generally feature smaller spring-fed rivers and creeks where casting distances aren't great, and neither is the distance a hooked fish would be expected to run. Indeed, one reads about these trout and their habits of "burying" in the weed beds. Some fish instantly dive head-first toward the bottom, entangling themselves in weeds, where they have to be levered, kicked, or scooped out with a net. Long, sizzling runs do not sound like the rule, from all I've read.

The big rivers of the West are another matter, especially the wide-open prairie fisheries like the North Platte, Big Horn, and Bow, and "wind tunnel" mountain rivers like the Yellowstone and Madison. Punching out casts into the wind is a daily reality. Trout can be big and make long, fearsome runs. Twenty-inch-plus fish are routine possibilities, and they have the sea room to show you your backing.

While the nuances of distorted surface currents are similar East and West, the wind and distance casting can throw another curve into Rocky Mountain fly presentations. Here, thirty miles per hour is a breeze, especially along the "East Slope of the Rockies" from Calgary to Denver. Forecasts of fifty- to eighty-mile-per-hour winds don't raise any eyebrows amongst the locals, though hometown fly fishermen are likely to sit such days out.

These conditions of big, fast, far-running fish and larger windswept rivers have shaped the equipment used in the West. One only has to look at an Orvis catalogue to see how the difference in geography has manifested itself in tackle terminology. There are slight and shorter rods designed for classic eastern streams, and the "Western Series," named for different Rocky Mountain rivers and their various casting demands. Rods designed in the West, such as Sage and Loomis, built their market success on being powerhouse tools that could tackle any condition. They've even had to back step a bit from power into the lighter-line, fine-tippet, and finesse realm. Power *and* delicacy are those conflicting demands.

Reels and lines, too, were defined by the special requirements of western waters. Fast and far-running fish on light tackle demand fine-machined and smooth-running reels. Climatic conditions often call for pounding casts into sweeping breezes while also landing #22 flies delicately with on-a-dime precision. Speed, power, and delicacy must all be well balanced here for maximum results.

Fortunately for fishermen, the highly competitive tackle market has produced the equipment to solve most western fishing problems. Smaller and better hook designs, stronger and finer leader material, and powerful yet supple rods are meeting market demands. Such quality equipment is a major investment these days. It's easy to drop more than six hundred dollars on a rod and reel purchase. The extra dollars spent buy many additional moments of content, though, when it comes to performance and control, especially in demanding situations. And nowhere is performance as critical as in the presentation of small flies to big surface-grazing trout.

Rods

The rod's function is the delivery of line and its manipulation in the form of mends. Because typical western conditions feature larger rivers (as well as numerous small streams) and wind, eight-and-a-half- to nine-foot models are most popular. These can cast far with less effort and mend more line across broad waters than a shorter rod can. The effects of reach casts, stack mends, and so on, are maximized with increased rod length.

When float fishing from a drift boat, the eight-and-a-half- to nine-plus-foot rod also keeps flies well above the heads of others in the boat. This is an important safety consideration. Today's more rigid rods also pick line off the water more crisply than soft rods do, which helps make those high-altitude backcasts possible from your elevated position in a boat. Short, soft rods tend to produce low and potentially dangerous backcasts that could hook others in the craft. Picking line crisply off the water helps in drying flies with fewer false casts, and also makes casting when deep wading or float-tubing easier. Longer rods can propel backcasts higher over streamside brush.

Short rods can have advantages in the close quarters of a bush-bound stream, the kind where willows and beaver ponds flourish. Stalking anglers fishing directly upstream find quick, short rods to be effective close-range tools. One can even make a case for using short rods in the wind, for there is less wind just above the river's surface due to its friction against the water. (Some ancient mariners were known to dump cargoes of olive oil on the sea in fearful storms. The oil acted as a lubricant between wind and water, reducing wave height and turbulence!) Anglers often cast sidearm to beat the wind, though this is a dangerous habit in a drift boat! Overall, the eight-and-a-half- to nine-foot fast-action rod is the ideal tool. Any longer and a rod starts being a workout to cast. Shorter rods certainly have their place and are

Eight-and-a-half to nine-foot rods have the power to deal with a variety of western conditions while retaining the ability to ply small flies as well. Drift-boat fishing, wind, and long required casting distances are common demands, and the extra length and rigidity of these rods then come in handy.

a pleasure to cast in the right situations. If I were to carry but one rod on an outing, though, the nine-footer would be my choice.

The evolution of graphite has revolutionized casting for the average angler. Those slow, lagging casts of old have been replaced by crisp, high-speed deliveries with increased distance potential and accuracy. The amount of time the fly spends in the air has been reduced, the time it can spend on the water in front of fish increased. This is one aspect of graphite that not all anglers have maximized yet. If it takes multiple casts to fool the average selective rising trout, then eliminating "air time" (the time your fly spends going back and forth on casts and false casts) is the one downtime factor you can reduce in order to catch more fish. You might be able to reduce the length of your fly's drift over the trout a little, if you're a careful and precise caster. Low, quick, and delicate landing presentations can be dropped a little closer to a trout's nose than you might think, but the slightest mistake will end the game. No, it's in the air, between deliveries, where the most time can be saved.

Being as close to your fish as possible aids here, because it takes less time to cast a short line than a long one. If it takes ten to twenty casts to fool a wary trout focused on dense hatches of small flies, and you can reduce the time spent recasting by just a couple of seconds, this adds up to a much better catch rate by the end of the day. Older rods and slower casters can spend five seconds or more between deliveries. Graphite speed casters take only two to three seconds. This might not sound like much of a difference at first, but it often translates into a twofold increase in the catch rate over the course of the day. Twice as many fish is a considerable gain. From my guiding experiences, this works in reality as well as on paper.

Lee Wulff clocked some of his casts at close to ninety miles per hour with a short bamboo rod. There is no doubt that high-modulus graphite can propel line at over one hundred miles per hour. It doesn't take a superhuman effort, either, just a rethinking of how a rod works. Speed casting may take less overall energy, since the time you spend casting and false casting is reduced. The time your fly spends in front of fish increases. The need for false casts is also reduced, because the high-speed turnover is more effective at drying out your fly. Let me take a moment here to describe a method of short-line speed casting that may be new to you. It only works well with more rigid graphite rods. I call it, for lack of a better term, "forcing a load."

Late-generation graphite rods can be so rigid that they hardly load under the weight of a short to medium length of line. If one casts slowly, as if he were casting bamboo or early fiberglass rods, the lack of a "load," or the line weight's ability to bend the rod, is even more apparent. Since the rod works like a bow and arrow, with the *unbending* of the rod the force that propels the line (*not* your arm's motion), this is of critical importance.

The traditional casting method with softer rod materials saw the backcast made, the angler waiting for the backcast to fully extend and begin loading the rod (or bending it backwards), the forward cast commence, and another pause taken while the fly line extended in front, and so on. The pattern here was backcast, pause, forward cast, pause, backcast, pause, final delivery. The softer rod throws a slower line, and more waiting is involved while the line extends in the air.

Forcing a load with a rigid graphite rod eliminates those pauses on short- to medium-range casts, and thus greatly reduces time spent casting and false casting. This time saved is put to use with additional numbers of presentations over the fish. Here's how it works.

The rod doesn't need any line to make it bend. Just waving it back and forth rapidly puts a perceived load on it. With rigid graphite it takes more speed, however, to get the rod to achieve the same arc or bend as a slower rod. It straightens, or "dampens," much more quickly, as well.

There are two techniques that will combine in making this forced-load speed cast. One is to cast in slight under (backcast) over (forecast) ovals, rather than back and forth on the exact same plane. These can be very tight ovals resulting in tight high-speed loops on the turnover.

The second and more interesting technique is that of forcing the load on the rod instead of waiting for it to load in the traditional manner. Rather than letting the line's pace be the lead in this dance, the rod will force the action. You push out a forward cast with great but smooth speed. The act of casting loads the rod, line or no line. The line just follows the rod's lead and doesn't dictate the pace. This is where the oval line path comes in. Now you can backcast with no pause at all, having described an oval turnover path with your rod tip. This allows the line to come and go without ever crossing itself, thus eliminating tangles and the need to pause or wait for the backcast to extend. The same goes for the next forward cast—no pause, just a high-speed continuous oval motion. The line will travel as fast as you can move the rod tip at shorter lengths. The faster you move the rod, the greater the load and the higher the line speed. Again, there is no pause, just a high-speed, continuous tight-oval looping of the line—you're like a high-tech rodeo lasso artist.

As line length increases, there comes a point where air resistance does start affecting line speed. This becomes noticeable at midlength casting distances

High-Speed Casting—The Oval Flight Path of a Forced-Load Cast

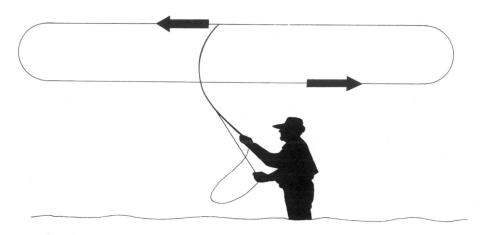

Short- to medium-range casts with rigid rods can be made as high-speed, nonstop ovals. Drop the rod arm and cant it off to the side a bit to get a lower backcast elevation. Bring the forward cast up and directly overhead for maximum accuracy. The speed used for the forward and backcasts loads the rod—the fly line's weight does not. You can cast with a rapid, oval, and nonstop motion of the rod tip, greatly increasing presentation speed. The more rigid the rod, the faster you can force it.

but varies from rod to rod, depending on rigidity. Now you do have to begin pausing as the line shoots back and forth, though not nearly as long as you would with a slower, softer rod. The line speed is much greater.

Forcing a load or speed casting at shorter delivery distances is merely a way to increase your casting and presentation efficiency, especially if you've already paid for a rod that can do it. It is common on-stream to see fishermen who proudly display their latest graphite rod but still cast as if it were soft as a noodle. This is a case of technology outstripping habit. You might remember that when graphite rods first hit the scene, anglers bought fly line that was one weight heavier than the rod manufacturer suggested. This was and still is a widespread practice. Here the manufacturer presented us with the latest technology, but anglers on the whole slapped on the extra heavy line to make the new rod cast like their old, softer favorite! They purposely slowed the fast rod down because they didn't understand its potential or how casting styles might change to match the improvements in equipment. The grace of the old slow-motion cast has been replaced by the simple elegance of efficiency.

This speed-casting technique doesn't work well with softer rods. They tend to wobble when pushed too far. This wobble transmits itself into the line's flight path, causing tangles. You have to slow down and smooth out a soft rod's power strokes.

One alternative is underweighting your rod by using a fly line that's one to three line weights *under* the recommended one. In other words, you could take an older, semirigid 6- to 8-weight rod and fish a 4- to 5-weight line. This setup would work where selective fish plus a dense hatch equal repetitive presentations for success. Speed casting hastens your victories. The same rod could then be weighted with its usual line for casting larger flies and streamers. The light landings and speed-casting potential of the underweighted line is just another way to maximize your equipment's potential, both in effectiveness and in a dollars-and-cents way, too. There are no hard and fast rules or limits, for enough speed will load any rod, and a limber one can cast the

High-Speed Casting with a Too-Soft Rod

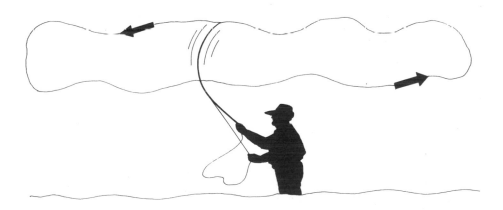

Trying to force too much speed out of a soft-action rod produces rod wobble. This transmits itself to the line, causing an uneven flight path, and often ends in tangles and tailing loops. More rigid rods allow higher-speed casts, which translates into more drifts of your fly over a picky trout's nose in a given period of time. This is one of the great but unheralded benefits of the modern graphite rod: maximum possible presentations per hour.

lightest of line weights. This allows anglers who can't afford to buy a rod for every purpose to vary their line weights and casting styles, maximizing one rod's utility.

The casting-in-ovals technique of speed casting can be used in other ways, too. When waiting for a rising fish to show again so I can get a perfect mark on its position, I'll shorten up my line and cast it in big, open, slow ovals, or even a horizontal circle. This keeps it out of the trout's view and keeps the fly dry, weed-free, and ready to be punched out instantly when the trout gives its position away. Being a self-taught and admittedly rude caster, I've found that keeping my forward and backcasts going on different planes— in ovals of various degrees of openness—helps immensely in avoiding tangles or tailing loops. When cast at high but smooth speeds, lines maintain their aerial tracking better than when cast slowly.

Where anglers have the most trouble with some of today's ultrarigid rods is on the hook set and the playing of big fish on light tippets. Being so stiff, the rod doesn't absorb shock as well, especially at close range. Break-offs are common if the angler can't control his nerves and reactions.

Since a large amount of focus has gone to the fishing of smaller flies across the West in the last decade, graphite-rod makers have developed "light line" or "spring creek" versions of rods, stepping back from the ultrarigidity a bit to meet these special demands. Other manufacturers, and perhaps most notably Winston, have built a reputation on softer-touch graphite rods. The idea here is to have the power through the butt and midsection for some distance and wind-fighting ability (which is no small matter in the West) while still having a soft-enough tip to accommodate shorter casts and shock absorption during light-tackle fights.

Anglers who like the most rigid of casting tools must modify their fish-striking and playing strategies to overcome this lack of flexibility. They must steel their nerves so as not to overreact on the hook set. A mere tightening on the fish with a small supersharp hook will do it. When the fish runs or lunges, line must instinctively be given from a high-quality and smooth-feeding reel.

The other option is to use extrastretchy leaders. Braided butts and bungee butts can be employed, the latter being a rubber-bandlike butt segment designed to absorb shock during light-tackle fights. Some makes of leader have more elasticity than others, too, and by lengthening leaders and tippet sections, a little more stretch and strength is gained. Tippets of three to four feet are not uncommon with small-fly work. They should be changed often and routinely checked for abrasion, for even the normal absorption of water weak-ens them.

Skilled anglers combine these elements so as to be able to use the fastest of rods. These help in making quick, accurate presentations as well as in fighting the wind. Extra distance and control can be achieved, too, and there are al-ways some fish on our broad rivers that seem just out of reach. These are often trout that rarely see a fly and are easier to fool if you can only reach them!

Small-fly work favors lighter-line rods of 3- to 5-weight. The 1- to 2-weight rods on the market are fine for smaller waters and ideal (windless) conditions, but get them out on a broad tailwater in your average twenty-mile-per-hour breeze and they begin to bog down. That's my experience anyway. Even in rela-tive calm periods on big water I've found that it takes me longer to get the fly to my target with the ultra, ultralight rods. To me, this is merely a waste of time with no advantage gained. A stiff 3- to 5-weight will rocket out line fast. Only when your fly is going over a trout's nose are you fishing! Everything in be-tween is downtime, the greatest obstacle to catching fish.

If I were to have but one dry-fly rod, it would be a crisp eight-and-a-half-to nine-foot, 3- to 5-weight, high-modulus rod fishing a weight-forward line. Such a rod can do just about anything, including fight stiff breezes. If an ul-tralight landing presentation is needed to avoid spooking fish, I'll lengthen the leader and tippet a bit, from twelve up to fifteen feet, and perhaps apply some leader sink to eliminate that great nullifier, a floating, surface-contort-ing tippet.

Reels

As I've mentioned more than once, any smooth-feeding high-quality reel is suitable for small-fly fishing. If it has an intricate drag system, be sure to leave it on a minimal setting, as low as it can go without overspooling. There's nothing worse than finally duping a big trout in the shallows, only to find your drag's set on high, intentionally or not. Perhaps you were just streamer-fishing with a heavy leader, or it just mysteriously got turned up to the max. In any case, a break-off on the first run is likely if you don't have the lightning reflexes to find and reset your drag mechanism in a microsecond. You're better off with no advanced drag system at all for this game, rather than one that occasionally defeats you.

Reels of at least medium diameter are recommended. Too small a reel won't feed out line as quickly because the drum diameter is so small. Reeling

in line quickly in a battle is difficult, too, since each turn of the handle brings
in very little line. I have a very small Hardy that I occasionally get into trouble
with on hot edge-water fish. It just won't unspool line fast enough because the
drum is so narrow. You can file down the mechanisms or otherwise modify the
drag systems on some reels, but most anglers expect a quality production reel
to be suited for the job. With small-fly fishing on broad western rivers this can
mean letting a big trout run one hundred feet of line out in a matter of seconds
on 6X tippet, and smoothly enough not to snap the leader. Nothing else really
matters. The Swedish loop reels are an interesting design in this respect, and
have a wide diameter and low start-up inertia to protect light tippets.

Jim Williams, proprietor of Just Reels, in Muskego, Wisconsin, suggests
the following reels as tops in smooth-feeding performance: ATH, Aaron, and
Ascent. He also noted that many reels excel in some regards, but very few excel in all regards.

Sometimes I think it would be interesting to have a high-tech automatic
reel that could be used like a single-action one, or could be spring-loaded to

*The biggest rising fish have moved into the shallowest, slowest water to surface-graze on
Trico spinners. When hooked, such fish can be expected to bolt for midriver. A high-quality
reel with a smooth drag system (set light!) is a great asset in this situation.*

suck in line more quickly when a trout runs right at you. There are western fishing situations where trout running toward you are common and where it's impossible to reel in line fast enough to take up the slack. Such situations include catching bank-feeding trout from midstream positions while wading or drift-boating. The trout usually runs for the sanctuary of midriver when hooked, which in these cases is right at you. Perhaps such a quality reel is a technical impossibility, would be too heavy for pleasant use, or too complicated to master when split-second decisions are called for. I'd sure like to try one, though!

Much is often made about whether you should reel right- or left-handed. Older theory stated that because a right-handed angler has more dexterity with his right hand, that is the one he should reel with. Modern theory states that it makes more sense not to have to pass the rod from hand to hand, so a right-hander should reel with his left. The implication here is that you're too stupid to pass the rod from one hand to the other without breaking off fish. This can happen, too, since the moment in which the rod is passed coincides with those early critical stages of the fight, when the trout is fresh and capable of wild runs, lunges, and jumps. If you prefer to reel right-handed, the trick is to pass the rod over in a noncritical phase of the fight, as when the trout is running line off the reel or just holding in midriver. Worst times to switch hands include when the trout's running out slack line that needs to be carefully attended as it flows through the rod's guides and your hands, or during any wild gyrations, jumps, or head-shakes by the fish. As long as one remains aware of the trout's behavior and the necessary responses to it (such as releasing the reel handle for a hot run or dipping the rod during a jump), one can switch rod hands safely. The thing to avoid at all costs is clamping the line down against the rod handle while changing hands, which makes the feeding of line momentarily impossible. This is when a lunge by the fish will break the tippet.

With practice and experience one can reel with either hand. What I find more useful is being able to cast with either hand. There are times, wind directions, and places where casting with the other hand is beneficial. I find that once one fully understands the mechanics of casting, it's easy to do with either hand. I have more trouble with line manipulation, such as stripping and getting line on the reel, with my right hand, even though I'm right-handed! Practice your casting and line manipulation with both hands, for situations will arise where the benefits of being ambidextrous become instantly apparent.

Lines

Choosing fly lines for small-fly work includes several factors. On western waters, where winds rip and rivers can be big, weight-forward lines have an advantage. Traditional thought leans toward double tapers, both for their light landing qualities and the economic advantages of being able to turn the fly line around on the reel and get more life out of it. The fastidious angler brings both kinds and is ready for any eventuality.

I prefer weight-forward floating lines for their added wind-fighting and distance-achieving capabilities. I find that it takes me fewer casts to work a weight-forward line out to a target, which thus eliminates more of that counterproductive downtime. The lighter weight-forward lines (3- to 5-weights) don't land all that heavily on the water anyway, especially when one uses a reach cast, which tends to float down quietly. In critical situations a few more feet of leader and tippet can be added to distance the line from the fish.

I found it amusing to read in Vincent Marinaro's classic *A Modern Dry-Fly Code*, that he evolved his small-fly fishing gear toward stiff rods and heavy fly line (with a belly dimension of .070 inches, or triple A, circa 1947). He noted that "This was variously described by my friends as clothesline, bull rope, lariat, and so forth; but I can truthfully say that I never enjoyed a more successful season with these difficult fish, and I ascribe a great measure of this success to the use of this [heavy line, stiff rod] combination, simply because I can throw a better slack line presentation." Here Marinaro found the heavy line a benefit when casting cross-stream, bounce-back, slack-line presentations. Lighter fly line, he stated, wouldn't achieve the same bounce-back, slack-giving landings. Consequently, he couldn't get as long a drag-free drift to the selective trout of the Letort. So here we have the angler who started the East Coast small-fly craze actually going the opposite way with rod and line than expected, and with good reason. This was on small water, too.

My thinking falls somewhat along these lines, but for a slightly different reason. While it might initially seem that a 2-weight double-taper line would be best for small-fly work, its casting limitations can slow down your presentations. Working out fifty feet of a 2-weight double-taper in a breeze takes much longer than does zapping out the same length of a weight-forward 3- to 4-weight. The 2-weight man might still be working his line out while the heavier rod has already put a couple of drifts over the fish. That heavier rod can perform a slack-line reach cast with speed and authority with the addition of an extralong fine tippet to fool the fish. Yes, if I were to travel about with only one fly line (and I usually do), it would be a weight-forward 3- to 5-weight, punched out with a rigid rod.

Small-fly nymphing is done with the same floating line. Remember when Sink-Tips came out and were the rage for about the usual amount of time allotted to new products? Since then, most anglers find they have greater control and mending capabilities with floating lines. Leaders can be lengthened or shortened and weight added or subtracted to gain the depth of drift needed. Line pickup for the recast is easier, too. This also eliminates the need to carry around extra spools. The need to switch from dry to nymph and back again can be quite frequent over the course of the day. Having to change lines would be a decided nuisance.

When fishing from a drift boat, I take two to three rods for each angler that are prerigged for varying happenstance. One will be set up with tiny match-the-hatch drys, another with a two-fly rig or indicator nymph, and a third with a big, hideous Woolly Bugger or crayfish imitation. This is one benefit of drift-boat fishing, for you have a built-in "rod caddy" and room for an arsenal of gear that you don't have to carry. I hate fishing without my boat!

And speaking of Woolly Buggers, this is one area in which weight-forward sinking-tip fly lines do have a benefit, and why I carry one along. Not only do they get flies down a little deeper, but their added weight also punches out and turns over in the wind better. The wind is no stranger to the East Slope of the Rockies, either, where many fabled trout rivers flow, from Alberta to Colorado. One could slow-fish small nymphs on a sinking tip on windy days, especially if imitating swimming nymphs (such as *Baetis* and *Callibaetis* nymphs) or crustaceans. Still-water fishermen also use full-sinking lines in some lake-fishing applications. From a stream-fishing small-fly point of view, though, the floating weight-forward line is most commonly used, with the double taper coming in a close second. I've also used the Lee Wulff Triangle Taper and find it to be an excellent casting tool. The one minor problem I found with these is that their extrathick midsection catches a little more wind. Outside of that, the design is superb.

The color of fly lines is something many anglers don't think much about. Often a bright color is chosen for easy viewing, as sort of an extended-fly directional pointer and strike indicator. The only place I've seen fly-line color seriously scrutinized on a daily basis is in New Zealand. There, anglers go so far as to dye their lines gray or green so the big clear-water trout don't see false casts in the air or line across the water. Fortunately, today's manufacturers have taken this into consideration and produce lines of various colors, tones, and hues.

One interesting treatment of line color is analyzed in the British team of

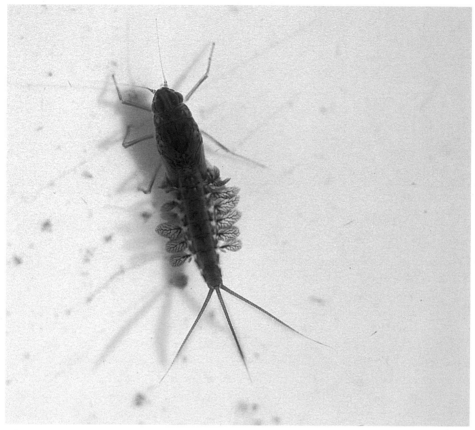

This Callibaetis *nymph, as well as* Baetis, Siphlonurus, *and damselfly nymphs, is among the swimming naturals that can be imitated with movement on a floating or sinking-tip line.*

Brian Clarke and John Goddard's modern classic, *The Trout and the Fly.* This excellent book gives views of fly lines both in the air and on the water. The most notable zone in which fly-line color is apparent to trout is not in that infamous "window," or in the air (you shouldn't be false-casting over fish anyway!), but across the surface beyond the window. This area, which a trout sees as a mirror actually reflecting the river's bottom or green depths, is where a white or bright-colored line stands out like a sore thumb and a medium to darker green one blends in nicely. "Streambed brown" would be a good line color addition, to match that lovely cobbled gold-brown you see reflected up on shallower streams under the midday sun.

Any color fly line is highly visible in the trout's window, and it shouldn't be there anyway. Clarke and Goddard assert that white or light bright-colored lines should not be used when trout are close to the surface. Since trout can see farther across the surface the deeper they are, one would expect this reasoning to carry over and perhaps be of greater importance when deep nymphing (though some trout nymphing hard will have such a "nose down" attitude that they scarcely notice any goings-on overhead). Using extralong leaders of twelve or more feet should keep your fly line completely out of a surface-feeding trout's view.

Another point of interest concerning the trout's window and beyond is the visibility of your leader. Here again the Clarke-Goddard book has an excellent photo showing how visible floating leaders are compared to sunk ones. An application of leader sink such as Orvis Mud helps disguise your tippet, while high floating leaders telegraph your furtive designs. It's the surface distortions created by the leader that really show up as a combination of glare spots and shadows. These are highly evident to fish. Sunk leaders are *much* less noticeable.

New on the scene are sinking leaders make of fluorocarbon material. These are available down to 8X and have some pluses and minuses in the performance department. Pluses include the sinking capability. This material is supposed to be less visible to fish, as well. It is a little stiffer and more abrasion-resistant than nylon. It doesn't absorb water and weaken as fast as nylon does, and it has good ultraviolet radiation resistance.

On the down side, it has a little less stretch than the best nylons do, and slightly weaker breaking strengths per diameter. If minimizing your leader's visibility means fooling more fish, then these semimarginal weak points can be overlooked. One will just have to use his fish-fighting skills all the more conscientiously.

Although this has nothing to do with fly lines, I must mention one further use of the trout's window that Goddard and Clarke mention in *The Trout and the Fly* before leaving this subject. This is the possibility of trout using the mirror to see food items that aren't in direct view, for instance on the other side of a weed bed. The authors credit the Flashback Nymph's attention-getting qualities in part to the trout's use of the mirror's surface in seeing it. The trout in effect sees the top of the nymph, which is catching sunlight and glistening brightly. Today's Beadheads give similar mirror-image advantages. In open water the trout see two images of the same food item, the reflected one above in the mirror, and the direct side view. If nothing else, it sounds alluring on paper!

Fly-Line Color and the Trout's Field of Vision

Beyond the window, the trout only sees the surface as a mirror reflecting the streambed. This is where fly-line color is most noticeable.

The window, through which trout can see into the upper world.

Trout can even see *over* weed beds they can't see *through* using the mirror.

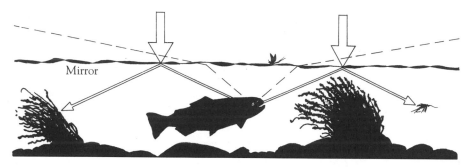

Mirror

Fly-line color is most visible to a fish beyond its window, for it then lies across the mirror. Fly line colored to match the streambed makes the most sense here. A bright line is highly visible. Fly-line color is of less concern in the trout's window. But it shouldn't be there anyway!

Leaders and Tippets

Now we're getting critically close to the trout and working toward the weakest link of the angler's chain of contentment. Leaders receive no end of scrutiny, theorizing, and adjustment. From butt section to tippet, all is subject to constant and historical tinkering. From horsehair to braided Kevlar, every generation looks for a better way to dupe and avoid losing fish. Higher strength and thinner diameter are the goals in leader material. Excellent turnover, elasticity, abrasion resistance, tensile and knot strength, and camouflage are manufacturer concerns. Most modern leaders are excellent, with some excelling in certain respects but seldom in all. It's the angler's physical reaction to the take and battle that tends to break tippets—plus a little luck, power, and evasive entanglement on the trout's behalf.

Leaders play a threefold role in the capture of trout. First, they must cast well and are built to turn over and straighten out in a variety of conditions.

The Trout's View of a Nymph, Using the Mirror

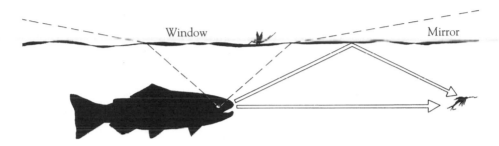

Trout can actually see two images of your nymph in the flatter water where small flies are important. They see the direct side view, plus a second image reflected on the underside of the surface beyond the window, where it acts as a mirror. This allows them a double scrutiny of your fly and has been posited as a reason why Flashback Nymphs (and now Beadheads) are especially effective. The reflected view is particularly bright and attractive. Broken water obviously disperses the mirrored view to varying degrees.

Second, they must be thin and camouflaged enough to fool the trout into disregarding them. Third, they must have the elasticity and strength to land fish—big fish, sharp-toothed fish, jumping fish, and entangling fish. At least in the last case we have reels that can feed out and draw in line. Consider our earliest fishing forefathers, who had to chase big fish around on a fixed and relatively short length of horsehair! Now that's sport!

Butt sections are traditionally stiff, acting as a power transmitter from fly line to lower leader. Good turnover qualities are the primary goal here, and more rigid European leader material is customarily used, including the Maxima and Mason brands.

In the last ten years or so, new trends in butt-section composition hit the market. In part, these were a response to the production of more rigid and powerful rods. Ultralight leaders and very rigid rods are obviously not a good combination unless a device is used to absorb the shock, for the rod no longer does to the same degree. More-elastic butt sections are a solution. Used in conjunction with stronger and more-elastic leader and tippet material, they give the shock absorption necessary to quell big fish.

Braided butts and bungee butts are the commercial response to this modern angling need, with the former getting the lion's share of the market. Braided nylon butts stretch up to four times more than standard mono butts, don't have "memory," or coils, resulting from reel storage, and do a good job of turning over a leader. They are available in floating and sinking models and connect to the fly line with glue or special sleeves.

Bungee butts have made less impact on the market. Their extrastretchy qualities protect fine tippets, but they deteriorate from ultraviolet radiation at a more rapid rate. I have heard of bungee failures on stream, see very few of them when guiding, and see none advertised in any of the big mail-order catalogs.

Since many manufacturers tout the advantages of loop-to-loop butt and leader connections, I'll throw in my two cents worth here. Loop-to-loop connections are designed to make it easy for fishermen, and particularly novices, to attach or change leaders, since no knot need be tied. In my estimation, this is a market ploy. The easier it is to rig up, the more people will fish, and the more they will buy the particular product.

My guiding experiences in the windy West have repeatedly shown that loop-to-loop leader connections work like magnets in attracting light-tippet tangles. The finer the tippet, the more exasperating the tangle that the wind (or poor casting techniques) wraps around your marvelous loops. Their bulk is what attracts these added tangles. I see and undo them on a daily and sometimes hourly basis. It takes much longer to repeatedly cut apart and retie a tippet or lower half of a leader that's tangled in loop-to-loop joinery than it does to tie a clean butt-to-leader blood knot in the first place! You can't escape the wind here, and the cleanest, smoothest knots you can tie will help in reducing the number of wind knots and tangles you have to deal with throughout the day. I routinely see anglers spend as much as a third of their total day (which is usually twelve or more hours on the water when I'm guiding) untangling, so this is no small matter.

This might lead you to think that knotless leaders would be better, but in general their casting qualities are inferior to well-designed knotted leaders. This is because leaders constructed from a combination of hard, medium, and soft or limp mono can provide superior turnover and fishing qualities than can leaders made from just one kind of nylon. They can be adapted to different conditions and purposes. You'll have to tie knots anyway, so don't fall for the loop-to-loop gimmick when it comes to serious small-fly fishing.

If you were just streamer-fishing or using extralarge dry flies, it's not such a problem. The stronger and thicker-diameter leader and tippet used in these cases doesn't tangle so badly. It's that ultrathin, limp tippet needed for small-fly work that loves to entwine itself about a loop-to-loop connection. Enough said.

Other butt materials in use include Hi-Vis (bright yellow or orange) mono, which gives a strike-detection advantage, and flat or oval mono butts, which are supposed to turn over and track better. The Hi-Vis butts come in both flat and round mono. These are fairly common, though, on the whole, flat and oval mono hasn't really caught on.

Whatever kind of material you end up using, be sure to rely on your "nerve control" more than anything. Get your physical reactions to the take of the fly and ensuing battle under mental control. A tarpon hook set will break any leader connected to 6X tippet and a good fish!

The rest of the leader is tied of conventional mono or perhaps a new product like the fluorocarbon leader material, which sinks. By the time this book comes out, several new products will no doubt have hit the scene to capture the imagination of the ever-tinkering fly fisherman.

While the more proper British and East Coast fly fishermen tend to tie up leaders to stringent section-length specifications (perhaps because they have a long closed season to while away), most western anglers I know seldom bother with such intricacies. This is due in part to the different casting distances, styles, and wind conditions. The classic style of elbow-tucked-to-side, short-stream, direct up-and-over the fish presentation calls for a smooth and calculated transmission and turnover of line and leader. The fly is gently tossed over the back of and just in front of the highly educated trout's nose. A relatively short cast is generally used Back East, so the traditional double taper needs a good continuance of calculated taper to achieve just the right delicate turnover and presentation. Shorter, softer rods are also more in vogue.

Western guys tend to be rowdier. Big water, big skies, and big wind are here to buck genteel casts. Enough power and pull-back will turn over anything! I've become more accustomed to the down-and-across slack-line reach cast than to upstream presentations as a consequence of the waters I fish. This allows the extra-power pull-back reach maneuver to straighten out the longest tippets. Imprecise leader "formulas" turn over just the same. It's a whole different way of casting that looks a little more vigorous on stream. That ultrarefined style of the East is often replaced by a "slam it out there" attitude that combines speed, distance, and accuracy in an off-the-hip method that works. Sure, there are many close-up situations where refined casts are needed, but because down-and-across reach casts aren't cast over the trout but rather well above them, more latitude is allowed in getting the fly to its drift lane. Trout are less likely to be scared by the cast itself. I probably pay less attention to my leader than the average angler does, and just keep adding tippet or rebuilding leader sections as needed on-stream without any real formulation. As long as it's gradually tapering and is long enough, the job gets done. My rude and overbearing style punches the fly out there, precise leader formula or not. If it's in the trout's lane, I'm happy. Consequently, I won't bother offering any leader-tying formulas here. I've never used one. They are readily available in numerous angling books, should your casting style be purer than mine. Maybe one day I'll advance to that level. In the meantime I just greet defeats with profanity.

When I do build a leader from scratch, I'm habituated to using what I jokingly refer to as an "Axis power" leader. The butt section and first few segments are tied of stiff German material—Maxima; the rest is constructed of softer Japanese mono such as Dai-riki, Orvis, or Umpqua (one should never forget the lessons of history). This is a typical arrangement for good turnover plus enough subtlety at the fly end of business to fool fish. Such pretied leaders are offered on the market, too. One can add an extralong tippet, three to four feet, for added insurance.

The new fluorocarbon material (which I'm just now toying with) could be just the ticket for spooky trout. This tippet material sinks, which should help alleviate those floating leader situations that can scare educated trout before they even bother looking at the fly. As mentioned earlier, its strength and elasticity rates a little lower than the best nylon leaders, when they are fresh. The benefits of being less visible and more abrasion-resistant could be enough on the plus side to be worth the ten dollars-a-spool price (as compared to three dollars a spool for regular tippet material). Price-resistance will no doubt keep a number of anglers from using such new products, but who will fool the most trout? You could save the expensive stuff for those single big-fish encounters when only the best is likely to dupe them.

Overall leader length will vary with circumstance. I find twelve feet to be a good starting point with small flies on flat water. If a wind chop is on the water, I'll shorten up a couple of feet and ease up on the tippet an X. Broken surfaces mask your leader (and mistakes) much better than slick ones do, especially under the midday sun. With ultraspooky fish, I might stretch the leader to fifteen feet using an extralong and fine tippet. I prefer medium casting distances and speed in deliveries, which turn over twelve- to fifteen-foot leaders in a satisfactory manner. In the wind, extra speed and an extrahard yank back with your line hand might be necessary to turn the leader over. The triple haul will help put the fly on the water where you want it.

When it comes to leader and tippet knots, the latest reports I've read found the surgeon's knot to be definitely stronger than the barrel or blood knot when tested on most every brand of leader material. The blood knot proved even weaker than wind knots! Blood knots give a smoother finished look, though, which helps in minimizing wind-related tangles. Ultraflimsy tippets will tangle around anything if given a chance. Leader knots and loop connections are common tangle sources. I use blood or barrel knots for the heavier butt section and first few leader knots, where strength isn't an issue and a smooth knot is. I use surgeon's knots for the last couple of leader knots, including the tippet connection, if for no other reason than because I can tie them faster on-stream. I was glad to read that they're stronger!

When it comes to knotting on a fly, I'm a creature of habit. There are plenty of good books and manufacturers' pamphlets on knots, so I won't go into any detail in this department here. I will only mention the knot I use, for I see very few freshwater anglers use it. It's called a trilene knot and is nothing more than an improved clinch knot with an added pass of the tippet through the eye of the hook. You go through the eye twice instead of once. This is exactly where most tippets break, and this knot spreads line stress a bit more around the eye, making a stronger knot.

Some anglers prefer loop-type knots that don't bind the fly and allow nymphs to wiggle in a more alluring fashion. I don't have any personal experience with these, though I would initially think that if one piece of ultrafine tippet can put off fish, a loop of it could only be worse. Perhaps it doesn't work out that way in practice, especially with sunk flies, where leaders are less visible.

When you pull your leader off the reel at the beginning of the day, it will have "memory" coils. These should come out when you stretch the leader once. I'll grab a three- to four-foot section at a time and stretch it as hard as I think it should be able to take. One stretch will straighten good leader material. If it doesn't straighten after a couple stretches, change it. Anglers used to use a piece of rubber to rub the line with in order to straighten it, but that's one less piece of equipment you need to carry.

While stretching all of the leader in turn, I also check for weak spots. I stretch it to near its capacity, and if it breaks I rebuild it from there. Feel for abrasions, too, especially in the fine-diameter segments and tippet, which are the weak links to big trout. It's not a bad idea to put on a fresh piece of tippet every time you start out. Fine nylon ages and wears quickly and soon starts weakening just from water contact and absorption. It's worth the extra couple minutes it takes to tie on a fresh tippet so as not to lose prize fish.

Check your leader and tippet for frays after every encounter with a trout or streamside vegetation. A trout's teeth will commonly rake the leader as it's played. A tangle in the bushes or boat can abrade line, too. As weak as 5X to 8X tippet can be after the knots are tied, you don't want to let nicks and abrasions further jeopardize your chances. Checking for frays should become a habitual part of your fishing routine.

When I start casting to a fish, I use the heaviest tippet I think might fool that particular trout in that particular situation. Dry flies generally require a tippet of at least one X narrower diameter to fool fish than a nymph needs. With dry flies in the #16 to #20 size range, I often start with 5X and work down from there if it seems the tippet might be the problem, not necessarily the fly pattern. I might change patterns a couple of times before decreasing the tippet size. Downsizing, however, can be the key. Going from 5X to 6X can be enough to fool a fair percentage of picky fish. You might have to go thinner than that, too.

With #22 to #26 and smaller dry flies, 6X is in order as a starting point. Don't be afraid to go finer if a few fly changes produce no results. Just be prepared to do a masterful handling job with the fish! Try to sink your tippet, too, or try the new sinking fluorocarbon material.

When fishing subsurface, you can usually go up an X in strength when fishing to the same fish, for a sunk tippet is much less visible. Go finer if you need to, though, and be mentally prepared to control your hook-set reactions on the take. Steadily porpoising trout, which are often taking small emergers just under the surface, can require the finest of tippets for this subsurface work. If a big slow-rising trout constantly shows you his dorsal fin and tail, expect this to be the case, especially if he's not leaving an occasional bubble behind. You can try 5X for a while, keeping your leader just to your side of him, but go down in tippet size before you spook him if no takes are forthcoming. These fish can be ultraselective about pattern anyway, and these two factors—pattern and tippet diameter—need to be juggled in a conscientious way. Either or both could be the reason for defeats. Some trout are just about impossible at times, too, and there are occasions when it's a better use of time to go look up another fish.

When fighting a fish on the lightest of leaders, you'll have to let it have its way much of the time. The first few runs must be uninhibited as you feed out line as smoothly as possible. Jumps, head-shakes, thrashes, and entanglement are all critical moments requiring the proper angler reaction but often given over to luck. You can only pressure a trout so hard on the finest tippet, and you'll want to learn by experience just how hard that is with varying strengths of leader. You also need to know when to let off pressure. Any time the trout slows or sulks, maximum pressure should be put on. Practice will certainly be needed to fully comprehend the limits of your equipment.

Having reached the fly end of the game, it's time to jump chapters. For all your pains to get the fly over the fish without spooking it come to naught if he turns down your pattern at the last second. And be assured, many of them will.

Small-Fly Patterns

B ack in the 1960s a new fly-tying concept was slowly formulating, fermenting, and imprinting itself in the minds of fly-fishing's makers and shakers to be. This direction change, popularized by Doug Swisher and Carl Richards's *Selective Trout* in 1971, and Al Caucci and Bob Nastasi's *Hatches* in 1975, combined new generalized tying styles with an intricate study of aquatic insect species. The proper imitative form was captured in a few pattern styles and then adjusted in color and size to match various hatches. Out the door went the helter-skelter assemblages of attractor drys and regional oddities, many of which had no natural parallels on stream and were mere tyer's fancy. That they worked on regional streams was often a testament to the gurgling freestone nature of the water and naivete of their innocent trout. One can still go around fishing "non match the hatch" patterns and catch all the fish one wants on some waters.

But these authors weren't after dumb fish. They were after smart ones. Perhaps this could be viewed as a historic necessity, since the overpopulating of the world, diminishing river resources, and greatly increased numbers of fishermen were educating trout on a never-before-seen scale. The damming of rivers for power and water storage inadvertently created a new breed of trout, too, the tailwater trout. Steady conditions, low river gradients, and rich dam release water turned big marginal rivers into giant spring creeks. Smooth surface flows and tiny insect hatches bred huge numbers of selective fish that can surface-feed all year. *Selective Trout* and *Hatches* concentrated on choosy trout wherever they might be found and came up with more realistic impressionist ties that would appeal to trout rather than to the angler's eye.

Now, one could go back through fly-fishing history and justifiably say that using one tying style and adjusting it to meet many hatches was nothing new. From the old English days on, a few tying styles dominated each epoch and were varied in size and color to match different hatches in their own way. This was especially true in England, where matching the hatch was a fully realized practice from the 1400s on.

Things fell apart a little in the eastern U.S., where brook trout were hungry and any fly would catch some fish. Early American anglers saw little need to match hatches and also lacked the historical background and scientific data on insects that the English had already accumulated. Many Yanks just used British and Scottish patterns. New England fishermen tied flies to please their own eyes and slapped themselves on the back when a brook trout jumped on it. (The same thing can be said of some western cutthroats.) A boxful of fanciful patterns was often the end result.

There were of course more serious students of aquatic life and trout behavior in the Northeast, and the classic Catskill fly-tying style evolved, producing elegantly tied patterns to imitate various hatches. This style was productive and was used to match various naturals using the same basic design.

As the fishing got tougher and the fishermen more numerous, newer, more realistic and smaller patterns became necessary to fool fish in different quarters. And that is where the latest trend toward hatch-matching asserted itself. As the fishing focus spread with the mobile, gas-consuming, traveling public, the West began to dominate the trout angler's imagination. A huge expanse of land, thousands of river miles and hundreds of streams, big fish, and most important, unpopulated countryside, promised glory on-stream in both setting and result. Here, too, the fish are picky, though, sometimes in the extreme. The new West became dominated by serious students of the hatches while still having rivers where attractor flies catch plenty of fast-water fish.

As fishing pressure continues to grow in the West, hatch-matching and new tying styles exert themselves relentlessly and are supported by a growing industry that provides the right products. Smaller and better hooks, an infinite variety of natural and manmade tying ingredients, better rods, reels, lines, and leaders all add up to a level of stream knowledge and expertise that has never been seen before on such a broad scale. Duns, stillborns, emergers, cripples, spentwings, larvae, pupae, nymphs, and worms, there is no aspect of an insect or trout's life cycle that goes without scrutiny. Underwater photography, video, computer programs, and specialty travel agencies all go to show that fishing is indeed ready for the twenty-first century. Creative fly tying goes on at a feverish pitch, and several young tying greats are associated with flat-water, small-fly, selective-trout scenarios.

We will look at fly patterns from two points of view. First we'll consider widely adaptable and general tying styles that are commonly used to match various western hatches. Second, we'll note some specific patterns and include their tying ingredients.

As a last note here, I think it's safe to say that today's angler is less inclined to spend a fishing lifetime depending on a few old favorite patterns. He tends to have current favorites that now change more rapidly. He expects new and more effective patterns to evolve, in some cases knowing that heavily pressured fish can respond well to something realistic and new. When everyone comes to use this new pattern the trout grow weary of it, and yet another new concept will arise to take its place.

Color Groupings

Before looking at tying styles and patterns, let's consider the general coloration of flies, for this is somewhat regimented no matter where in the West one goes. This is especially true of the prolific and widespread hatches of small flies.

There are several color groups, which as we saw are seasonal variations evolved in response to temperature, water level, and sun intensity. The early- and late-season hatches tend to be dark. High-water freestone hatches feature the largest aquatic insects. Mid- to late summer's low-water hatches lean toward lighter-colored insects of smaller sizes. These are fairly universal traits.

Of the color groups, the first is of great importance on a seasonlong basis, and that is the blue-winged olives. The olive body and medium gray wing coloration includes the prolific *Baetis* and *Pseudocloeon* mayfly hatches, plus several *Ephemerella* species, including *tibialis*, *margarita*, and *flavilinea*. Olive nymphs are common, too. Shades of color and tone vary, even among the same species and same dates of emergence, but this general coloration scheme is seen on the water from March to July and again from September to December. Even when PMDs and Tricos dominate the hatch scene in July and August, *Pseudocloeon* mayflies (or tiny BWOs) can put in a showing on rainy and cooler days.

The earliest and latest hatching *Baetis* tend to be the darkest and largest, often appearing a dark gray on the water. Body color can vary from olive toward gray or olive-brown, with hints of olive generally present. The wings are a medium gray, though they can look darker on glaring water.

As spring blooms into summer, the BWO coloration generally lightens. Some late-summer *Pseudocloeon* mayflies feature bright, almost lime green, bodies and pale gray wings. There are lime green summer midges, too, not to mention a variety of olive-green-bodied caddis. Other Pseudos become almost tan.

The *Ephemerella* genus of mayflies features several smaller species with rather *Baetis*like coloration, ranging in size from #14 to #18. Their more developed hind wing is a key in identification. *Baetis* vary in size from #18 to #22, and *Pseudocloeon* from #22 to #26. As you can see, having a variety of BWO-colored mayfly patterns and tying styles from #16 to #24 (and on up to #10 for green drakes and other swift-water mayflies) will cover a good percentage of the season's hatches. Dubbed bodies of gray to olive to olive-brown are used to match these hatches with a variety of wing colors. Some wing

Baetis duns, *also known as olives, little blue-winged olives, or BWOs, are western angling mainstays. Their generally gray appearance on the water masks subtle olive or olive-brown undertones. Have plenty of #16 to #22 patterns on hand.*

materials are meant to match the hatches' color. Others are geared to easier viewing by the angler, for gray wings on a small fly have a way of disappearing on broad waters. White, Hi-Vis orange or chartreuse, and black are among the wing-color options. Olive and olive-brown nymphs are very common in rivers, too, and in a wide variety of insect families and species, including midges, mayflies, caddis, and stoneflies.

The second important color group to fishermen is the pale yellow-green or PMD variations. Prominent hatches of *Ephemerella inermis, infrequens,* and *lacustris* dominate this summer color scheme on most small-fly waters. Some species of *Epeorus* and *Heptagenia* mayflies, which dwell more in swift-water streams; little yellow and brown stoneflies; some smaller caddis; and even midges fit into this general color scheme, too. Most of these lighter-colored hatches begin toward the end of June in the Rockies, and carry on till August or early September. From late June into August the PMDs dominate much of the fishing day. On some rivers late-morning hatches are best, in others early evening is better. PMDs, Tricos, caddis, and midges make up the bulk of the midsummer insect stew on the Missouri, where I spend most of my time.

The trick to this coloration are the other subtle color hues that can be mixed in the natural. Tones of pale green, light orange, and gray are common and are considered to be reasons why matching these hatches is at times frustratingly difficult. While appearing pale yellow on the water, the undersides (which the fish see) can vary widely when viewed close-up. No end of profanity and vise time has been spent trying to design foolproof PMD patterns, and especially emergers. No one to my regionally limited knowledge has achieved total success. Flies in this color range vary from #16 to #24 with #18 to #22 being most useful.

The third color group is almost as important as the PMDs, and more so to some anglers. These are the black to dark gray hatches. Included here are midges, early winter stoneflies, a few very dark gray mayfly species, black caddis, beetles, ants, crickets, cicadas, and the magnificent summer *Tricorythodes* mayfly hatches and spinner falls. Numerous nymphs are nearly black, too, especially the stoneflies and some fast-water mayfly nymphs. At least one of these blackish food items is on the water every month of the year. Hatches of *Paraleptophlebia packi,* the dark blue quill showcase one vary dark, smaller mayfly that is prevalent on the Smith River, where I guide, and elsewhere around the West. In my region, these start hatching in late April and carry on into June, until runoff dilutes their localized importance. They can be mixed in with western march browns (*Rhithrogena*) and *Baetis,* which presents a mixed-hatch situation of darker early-season mayflies. Small black flies will often draw a midsummer trout's attention, too, and can be easier to see on the water in glaring and low-light situations.

The black color of male Tricos is one exception that bucks the trend of light summer coloration. Tricos hatch at the hottest time of year, with the males hatching the night before the next morning's spinner fall. The females hatch in the morning and are more olive than black, actually fitting into the BWO color scheme. The Trico's very short lifespan and small size obviously make coloration and dehydration a nonissue for this mayfly species.

Black-gray midges are found year-round and are of particular importance from late fall to spring. The black and dark brown little winter stoneflies are on the water in February and March, while the larger models become more gray to olive-brown and hatch from late March through July. Beetles and ants are on the water as soon as the spring sun starts beating down between the shoots of winter-browned grasses. They're on the water in good numbers from April on, though most anglers look at them as late-summer options. Beetles are among the most numerous insects on earth, with hundreds of species in the western

This spring Paraleptophlebia *mayfly, known as a dark blue quill, is very* Baetis*like. Note the large hind wing and dark color, which help to distinguish it from* Baetis *mayflies. It produces a common freestone-river hatch in #16.*

U.S. alone. Crickets, too, are common throughout the summer. Smaller black caddis are prominent on some fisheries from late spring into midsummer.

The black color group obviously covers many different insect shapes and silhouettes—in fact all that are to be found on water. Perhaps this is what makes black an attraction to fish. Flies of #16 to #28 are common, with larger patterns up to #8 imitating cicadas and crickets. Small black drys can make good midday summer searching patterns. Beetles are a favorite here. Black nymphs work well, too, in all sizes, from midge pupae to salmon fly nymphs.

The fourth major color group is the brown to tan spectrum. Important here are many caddis, a number of mayfly spinners, some mayfly duns, small stone-flies, midges, and some terrestrials. A great many nymphs are tan to brown too, including midge and caddis larvae and mayfly and stonefly nymphs.

Caddis are most common here, and their often-mottled forms are matched by #16 to #24 fly patterns. Body color can vary from wing color, so look closely at the naturals if you can catch one. The smallest caddis patterns can be used for midge imitations, too, or small terrestrials.

Rusty brown mayfly spinners seem prominent worldwide. In the West, male PMD spinners (and the majority of *Ephemerella* spentwings), *Baetis*, *Heptagenia*, and other spentwings come in shades of rusty brown to tan. Some have pink hues. Variation in color between the sexes is very common in mayfly spinners. Basic reddish brown mayfly spentwings are common in sizes #18 to #24, with some larger models found on swift freestone streams. Paler tan examples are very common in the wild, too.

There are some prominent brown or olive-brown mayfly duns as well, including species of *Rhithrogena*, *Ephemerella*, and *Paraleptophlebia*. Some Pseudo duns are almost tan in color and are as small as #24 to #26.

Notable brownish mayfly duns include *Rhithrogena morrisoni*, known as the western march brown; the brown drake, *Ephemera simulans*, *Ephemerella doddsi*, *coloradensis*, and *tibialis*; and *Paraleptophlebia debilis* and *bicornuta*, which are often called mahogany duns. Most of these are medium to large mayflies, running from #18 all the way up to #10. As with most large-fly hatches, their emergence dates and hours tend to be of much shorter duration than the tini-est fly hatches. Overall, they are of less importance than the BWO, and PMD color groups, but the larger brown duns can certainly be regionally and sea-sonally important. It is the mayfly spinners and nymphs and caddis that give the most action overall in the brown to tan color range.

There are color tones in mayflies that transcend these basic parameters—flies or spinners that are pinkish, subtly purple, and almost pure white. These

Tan- to brown-winged caddis are common and can have bodies of various colors.

are of very limited use to most fishermen. Pale gray is not uncommon and includes a few prominent hatches like *Callibaetis* (speckled dun and spinner) and *Siphlonurus occidentalis* (the gray drake).

The practicality of generalized color schemes is demonstrated in tying particular pattern styles to fish varied waters and hatches. For instance, one can use the thorax tie, a superb mayfly design (which can also pass for a spentwing in a pinch), and tie a dozen in four colors and three sizes each. Let's say you'd tie BWOs in sizes #24, #20, and #18; PMDs in varying hues in #22, #20, and #18; black in #24, #22, and #16; and three brown tones in #20, #18, and #16. Here you have used one tying style to cover the majority of important western small-fly hatches. Color and body tone can be varied for more exacting situations and is something you build on with experience. Wings can be tied to suit different viewing conditions. The tails can even be snipped off the tiny black models on-stream for use as midge and beetle imitations.

This whole color-pattern style approach is an option for fishermen who aren't up (and perhaps don't plan to be) on the entire Latin entomological scene. Understanding all the families of aquatic insects, their emergence schedules, and Latin names does take a degree of study, and time that many fishermen don't have to invest. Instead, observant anglers can just juggle around a few basic tying styles, their sizes, and colors to match what he sees on-stream. This simpler approach will catch a lot of fish. He may even come to know the naturals by their Latin names since so many other fishermen are using that nomenclature for accuracy and universal understanding's sake. For instance, most of today's fly fishermen use the term *Baetis* for a *Baetis* hatch, since it's become common fly-shop lingo. It's also shorter than saying little blue-winged olives. Twenty years ago this wasn't the case. Most anglers were still in the "old favorite" game of buying an assortment of patterns, many with nonhatch-matching origins. Knowledge of western hatches has advanced greatly and been widely popularized.

Imitative Tying Styles to Meet the Hatches

There are a number of prominent tying styles that can be juggled to meet various hatches. Most of these are mayfly and midge patterns, since these are the small-fly types that have the longest and most predictable emergences to bring up the steadiest-rising fish. Also included are a few caddis, emerger, and nymph designs to round out your stream-fishing needs.

Mayfly Duns: Traditional (Catskill Style)

Traditional ties feature a well-balanced formula of tail length, thin tapered body, dual wings, and front-loaded hackle. The tail is generally tied about the same length as the body. The hackle extends just beyond the hook gape in length and is concentrated in the forward third of the fly, right up to the eye. Two hackles are often used. Two wings are set back about a quarter of the way down the shank from the eye.

Common problems beginners have here are proportion, wing placement, a neat job of hackling, and crowding the eye with materials.

Many western anglers have drifted away from this tying style, though it produces some elegant and beautiful dry flies. They have gravitated to some of the following styles because they're more realistic and easier to tie. Some use less-expensive materials, as well, or less of them, a practice that is appreciated by many thrifty commercial tyers and fishermen.

Mayfly Duns: Thorax

Thorax flies feature a single upright wing in the center of the shank (or one-third of the way back from the eye), and a single hackle, center-wound. The bottom hackles are clipped so the fly sits flat on the water, more like a real dun. It can also pass for a spentwing, and the wing can be trimmed off. The tail is usually split into a V for added realism and flotation. This fly usually lands right-side-up due to its design, more so than traditional ties do. The proportions are more realistic, too.

Thorax flies are easier to tie than are traditional drys. The one wing and centered sparse hackle give tyers plenty of working room, even on the smallest patterns. Crowding the eye is obviously not a problem. Only one hackle is needed, and this is often tied in sparsely for added realism on flat water, for the naturals only have six legs, not one hundred and six. This is one of the best, most natural looking all-around mayfly patterns.

Mayfly Duns: Comparaduns

This now classic Caucci-Nastasi pattern was formulated to match various hatches. Its simplicity, ease of tying, and durability make it a popular small-fly choice. It floats well, takes repeated chewing by trout, and is very inexpensive to tie, for no expensive hackle is needed. This last point alone is the deciding factor for many!

Comparaduns are updated versions of the older Haystack pattern. They feature a V-split or fanned tail, dubbed body, and deerhair wings. What could be simpler? As with all these stylized patterns, body, tail, wing color, and size are adjusted to meet local hatches. Many anglers agree that size is often the crucial factor.

After you get the hang of keeping the dubbed body thin and wedging the wings in properly, there can hardly be a fly so easy to tie yet so universally effective. These, too, can be taken for spentwings (and also emergers and cripples), for the underside silhouette shows a trout just that shape.

Mayfly Duns: Sparkle Duns

Sparkle Duns are a more recent variation of Comparaduns featuring a Zlon tail that's meant to imitate a nymphal shuck. This surface emerger has really caught on in the last five years or so.

Like the Comparadun, this style is easy to tie and is durable, though Zlon seems a little overpriced. It doesn't take much as a tail/shuck on a #20 Sparkle Dun, though. Although this Z-lon tail looks nothing like a half-empty nymphal shuck in reality, it pleases the modern angler's technical mind and catches a lot of fish, making these patterns small-fly mainstays of late.

Mayfly Duns: Hairwing

These are sort of a mayfly-caddis cross in style and are now tied to imitate a variety of mayfly hatches. This modern dressing was preceded by a similar pattern called the Colorado King. It had a fully palmered hackle and split peccary or moose body hairs for tails. Today's popular ties feature hackle just around the thorax and tails of split Micro Fibetts or hackle fibers. The hackles can be trimmed from the bottom, if desired, for flat-water work. The wing is tied Elkhair Caddis style and can be varied in coloration to match the hatch or provide better viewing. Since mayfly wings are actually raked back, and don't stand straight up, this gives a realistic silhouette. The dubbed body should be kept on the sparse side and colored to match the natural. This is a durable and easy tie that also floats well on rougher water.

Mayfly Duns: Swisher-Richards No-Hackles

These exquisite-looking patterns are excellent match-the-hatch flies, especially in smaller sizes, but lack the durability of most other patterns. The duck-quill wings can get haggard after a couple of chewings by trout. It's good to have a couple on hand, though, when dealing with that one extra-picky rising fish. In my years of guiding I'd have to say I see fewer anglers using these patterns compared to some of the others mentioned. They aren't too difficult to tie, though the wings take a little finesse. Otherwise the materials are cheap, and the fly is easy to tie and effective. I sometimes use duck quill for *Baetis* wings on thorax patterns, for I can obtain shades of gray that almost exactly match the natural.

The tails are a V on these No-Hackle ties. They look realistic that way and are often spoken of as "outriggers." These are tied from hackle fibers or Micro Fibetts, a synthetic substitute. The fur-dubbed bodies should be kept trim and altered to match local hatches. Gray, olive, olive-brown, and PMD blends are among the most common colors used.

Mayfly Duns: Parachutes

Parachute ties are among the best and most widely used dry-fly patterns. Their effectiveness on fish and evident visibility for anglers is a great combination. They are easier to tie than conventional dry flies, having a single upright wing. Crowding the eye with materials shouldn't be a problem. Since the fly's body sits in the water, it can be taken for a dun, emerger, cripple, or spentwing by fish. I find that a lot of trout will take them at the tail end of a Trico spinner fall, where even oversized ones are apparently taken for leftover spentwings.

Parachutes are tied to match most hatches, even as small as #24 Tricos and Pseudos. There are also Parachute caddis and hopper patterns. The Parachute tie of winding hackle horizontally around an upright wing post provides excellent buoyancy. The splayed hackles can pass for legs or spentwings to the trout and can even be trimmed to form more realistic spentwing shapes.

I vary the wing color to meet different viewing criteria, as discussed earlier. Variants of Parachute Adamses are among my most commonly used dry-fly patterns, in all sizes.

Mayfly Duns: CDC ((ul de (anard)

Cul de Canard dry flies are an old Swiss creation that was popularized in France. The naturally oily feathers found around a duck's rump are what the name suggests. These few feathers that surround the "preen gland" have an innate buoyant quality until sunk by a fish or by prolonged use. Dry-fly crystals can help bring sodden flies back to life, but floatant isn't used on them.

The bodies of such flies are generally match-the-hatch dubbing, and the tails are of hackle fibers, CDC feathers, or Z-lon. The CDC wings are tied in a variety of ways, including swept-back, spent, and Comparadun style. These

patterns often transcend the
dry-fly realm and are frequently
used for surface emergers, where
the body is half-sunk and the
CDC wings are floating and
dancing above. Cul de Canard
feather fibers are wispy and give
subtle movement on the water,
which could be one ingredient
in their success. These patterns
have gone through a rapid evo
lution in the U.S. after having
been ignored for so long.

Mayfly Emergers

Trout are often said to eat 80 percent of their food subsurface. With
mounting fishing pressure, trout grow leader-wary and can shun dry flies because the tippets are so visible on the surface. In the last decade or so,
emerger patterns have carved themselves a large chunk of the fly market.
This stage of the natural, between nymph and fully winged adult, is particularly vulnerable to predation by trout. Nymphs that tried to stay hidden most
of their lives swim up in front of the trout's nose, hesitating at the surface to
molt and then climb up on top of the surface film, where they meet new foes
in a brave and arid new world. Imitating this transition phase now takes up
much of a serious fly tyer's time.

There are hatches where emergers are generally preferred over duns. I find
this particularly true of PMDs (especially toward the end of their seasonal
emergence period), and with caddis. There are even some mayfly species reputed to shed their nymphal shucks near the streambed and rise to the surface
as already winged adults. These tend to be medium-sized swift-water species
(some *Rhithrogena* and *Epeorus* mayflies), and are fairly well imitated with traditional wet flies, Soft-Hackles, and now Beadhead variants. The following
emerger tying styles are productive on varied waters across the West.

Mayfly Emergers: Traditional Wet Flies

This classic configuration still catches plenty of fish, especially in swifter
rivers. Certain species of *Epeorus* and *Rhithrogena* mayflies are known to swim

to the surface as winged adults, having already shed their nymphal shucks near the bottom. This shape can also pass for a caddis emerger or sunken dun or spinner. Traditionally, these patterns were tied in medium sizes, #14 to #10 or so. I can't say that I've seen too many people fish miniature models in the #18 to #22 range. Such miniwets could be fished as "cripples" as well, mayflies that have been unsuccessful in hatching and remain trapped in the river's surface grip. This is common with some hatches, including those of *Baetis* and *Ephemerella* species. I tie tiny wets down to #24, using partridge for wings, almost like Soft-Hackles. I have found these to be attractive to selective fish, even if they are surface feeding. A slight down-and-across drag that swings into their view often brings a veering take. I have beginners use these as droppers at times, especially if they can't get drag-free drifts at critical moments.

Whenever trout shun larger flies and popular ties because of fishing pressure, going small can be enough for added success, even using the exact same patterns of old. Size is often the key ingredient. Beadhead versions of traditional wet flies would have obvious advantages in deeper broken freestone runs. A size #18 is about as small as you can tie Beadheads, because it's hard to get the bead round the bend of a smaller hook.

Mayfly Emergers: Soft-Hackles

Soft-Hackles are another old and traditional style that has had a rebirth in popularity of late, due in part to the promotion of Sylvester Nemes. These simplistic emerger patterns work through their swimming movement in the water. The soft partridge hackle pulses in a tantalizing fashion. These, like traditional wet flies, are fished down-and-across in a controlled drift, not too fast, and swung in front of bulging, rising, or imagined trout. They can be fished dead-drift in the surface film to imitate emergers or cripples. Here is another case of an inexpensive, simple, yet universally effective fly that's fun to fish. Beadhead versions are doing excellent business as well, and can be allowed to sink deeply before line pressure slowly draws them to the surface on the down-and-across swing. Takes by fish on tight lines can be bold. It's best to up your tippet strength an X when swinging wets and Soft-Hackles in the currents. Trout can take sinking Beadhead models for diving egg-laying caddis, too.

I often have beginners swing Soft-Hackles from the boat right in front of ultrapicky and spooky surface-feeding trout. A percentage will move for the subsurface Soft-Hackle and hook themselves on the lunge. I tie them down to

#24, though at that size you can't always wind the hackle on in the traditional way. I just clip bits of partridge and piece them in because ultrasmall Soft-Hackle feathers are not always at hand. One can substitute any soft and even downy feather to match a desired color scheme. In that way you can even swing them in front of Trico-feeding trout, as Syl does on my home river.

Mayfly Emergers: CDCs

Cul de Canard emergers have proven their effectiveness time and again. These can be tied just like CDC drys, but with shortened wings. One can match the nymph's body and tail coloration, but not the dun's, for you're imitating the emergence process. These, too, have some built-in motion, for CDC fibers are very supple and independent. They are easy to tie and are workable down to the smallest sizes. The length of the CDC feathers can be varied to imitate a fresh emerger, cripple, or dun while using the same basic design. One can use dubbing, pheasant-tail fibers, or wound marabou in an attempt to get a good nymphal imitation out of the body.

Mayfly Emergers: Hairwing Cripples and Emergers

These flies are tied to imitate the dun trying to escape its nymphal shuck at the surface. A deer- or elkhair wing points forward and supports a more water-absorbent body and tail. On the water the hook and tail end should sink, leaving the wing pointing up, like a natural. The wing and thorax are colored to match the dun, the rest of the body and tail to match the nymph. These are tied to match hatches varying from PMDs all the way up in size to monster *Hexagenias*. They have proven effective on a variety of tough western waters from California to Idaho and beyond.

Mayfly Emergers: Parachutes

These are basic offshoots of Parachute drys but are refined for picky fish concentrating on surface emergers and cripples. Instead of a full-fledged wing, a ball of dubbing or foam is used. The unfurling wing can be tied in a match-the-hatch color, though with the BWOs this makes them fairly difficult to spot on the water. The other option is to use a white or Hi-Vis colored wing clump. One can also take a standard Parachute fly, trim down the wing, and thin out the hackle a bit. The Parachute-wound hackle on these floating nymphs is generally wound very sparse for realism. The tail is usually in a V for looks and "outrigger" support.

One effective variation I've used in Montana and New Zealand features a pheasant-tail-fiber body. That coloration matches many nymphs, emergers, duns, and spentwings. Fish like it!

Mayfly Emergers: Beadheads

Beadheads seem to catch fish no matter how they're tied. Some like to think the bead imitates the now legendary gas bubbles that develop under the nymph's shuck and help buoy it to the surface upon emergence. Others have derided the bubble theory based on years of their own tank observations and photographs. There are mayflies and caddis that crawl

or dive underwater to lay their eggs on the bottom or beneath streamside debris. These *do* trap bubbles of glistening air when descending, which would be highly visible to fish. I have seen both *Baetis* mayflies and caddis do this.

Regardless of the reason, fish are attracted to Beadheads. Perhaps it's just their visibility and the fact that they can drop down deeply, in the trout's face. That's all that is needed sometimes to fool a good percentage of fish. Beadheads added to nymphs, wet flies, Soft-Hackles, and emergers are worth having on a percentage of your flies, especially in nonhatch periods.

On big tailwaters, freestoners, and spring creeks, trout will settle into summer residences and can be relied on to be there once you know a river well. Deep-sunk Beadheads fool many such fish, whether the angler is wading or fishing from a boat.

Mayfly Emergers: Mayfly Nymphs

Mayfly nymphs have a generalized shape that fits into stylized tying quite well. Size and color can be adjusted to imitate most species. Tan to brown and pale to dark olive covers a high percentage. Throw in a few offshoot tones like amber, reddish brown, olive-brown, to black and most all fish can be fooled. Wing pads on the naturals tend to darken just prior to emergence.

One notable generalization that can be made is that fast-water mayfly nymphs tend to be wide, with prominent legs and gills, while slow, rich water mayfly nymphs are usually smaller, thinner, and more streamlined. Fast-water models are "clingers" and "crawlers." Slow-water ones are usually swimmers who tuck their legs in and use body undulations to swim among weed beds and cobble.

Frank Sawyer, the infamous British riverkeeper and designer of the world famous Pheasant Tail Nymph, purposely left legs off his pattern after noting how the natural *Baetis* nymphs he was imitating tuck their legs in and out of view when swimming. He tied copper into his nymphs to get them down quickly, and used an "induced take," or slight swimming motion in front of visible trout to get them to take. This was a pure sight-fishing game. The reddish brown color and segmented effect matches many mayfly nymphs around the world, particularly in spring-rich drainages.

On the faster-water side of the hill, the Hare's Ear is the classic configuration—wider and scruffier to imitate the configuration of most swift-water nymphs. All that protruding hair and the disheveled look imitates flared gills and prominent legs. The New Zealand version of this fly, the Hare and Copper, takes this scruffiness to extremes, and the trout love it!

Slower-paced rich-water mayfly nymphs are small on the average, ranging from #18 to #24. There are larger slow-water mayflies, as well, including the biggest, brown drakes and *Hexagenia*, which are as large as #8. These burrow tunnels in siltier substrate and are not readily available to trout. *Callibaetis* and *Siphlonurus* nymphs might also be found. These, too, are active swimmers in the medium- and large-size range, respectively, #18 to #14 for *Callibaetis*, and up to #10 for the gray drake, *Siphlonurus*. These are nowhere near as numerous as the smaller *Baetis*, *Pseudocloeon*, and *Ephemerella* nymphs, which make up the bulk of a summer trout's diet. These nymphs, by the way, can show a great latitude in color variation within the same species, from amber to brown to all shades of olive.

Swift freestone river nymphs average larger. Individuals #18 to #14 are common enough to keep trout happy. There are smaller immature ones, and those giants of the streambed, salmon fly nymphs, as well. The big stonefly nymphs actually bury beneath the streambed in many instances and are not as available to trout as are the multitude of medium-sized naturals come midsummer.

Spentwing Mayflies

Spentwing mayflies present a very basic shape to fish, one of trim body, long tails, and splayed clear wings. The delicate nature and glass-clear wings have always presented tyers with a subtle challenge, and anglers with an absolute necessity of dead-drift presentations. Various wing materials have been used over the years, including clear plastic sheeting, hackle fibers, hackle tips, and as of late, CDC and Z-lon. White polypropylene fibers have long been a standard spentwing material. The natural's clear wings often look white when they have pockets of air trapped between them and the surface. Parachutes, Comparaduns, and Thorax Duns can also pass as spinner patterns because they give the right silhouette when viewed from underneath.

Spentwing Mayflies: Poly Wing Spinner

This old-time tie is still very effective when tied on to the perfect drag-free drift! Size and often color need to be close to the natural. Long split tails, often using the exact number of fibers as the natural's tail, are features here (mayflies have either two or three tails, depending on the species). Dubbed or quill bodies are kept very trim. In the smallest sizes, only tying thread need be used. The wings are tied about one-third to one-fourth of the way down the shank from the hook's eye. These lie out flat, tied at a ninety-degree angle to the shank. Because these flies lie flush on the surface, they can be hard to see, especially in the smallest sizes used for Tricos and Pseudo spinners, #22 to #26. This is why some anglers use tiny Parachutes for spinner patterns or use a larger fly as a strike indicator.

Midge Dry Flies

These patterns first evolved on British chalkstreams, where midges were known as "smuts" or "the angler's curse." In the old days, hooks weren't manufactured small enough to make realistic imitations. Failure during midge hatches was the rule, even though the hatch was well enough understood. By the beginning of the twentieth century smaller hooks were being made, but still not small enough for routine midging success. Today's angler is blessed with quality hooks to the smallest sizes, #28 and even #32. Now there's no excuse!

Midge Dry Flies: Traditional

Traditional midge drys are tied like minimayflies minus the wings. Size can be the over-riding factor with midge pat-terns, and these can work well if they are small enough for your fish's tastes. Although the natural midge lacks a promi-nent tail, it's included in these fly patterns for proper flotation. Trout can mistake it for a shuck, too, with the fly passing

for an emerger if you're the realist type. Modifications could be made to further enhance the tail as a trailing shuck, which is a very common phenomenon with the naturals on-stream.

The basic midge dry is often tied in black or gray. The body can be noth-ing but thread and the hackle tied sparse. Tiny traditional Adamses work well as midges, too, for the variegated grizzly coloration of the tail looks a bit like the segmented shuck of the real thing. The buzzlike gray hackle passes for the emerging midge adult.

Since midges can vary in color, including black, gray, olive, tan, cream, bright green, and even red, any tiny mayfly pattern of the proper color and size can pass as a midge at times. Trimming a fly down on-stream is another option. A small mayfly pattern can have its tail and wings snipped off, which can leave just enough body and hackle to give a midgelike impression. Some midges aren't all that small, either, especially if trailing a shuck that they can't quite shake off. River midges can approach #18, and lake midges come as large as #10.

Midge Dry Flies: Griffith's Gnats—Palmered Dry Flies

This tying style has been around for centuries. They were known as "buzz" ties in older English days. Today, the Griffith's Gnat has become the Royal Wulff of midge drys and is probably as popular as any small fly on the market.

Fished in sizes #16 to #26, dead-drifted, twitched, or skittered across the surface, these fully hackled little patterns have duped thousands of fish.

Common ties include grizzly, dun, or black hackle over peacock herl or black dubbing. Tans, grays, and bright green are also common midge colors where I fish, so I tie up those colors as well. Black models can be easiest to see in some lighting situations, and tiny Hi-Vis caddis-style overwings can be added if it helps you see your fly.

Since midges commonly skitter across the water, and generally in an upstream, back-and-forth manner, fishing them that way sometimes works better than dead-drifting them. Just a twitch or slight lift of the rod tip as the fly comes into the fish's view can be enough to single your midge out from the crowd. Certainly there are fish that favor dead-drifted ones, too. I'll use a Griffith's Gnat for a strike indicator and hang a tiny midge pupa below it as a dropper. This is a good system to feel out the trout's preferences. Each fish is his own man, though, and fly changes are often in order as one moves up and down the river fishing water of differing character.

Midge Pupae

Midge pupae represent a most important fishing stage of this incalculably profuse and diverse insect group. And talk about easy—the basic midge silhouette is as easy as they come. Even bare hooks have caught fish, with the eye of the hook passing as the midge's slightly bulging thorax. Historically, hooks weren't made small enough for realistic pupa imitations. That's not true today. More often it's the angler's attitude or lack of confidence in very small hooks that prevents him from fishing them. Hang one beneath a small dry fly, set the hook gently, and hold on! Midge fishing can be as simple as that. Other times find trout ultraselective to size, color, form, motion, translucence, or some other factor an angler can't quite put his finger on. Maybe it's that thirty-foot line attached to a man that bothers them! It might be time to look up another fish.

Midge pupa bodies are kept very thin and are tied of some fine material, very sparse dubbing, or just tying thread. Ribbing is often used for the segmented effect. The thorax is just a slight hump, usually tied with a twist or two of dubbing, built up tying thread or herl. Midges do have little antennae and some anglers tie wisps of Z-lon or downy fibers pointing forward at the eye. These also pass for emerging wings when fished in the surface film. In ultrasmall sizes such detail can be meaningless.

There are times when trout are fools for a good midge pupa pattern while anglers fishing larger standard dry flies consider the same bulging fish impossible. Because midges hatch twelve months a year on most waters, fishing them habitually is an excellent idea. They only take a minute to tie, and take so little space in a fly box. Considering the number of good fish they can fool, no other fly, by size, is so worthwhile.

Midge Larvae

Midge larvae are mere worms found attached to the streambed by the thousands, sometimes breaking free and drifting. These are secondary to pupae in actual use, though spring-creek and tailwater fishermen find them effective when hatches are sparse. It has become popular of late to fish one as a dropper off a more visible deep nymph such as a Beadhead or San Juan Worm. Jaded fish laugh at the larger offering and inhale the small one! Winter and early-spring trout seem to always have midge larvae in their stomach, and sometimes in good numbers, at least in the stomach samples I've taken over the years. Other

days or hours find midge pupae and adults getting most of the attention.

These #18-to-#22 flies can be tied on curved-shank scud hooks for added realism. Simple tubular bodies and a slightly enlarged thorax are all tied of the same material and color, be it tying thread, sparse dubbing, monofilament, floss, or what have you. Ribbing with fine wire for segmentation is an option. Common colors include black, olive, brown, and red.

Caddis Dry Flies

Caddis Dry Flies: Traditional Feather Wings

Many feather-wing variations capture the caddis silhouette and color quite well. The body color of the natural can be of concern, too, with shades of green, tan, amber, brown, and gray being common. Synthetic wing substitutes are popular, too, and look realistic as finished products. They hold up better after being chewed. The traditional hackling can also be replaced with a wing post and Parachute tie. In the smallest sizes, down to #24, one could drop the hackle and just rough-dub the thorax, picking out some hairs for looks and buoyancy. Such mininaturals are about in the summer and trout do cash in on them.

Caddis Dry Flies: Hairwing Caddis

Hairwing caddis are now western and world standards, with Al Troth's Elkhair Caddis the archetypal design. Dubbed, fully hackled, and sporting a buoyant elkhair wing, such patterns float high and catch a lot of fish. The hackle can be eliminated for flat-water work, for the dubbing and hollow elk (or deer) hair alone provides plenty of flotation, especially in smaller sizes. I tie them down to #24 and sometimes use them for midge patterns, as well, for the light coloration is easy to see when facing a dark bank-reflecting background.

The other result of hairtying is the Goddard Caddis. This tie features a body and wing shaped as one, using the spun-deer-hair technique (which is seen on the bodies of Irresistibles and the heads of Letort Hoppers). Hackle is added in the usual dry-fly location, behind the eye and hackle stem antennae, as well. These are highly buoyant, durable, and visible patterns, though a little tricky to tie in smaller sizes. The color of the spun deer hair is varied to match the hatch. Tan, brown, olive, and black are common choices.

There's another phase that most anglers don't think about—spent caddis.

These are not as numerous or synchronized as mayfly spinners, but they are on the water in a scattered sort of way. There are also spent aquatic moths, which can be more numerous. Some trout will target these. When photographing trout during Trico hatches, I watched a percentage of fish move for the spent caddis and moths while others stuck to Tricos. I often have anglers

with poor eyesight use an Elkhair Caddis for a strike indicator under these conditions, since the number of spent aquatic moths can be quite high, and trail a Trico spinner as a dropper. A good number of fish go for the caddis, too.

One could tie a little elk hair on each side of the fly, rather than over its back, for a better silhouette. The moths are almost white, about #16 to #14. A cream dubbed body works well. Spent caddis are a little darker. Natural deerhair wings and a green-olive, tan, amber, or gray body makes a good match. Their long antennae can be prominent, but I just figure my tippet can pass for that, and I leave an extra-long tag end off the fly's knot as the second antenna. These are secondary tactics, but there for those anglers with hyperactive entomological minds!

Caddis Dry Flies: Surface–Emergent Caddis

These flies are tied somewhat like Elkhair Caddis but with a trailing shuck of Antron or Z-lon. This style was popularized by Gary LaFontaine in his landmark book, *Caddisflies*. Antron filaments are draped around a dubbed body, with some left trailing as a shuck. These are intended to hold air bubbles when under water. An ostrich-herl head is added, and the elk- or deerhair wings are kept sparse. These are fished wet, just under the surface, and on the surface. Hackle can be added for more buoyancy, tied sparsely in the traditional manner or Parachute. Some modern tyers just add a Z-lon tail to a standard Elkhair Caddis. Deep and surface-emergent caddis patterns have proved to be deadly trout flies across the West, where such patterns were once more notable for their absence.

Caddis Dry Flies: CDC Caddis

Cul de Canard caddis ties depend on the natural flotation qualities of the specialized feathers and on their lifelike movement for added attraction. Bodies are tied of match-the-hatch dubbing or herl, and a few soft partridge hackles can be added at the throat. These are good flat-water patterns that can be taken as emergers or adults. They won't take the repeated chewings that an Elkhair Caddis will but are worth trying on extrapicky big-rising fish.

Emergent Caddis

Emergent Caddis: Traditional Wet Flies

Wet flies are often taken for caddis emergers. Scale down the size, throw in a little partridge round the throat, maybe a bead at the head, and you have a workable classic tie for rough pocket water and tailwater alike. Let it sink a bit, then give it the old down-and-across treatment and hold on. A great way to fish if you want to look around at the scenery and daydream too!

Emergent Caddis: Soft-Hackles

Soft-Hackles make good caddis emergers, too. Rougher dubbed bodies, a little Antron, and beadheads can be added for additional sparkle and depth. Peacock herl is another excellent body material when matched with partridge and other soft hackles. Down-and-across controlled drifts bring sound takes that can pop too light a tippet.

Emergent Caddis: Beadhead Caddis Emergers

Beadhead Caddis emergers have been working wonders. These can be nothing more than a rough dubbed body and a bead. Such simplistic ties have caught hundreds of fish, East and West. The addition of a little soft hackle for wings and Antron or Z-lon for a shuck can further enhance imagined effectiveness.

Swisher and Richards noted in their book *Emergers* that it is the swimming legs of caddis emergers that are perhaps most noticeable to fish. They even suggest rubber-legged emergers to imitate the natural's vigorous paddling leg motions during rises to the surface. Without saying as much, they contest the "gas bubble" theory that is the basis of LaFontaine's very successful Antron emergers. The Sparkle Pupa set out to imitate the alleged buildup of gas under the emerging caddis's shuck, which is supposedly glistening and highly visible to trout as it buoys the insect to the surface. While this might remain a debatable point, both types of pattern continue to catch lots of fish! A #18 is about the smallest hook you can slide a bead onto.

Emergent Caddis: Sparkle Pupa

Sparkle Pupas are Gary LaFontaine's effective patterns, which set off a mild revolution in caddis-fishing quarters with the release of his detailed book *Caddisflies*. The combination of herl head, dubbed body, Antron oversheath, and deerhair wing create a unique-looking fly that has proven to be a great deceiver of trout. Designed in deep-drifting and subsurface emergent varieties, they fool trout into the caddis hatches that dominate many rivers' ecosystems.

Historically, caddis imitations took a back seat to mayflies because the naturals lacked the long surface drifts, dense and predictable hatches, and graceful style of the mayfly, even though caddis are often the more populous insect of the two. Gary went a long way in ending that unbalanced fly scenario with his series of caddis imitations.

Caddis Worms

Caddis worms, or larvae, are innumerable on most streambeds, and worthy of imitation. Some are cased, some free-roaming, and some even spin webs like spiders. Most anglers have some imitations in their box, but they seem to take a back seat to more trendy patterns of the day.

Typically, they are tied on

curved-shank hooks, and often in green with a black head. They are kept thin and bounced along the bottom, where trout expect to see them. A bead head is an obvious option here, and beads come in black as well as in shiny tones. There are tungsten beads, too, that are heavier than lead. Caddis worm or larva imitations are usually fished in #16 and up. Smaller than that and they begin to compete with midge larvae.

Cased Caddis

Cased caddis imitations seem to come and go, rarely catching on in the average angler's imagination or fly box. Case materials of both the naturals and imitations vary because caddis use sticks, sand, pebbles, and other stream refuse to construct their protective homes. Some anglers have gone so far as to glue real caddis cases on hooks. The exposed head and crawling legs of the natural are usually imitated with a small amount of rough dubbing or sparse hackle. Weight should be built in, for these flies are bounced along the bottom. Trout eat lots of the real ones, especially when other hatches become sparse. You'll catch the odd trout that has obvious nose wear from grubbing them off the bottom. I've had success casting them to visible trout. I list this pattern in the next section, along with a series of proven small-fly patterns. Cased caddis patterns are usually fished in sizes #18 to #16 on long or curved-shank hooks, on up to giant #8s for October caddis.

A Select Group of Proven Small-Fly Patterns

The following are a chosen selection of small-fly patterns representing several tying styles. Tying ingredients are given, along with notes on tying and presentation. This is not a fly-tying manual, though, and beginners should get some instruction before tackling the smaller patterns. Many of the patterns are quite simple and can be tied with just a little practice, the right tools, and perhaps some magnification. Having broken that forty-year barrier, I now have to wear reading glasses to tie small flies.

There is no last word on fly patterns in the small-fly arena. Although some of these patterns may remain popular for decades, expect many new developments in theory, hooks, materials, and tippets to launch novel patterns that will have their own lifespans. An ongoing process of fooling pickier and pickier fish will no doubt be the future of fly fishing in most quarters of the globe, with small flies dominating catch rates as time goes on. Some of these

flies are already old standards, others are fresher on the scene. With such a selection on hand, you are likely to catch trout anywhere across the West.

A Note on Hooks

Hooks listed in the tying menus that follow can be found on the chart below. This will simplify things a bit, for there are many quality hooks on the
market today.

Hook eyes come in downturned (for added hooking leverage), straight- or
ring-eye, and upturned styles. Many small-fly anglers use straight-eye hooks to
gain extra gape distance between the hook eye and point. Every advantage
can help when one is fishing the smallest sizes. Shorter-shank wide-gape
hooks are popular, too, for the smallest models can have added hooking potential with a larger gape. In the chart below, straight eye hooks are marked
SE. Barbless hooks are marked B. Several manufacturers' hook models are
listed below, but this isn't intended to be a complete analysis of what's on the
market. And not all models go as small as some anglers would like.

Style 1: Standard Dry-Fly Hooks

Daiichi	1100, 1110 (SE), 1190 (B)
Dai-Riki	305, 310 (SE)
Mustad Accupoint	AC 94840
Mustad Standard	94845 (B)
Orvis	4641–00 (big-eye hook) (SE)
	4864 (big-eye standard)
Partridge	L3A
Tiemco	TMC 100, TMC 101 (SE), TMC 902BL (B)

Style 2: Short-Shank Dry-Fly Hooks

(These are better choices for some tiny drys, including midges, Trico spinners,
Pseudo duns, beetles, and so on.)

Daiichi	1310, 1480 (SE), 1640 (SE)
Partridge	K1A (down to #28)
Tiemco	TMC 921, TMC 501 (SE)

Style 3: Emerger Hooks

(These have short curved shanks and fine to medium wire.)

Daiichi	1140, J220
Partridge	K4A
Tiemco	TMC 2487, TMC 206BL (B)

Style 4: Standard Nymph Hook

Daiichi	1550, 1560
Dai-Riki	300, 060, 730
Mustad	9671, 3906
Partridge	L2A, H1A
Tiemco	3769, 3761

Style 5: Scud and Caddis Pupa Hooks

Daiichi	1130, 1140, 1150
Dai-Riki	135
Mustad Accupoint	AC 80250BR
Mustad Standard	37160
Partridge	K4A, K2B
Tiemco	TMC 2487, TMC 2457, TMC 205BL (B), TMC 206BL (B)

Style 6: Longer Curved-Shank Hooks

(These hooks are used for caddis worms, cased caddis, San Juan Worms.)

Daiichi	1270 (SE), 1273 (SE)
Dai-Riki	270 (SE)
Mustad Accupoint	AC 80050BR (SE)
Mustad Standard	37160
Partridge	K12ST (SE)
Tiemco	TMC 200R (SE)

These hook styles and models cover most tying situations. There are others to experiment with, but many of them don't come in the smallest sizes. Many fishermen just use dry-fly hooks for subsurface nymphs and emergers; the heavier-wire wet-fly and nymph hooks help get flies down a little deeper and have added strength.

Midge Patterns

Griffith's Gnat

Hook:	Style 1 or 2, #18 to #28
Thread:	Black 8/0
Body:	Peacock herl, various colors of dubbing
Hackle:	Grizzly, black, dun, barred ginger, or whatever matches today's midge menu

A now-classic seducer of midging and picky rising trout. Use this dead-drifted, twitched, or skittered. Some fish might demand "fly before tippet" presentations. Size 26 and smaller flies could be tied with just a pinch of rough dubbing.

Palomino Midge

Hook:	Style 2 or 3, #16 to #24
Thread:	Match body color
Shuck:	Micro Ultrachenile or New Dub in black, gray, tan, olive, green, red
Wing case/emergent wings:	Z-lon or poly
Thorax:	Dubbing to match or contrast with shuck

Tie to the smallest sizes and fish in the film. These have been inhaled by many a selective trout. Dead-drift, but don't be afraid to give the slightest twitch as the fly comes into the trout's view. Struggling midge emergers are familiar to trout. This is an easy fly to tie.

Serendipity

Hook: Style 3 or 5, #16 to #22
Thread: To match body color
Body: Z-lon in red, brown, olive, tan
Thorax/emergent wings:
            Natural deer hair

This is a fairly recent invention, and a very effective one. Dead-drifted, the fly hangs from the surface film like an emerging midge. Another of those easy but effective ties that serious anglers love.

Reverse Suspender Midge

Hook: Style 1, #18 to #24
Thread: Black 8/0
Emergent wings: Foam at bend of hook
Hackle: Grizzly, few turns at bend of hook
Thorax: Black and gray mixed dubbing, sparse, toward bend of hook
Body: Stripped grizzly-hackle stem or peacock herl, lacquered

There are several popular suspender midges around—this one is tied in reverse order and gives a good effect. Using a sinking leader or tiny split shot on the leader helps achieve the right drift. The eye of the hook should be sunk and dangling, the foam-buoyed bend of the hook should float. Trout do focus on midges as they struggle to escape their shucks.

Brassie

Hook: Style 1, 2, 4, 5, or 6, #16 to #26
Thread: Black 8/0
Body: Thin copperwire or ribbon in natural, green, or red
Thorax: Hare's-ear dubbing in black, gray, or natural, or peacock or ostrich herl. Keep sparse yet scruffy.

A Colorado classic. It seems all anglers are just born superior nymph fishermen there! Dead-drift down deep, in the trout's face. Added weight to the leader and a strike indicator are usually employed. We in Montana hang them as droppers off dry flies, too, for many of our targeted trout sit in one to three feet of slow, gliding tailwater currents. It's also become popular to use them (or other midge larvae) as droppers off San Juan Worms or Beadheads. The large fly works somewhat as an attractor nymph, but the wily trout who has been dodging larger flies for years opts for the conservative offering. Trout Psychology 101.

Michelle's Midge

Hook: Style 1 or 2, #16 to #28
Thread: Black 8/0
Rib: White thread
Body: Black tying thread
Thorax: Black or gray dubbing, picked out
Antennae: White thread,
a tag end after the ribbing is wound up and dubbed over.

I taught my wife to fly fish over midging and Trico-feeding trout, so I named this pattern after her. One might view this as a good way to end a marriage, but this pattern proved so effective in its time and place that catching midging trout was as simple as could be. The fish we cast to are visible trout that are bulging and rising to late-fall and winter midges. From late fall into spring, midge species seem fewer and relatively uniform in color: black-gray. We hang these pupae ten to eighteen inches below a Parachute Adams (for easy viewing) or a Griffith's Gnat. Since the trout are hovering just under the surface, I use dry-fly hooks. Trout will move farther from side to side to intercept midge pupae than they will for drys, for subsurface pupae are easier for them to see. They are taken dead-drifted and with slight drag.

This fly, like the Brassie, is a model of small-fly simplicity, using inexpensive materials and minimal tying time yet maximizing effectiveness. Simple midge larvae and pupae are tied in a wide variety of colors and materials while retaining the basic midge pupa silhouette. Tying time invested per fish caught is at its best in this department! The very smallest sizes, down to #28, can omit ribbing and just give the shape trout are so used to eating year-round. This is the trout's main food source on many rich waters over the course of the year.

Baetis, Pseudocloeon, and Other BWO Patterns

This group of insects is second in importance to trout on a seasonal basis, after the prolific midges. Consequently, they tend to take up a fair amount of space in a savvy angler's fly box.

Olive Thorax

Hook:	Style 1 or 2, #16 to #24
Thread:	Olive 8/0
Tail:	Dun hackles or Micro Fibetts, split
Body:	Olive, green, olive-brown, or gray dubbing, depending on hatch (can be adapted to PMDs, as well)
Hackle:	Dark or light dun, bottom trimmed off
Wing:	Teal flank, hen hackle fibers, turkey flats, duck-quill segments, or dark calf body or tail hair

Any light to dark gray wing material that ties in compactly and maintains a good silhouette will do. Only one wing is used. I often use black calf hair because it's durable, and black shows up well when contrasted against gray-sky-reflecting water, which can dominate on wide-open rivers.

This is one of the easiest hackled dry-fly patterns to tie in the smaller sizes, for materials are concentrated in the center of the shank. Crowding the eye isn't a problem. The hackle is trimmed from the bottom of the fly. The end result is Parachutelike, but these are a little easier to tie.

Pseudocloeon mayfly imitations are the smallest, in the #22 to #26 size range. These are a little lighter in color than *Baetis* mayflies, with medium olive or even bright green bodies and pale gray wings.

Baetis are larger, from #16 to #22. They range in color from medium to dark olive to olive-brown and gray. They often appear gray on the water but usually have an olive cast underneath. Wings are medium gray but can look dark against sky-glare backgrounds. Some small *Ephemerella* species are very *Baetis*like in coloration and can be a bit darker in body and wing. They also have more developed hind wings. These are slightly larger, in the #16 to #20 range. Olive Thorax variations are versatile fish-catching flies.

Baetis Parachute

Hook:	Style 1
Thread:	Olive 6/0, 8/0
Tail:	Dun hackle fibers, lifted and spread
Body:	Fine gray dubbing, sparse
Hackle:	Single grizzly or dun, Parachute style
Wing:	Black calf body or tail hair
Thorax:	Olive dubbing

This is a variation of a Parachute Adams I tie for local spring and fall *Baetis* hatches, which give a total of four-plus months of sport a season. I often use this pattern for a strike indicator when hanging a midge pupa below, for midges and *Baetis* are usually on the water at the same time. The gray-olive body follows an old theory of showing the trout a variety of colors in a fly, which, it is hoped, allows him to see the one he wants and take it. Other anglers mix dubbing colors together in a blender to achieve a similar result.

The black wing is for high visibility on glaring open water zones. It's not as easy to see against a dark backdrop like a wooded bank, though grizzly hackle stands out well enough. Cocking up the tail adds a natural look, for real mayflies tend to keep them lifted up off the water and have curved abdomens. Wrapping a turn or two of very sparsely dubbed thread under a hackle-fiber tail lifts and spreads it. One could substitute split hackle or Micro Fibbets.

Larger sizes of this fly work on less-pressured fish and in ripple lines and wind chop where the trout's vision is obscured a bit. I go small upon necessity, and there are plenty of picky fish around! I often think that obscuring the tippet can be more important than the pattern itself on ultraflat water. Going down in tippet size and sinking it can be every bit as important as changing or downsizing the fly pattern.

Traditional Adamses, Comparaduns and Sparkle Duns, and Swisher-Richards No-Hackles are extremely well suited for *Baetis* and *Pseudocloeon* hatches. We'll cover these ties under PMDs to save space and repetition. Of course, the coloration should match BWO hatches and be tied in #18 to #24.

H & L Variant

Hook:	Style 1, #16 to #22
Thread:	Black
Tail:	White calf body hair
Body:	Stripped peacock herl
Thorax:	Peacock herl
Hackle:	Brown or dark dun
Wings:	White calf body hair

Also known as Eisenhower's favorite fly, the H & L Variant is included here both as a tribute to the past and because it's one of those miniature attractor patterns that can work quite well, even on selective trout. Fished in the smallest sizes, we find it effective on *Baetis*-feeding fish, especially in ripple lines and wind chop. Even on flat water, some picky trout will take it. It's a good between-hatches pattern, too, when aimed at occasional risers or fished blind. Mini-Wulffs, H & Ls, Humpies, and other little attractors still catch a lot of trout on many rivers around the West and are easy to see.

RS-2 (or Rim, Style 2)

Hook: Style 1, #18 to #24
Thread: To match body
Tail: Two beaver guard hairs, split
Body: Sparse fur dubbing in olive, brown, gray, or tan
Wing case: Clump of down from the base of a pheasant body feather, or black Antron yarn

From Denverite Rim Chung comes this match-the-hatch *Baetis* emerger pattern that is now a favorite on the South Platte. An obvious variation would include CDC wings, tied in shorter or longer, to represent fledgling emerger or drifting dun. Since *Baetis* duns tend to drift so long on the surface before taking off, especially in cold weather, I find trout taking as many or more duns than emergers. This could certainly differ from locale to locale and even fish to fish. This basic shape and coloration signals "food" to trout.

Beadhead Pheasant Tail Nymph

Hook: Style 1 or 4, #16 to #18 (or the smallest hook you can get a bead on)
Thread: 8/0 olive or brown
Tail: Pheasant-tail fibers
Rib: Fine copper or gold wire

Body: Pheasant-tail fibers
Bead: Brass, copper, nickel, or black, in the smallest sizes

The classic *Baetis* nymph pattern has been made even more effective in many cases by the addition of the sinking bead. Go flashy, or black to match the darkening wing case of the pre-eminent natural. Whereas standard P.T.s can be tied down into the twenties, it's hard or impossible to get a bead over hooks smaller than a #18. The P.T. coloration matches many other mayfly nymph species, as well, including PMDs. The Beadhead P.T. has proven to be a killer pattern most everywhere it's fished.

Pale Morning Dun Patterns

This is one of the great summer hatches of the West and poses problems for anglers when the trout are tightly focused on the emergers or on some mysterious aspect of this fly's coloration or behavior. Some days your catch rate is good, other sessions it's dismal as the trout continue to heave all around. I think more energy is spent trying to master this emergence than most others combined.

PMD Sparkle Dun

Hook: Style 1, #18 to #24
Thread: Yellow 8/0
Tail: Brown Z-lon shuck
Body: Yellowish dubbing
               with subtle shades
               of pale green or
               pale orange
Wing: Natural deer hair,
               Comparadun style

Craig Mathews's adaptation of the Caucci-Nastasi pattern simply adds a trailing shuck of nymph-matching Z-lon. The idea is to present a fly that's still emerging at the surface, which can be a choice moment for trout to grab struggling naturals. Some species of mayflys have a harder time than others in escaping their shucks. The *Ephemerellas* tend to be strugglers.

The original Comparadun pattern features a split or fanned tail of stiff hackle fibers. Both these patterns are easy to tie, use inexpensive materials, and are very durable on-stream. This has made Comparaduns a favorite for twenty years now. They still hold a prominent place in the flat-water, selective-fish scene.

Swisher-Richards PMD No-Hackle

Hook:	Style 1, #18 to #22
Thread:	Pale olive 8/0
Tail:	Light olive or dun hackle fibers, split
Body:	Pale olive and yellow rabbit fur, mixed
Wing:	Light gray duck shoulder or quill, Sidewinder style

These beautiful patterns catch fish as well as the angler's eye. They are not as durable as Comparaduns, and the wings take some practice to perfect. Perhaps for those reasons they are not used commonly on-stream. But when one is up against that one big and most desirable flat-water riser, they are hard to beat for realism. A few hairs of dubbing can be picked out of the thorax to imitate legs and add flotation.

Swisher and Richards also have an emergent variation from their interesting book *Emergers*. The same dun style features a trailing shuck made of a reversed hackle segment. It provides a lifelike silhouette of a nymphal shuck and is fairly durable. Anyone caught up in the manmade material craze could substitute Z-lon, which doesn't really look much like a shuck in shape but has at least captured anglers' imaginations.

PMD Cripple/Emerger

Hook: Style 1 or 3, #18 to
            #22
Thread: Pale olive or yellow
Tail: Brown or olive-
            brown marabou,
            short
Body: Brown or olive-
            brown marabou or
            pheasant-tail fibers
Thorax: Pale olive and yel-
low dubbing, mixed, a pale orange-yellow mix is also used
Hackle: Ginger, sparse
Wing: Elk or natural deer hair, pointed forward

These emergers or "cripples" are meant to imitate mayfly duns still stuck in their nymphal shucks. The tail end of these flies absorbs water and sinks, with the fly, ideally, floating hook-down. This keeps the wing, which looks odd at first glance, pointing up once the tail end sinks. Some patterns omit the tail altogether; it can certainly be kept very short. The marabou adds life and motion to help imitate the struggling insect. One can also use pheasant-tail fibers or dubbing. Only the wing should be treated with floatant. This interesting concept has caught plenty of picky fish across the West and has been adapted to numerous hatches.

CDC Transitional Dun

Hook: Style 1, #18 to #22
Thread: Pale olive or yellow
Tail: Brown marabou or
            Z-lon
Body: Brown marabou,
            pheasant-tail fibers,
            or dubbing
Thorax: Pale olive and yel-
            low dubbing, mixed
Wing: Light gray CDC
            fibers

Here's another surface emerger using CDC feathers instead of the elk or deer hair in the previous pattern. The body represents the nymphal shuck and sits just under the surface. The CDC wing and dubbed thorax float. Perhaps you are beginning to get the idea that there can be some trick in fooling trout when concentrating on the PMD emergence process!

PMD Soft Hackle

Hook:	Style 1, #16 to #20
Thread:	8/0 orange
Tail:	Silvery sparkle poly, thin and short
Body:	Pale yellow-orange rabbit dubbing, sparse
Hackle:	3 to 4 turns of cream with rust or ginger-edged hen hackle
Head:	Same dubbing as body

This is Sylvester Nemes's variation of a PMD Soft-Hackle. He notes that many fish take it dead-drifted on the surface, again mimicking the PMD's trouble getting its wings in the air and fully hatching. The flies are also fished wet, with a controlled swing in front of bulging trout. Traditional Soft-Hackles lack the tail, and such patterns as the Partridge and Yellow have caught plenty of fish over the decades. Many just have a thin floss body, with a tuft of dubbing or herl at the thorax. Hen or partridge hackle is wound sparsely and gives the motion of life.

PMD Spinner

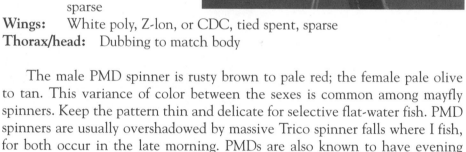

Hook: Style 1 or 2, #18 to
            #24
Thread: Brown or pale olive
            8/0
Tails: Light olive hackle
            fibers or Micro Fi-
            betts, split
Body: Rusty brown or
            pale olive dubbing,
            sparse
Wings: White poly, Z-lon, or CDC, tied spent, sparse
Thorax/head: Dubbing to match body

The male PMD spinner is rusty brown to pale red; the female pale olive to tan. This variance of color between the sexes is common among mayfly spinners. Keep the pattern thin and delicate for selective flat-water fish. PMD spinners are usually overshadowed by massive Trico spinner falls where I fish, for both occur in the late morning. PMDs are also known to have evening spinner falls, depending on conditions.

There are plenty of other good PMD patterns around, including traditional hackled models and Parachutes. Even tiny #20 Humpies can work as PMDs. No end of nymphs, emergers, cripples, and duns are experimented with, for there seems to be some spark to the creative process in standing among dozens of surging fish that won't touch your fly! Have several pattern variations on hand to lessen chances of total failure!

Trico (*Tricorythodes* Mayfly) Patterns

Tricos by the millions adorn late-summer rivers across the country. Here in Montana they bring up the most and the steadiest-rising fish to be seen all year. The morning hatch, and more importantly the spinner fall, lasts a solid two months, from early July to mid-September. The naturals are small and numerous, the trout picky. Obvious leader and tippet shadows and surface contortions under the late morning sun might be the biggest factor of all in the trouts' studious avoidance of your pattern. Long, fine tippets are recommended, better yet sunk.

Trico patterns are fairly basic. It's the repetitive casts, accuracy, and drag-free drifts needed to match the trout's rise rhythm that can be limiting factors. Rapid-fire presentations tend to catch more fish.

Here are some patterns that work. It's your job to intercept the trout in midrise with your fly!

Poly Wing Trico Spinner

Hook: Style 1 or 2, #18 to #26
Thread: Black or olive 8/0
Tail: 2 to 3 cream or light dun hackle fibers or Micro Fibetts, split and long
Abdomen: Pale olive thread wound halfway up shank
Wing: White poly tied spent, sparse
Thorax: Black dubbing, sparse

Fishing the classic Trico spinner usually finds the angler hunched over for better viewing of his tiny fly mixed with the thousands of naturals. Some think this is too much work. Others are addicted to it! Quick repetitive casts worked over a single fish will eventually intercept it. Trout often school up when feeding on Tricos, losing any territoriality with the superabundance of food. Sometimes just a few casts are needed, other times ten to fifty. Sometimes the trout just catch on to your game and dodge your casts. Down-and-across slack-line presentations might be needed to fool flat-water fish.

One gimmick we use is to fish tiny black nymphs or Soft-Hackles to fish that obviously have the "surface jitters." Fish that are spooked or wary of repeated presentations often resume feeding underwater before venturing back to the surface. I've witnessed this many times, especially when hiding in the willows on photo safaris. A sunk spinner is definitely an alternative.

CDC Trico Spinner

Hook: Style 1 or 2, #18 to
              #24
Thread: 8/0 olive or black
Tails: Cream or light dun
              hackle fibers, split
              and long
Abdomen: Black or pale olive
              dubbing, very sparse
Wing: White or light gray
              CDC feather fibers,
              tied spent or Comparadun style for added visibility
Thorax: Black dubbing, sparse

This is another Trico variation using the buoyancy of CDC feathers for flotation. Once it has been chewed, you need to switch flies and let the first one dry, or use dry-fly crystals. Tiny traditional Comparaduns and Sparkle Duns also work.

Parachute Tricos

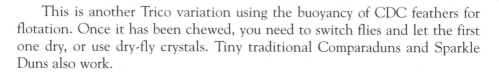

Hook: Style 1 or 2, #18 to
               #24
Thread: Black or olive 8/0
Tail: 2 to 3 cream or
               light dun hackle
               fibers or Micro Fi-
               betts, split and long
Abdomen: Pale olive or black
               dubbing, sparse
Wing post: White calf body
               hair or Z-lon
Hackle: Grizzly or cream, Parachute style
Thorax: Black dubbing, sparse

The advantage of the Parachute is its visible wing post. The tiny para-chuted hackles take a little finesse and refined tying tools to wind, but it isn't as difficult as you might imagine. I do it without hackle pliers. I have a bunch of leftover grizzly-hackle necks from which I only use feathers for #16 and smaller flies. The rest are intact!

One can use this same tie for midges by eliminating the tail. I've found that tails aren't that important to Trico-feeding trout, considering that you already have that one extralong one that connects to your fly rod!

Caddis Patterns

Although the majority of caddis seen around the river seem to be #16 to #14, there are plenty of miniature models that get the trout's attention at times. Caddis from #16 to #24 are common midsummer in shades of tan, gray, and black. Scaled-down versions of traditional caddis patterns work fine, and hackle can be eliminated for tiny flat-water imitations.

Elkhair Caddis

Hook:	Style 1 or 2, #16 to #24
Thread:	Black, brown, olive, tan 8/0
Body:	Dubbing to match natural, sparse but scruffy
Wing:	Natural or dyed elk or deer hair to match hatch

Mini-Elkhair Caddis work fine without hackle, especially in smaller sizes on flat water. Get the size right and many trout will glomp it on the first few drifts. Keep an eye on the surface for these little naturals. They're not as predictable as mayflies and can appear suddenly and catch you unaware playing with other hatches. These patterns are easy, cheap, and effective, just what the fly tyer who would rather fish prefers! Some tyers add a short trailing shuck of Antron or Z-lon as an emergent shuck. Amber, gray, and brown are typical choices for this.

Parachute Caddis

Hook:	Style 1, #16 to #22
Thread:	Black, gray, olive, brown, tan 8/0
Body:	Dubbing to match hatch, sparse
Wings:	Gray mallard quill, mottled brown turkey quill, or synthetic material to match hatch
Wing post:	Calf body hair or Z-lon, short
Hackle:	Black, brown, grizzly; to match hatch, Parachute style
Thorax:	Dubbing to match or contrast with body

Little Parachute Caddis are easier to see in ripple lines and against dark backgrounds. One can use the same basic tie with conventional hackling, or no hackle and picked-out dubbing at the thorax. In the tiniest sizes these can pass for midges. There are synthetic wing materials available, and some anglers use Z-lon or poly for wings. Cul de Canard wings can also be substituted, and hackle eliminated. Getting the proper silhouette and size are top priorities.

Peacock and Partridge Soft-Hackle

Hook:	Style 1, 2, 4, or 5, #16 to #22
Thread:	Olive 8/0
Rib:	Fine gold wire
Body:	Peacock herl
Hackle:	Partridge, 2 to 3 turns

This classic Soft-Hackle pattern can work very well during caddis emergences when fished dead-drift and on the swing. Variations include Beadhead models and two-tone bodies where the abdomen is thinner and of various match-the-hatch colors of floss or dubbing, plus a peacock-herl thorax. Another interesting variation is to point the hackles forward a bit. This increases the swimming motion when fished on the swing to imitate the emerging caddis's rapidly paddling legs.

LaFontaine Sparkle Pupa

Hook: Style 1, 4, or 5, #16 to #22
Thread: Brown 8/0
Sheath/overbody:
Strands of rust, grey, or amber Antron tied in at tail and pulled loosely over and around body, then tied in at thorax
Body: Brown rust Antron and fur, mixed, dubbing; also shades of green and yellow
Wing: Light deer hair, sparse, to bend of hook
Head: Brown marabou, fur, or herl

A highly effective pupa pattern that shook up the fly-fishing world. Intended to be fished deep, dead-drifted just above the bottom (Deep Sparkle Pupa) or just under the surface, where the natural can have some problems breaking through the film (Emergent Sparkle Pupa), these patterns have caught a lot of fish. Though the basic idea in fishing them is *not* the classic down-and-across swing, they catch fish that way, too. We've caught fish just standing in a riffle and letting the pupa drag in place downstream! A bead head is certainly an option for the Deep Sparkle Pupa.

Beadhead Caddis Worm

Hook:	Style 4 or 5, #16 to #18
Thread:	Black
Rib:	Fine copper or gold wire
Body:	Green, olive, or tan dubbing
Collar:	Scruffy black dubbing, sparse
Bead:	Black, tungsten, or shiny

The black bead is more realistic, the flashier ones perhaps more eye-catching. The trout eat both. This fly can be tied of nothing more than one-color dubbing and a bead and be just as effective. Tumble it along the bottom between hatches to pick up additional fish. You might also try a two-nymph indicator rig using a variety of nymphs. The Caddis Worm and a Soft-Hackle dropper would be a good freestone choice. A midge larva or pupa dropper might be a better tailwater second-fly option. Experimenting with two different flies at the same time is half the fun and can shorten the time needed to find the most productive deep pattern of the day.

Cased Caddis

Hook:	Style 4, 5, or 6, #16 to #20
Thread:	Black
Legs:	Scruffy black dubbing, sparse (in this case, the tail position is the head of the fly, at the bend of the hook)
Ribbing:	Fine copper or gold wire
Body:	Pheasant-tail fibers tapering thinner toward the eye over a tapering base of fine lead or copper wire

This is a simple pattern I've used successfully in Montana and New Zealand when fishing to visible trout in low, clear water. It would undoubtedly catch unseen fish, too, and should be bounced dead-drift along the bottom under a strike indicator if you can't see the trout take it. If it looks like the real thing to ultraclear-water trout, it can't be all bad!

Terrestrials and Crustaceans

In between hatches on hot summer afternoons, trout feed languidly on what drifts nearby. By late summer, nonaquatic insects begin playing a major role in a stream trout's diet, for many of the hatches are gone for the year, and so, too, the mature nymphs. Terrestrial insects help fill this void.

Bottom-dwelling crustaceans are also favorites, and will turn the trout's flesh orange or red when eaten in quantity. They're inhaled whenever one drifts, crawls, or swims a little too close. Spring-fed-lake fish make a steady diet of these, and spring creek trout eat their fair share, too.

These time-filler patterns can actually account for a large share of the day's action. Trout focused on a hatch are often harder to catch than are between-hatch fish trying to stock the physiological larder. These basic patterns and their offshoots and predecessors fool a large percentage of trout every season.

Foam Beetle

Hook: Style 1 or 2, #16 to #22
Thread: Black
Body: Black tubular or flat foam
Legs: Black hackle, elk hair, or moose mane
Indicator (optional): Hi-Vis hot pink poly tied in at top of collar

Trout eat a lot of beetles, especially toward late summer. They are numerous and constantly plopping into the stream. Bank-feeding trout are obvious candidates, but most fish will take a beetle that twirls a little too close. I guide skilled anglers who cast beetle patterns to visible fish, and others who use them as droppers off large attractor patterns in freestone rivers. Both techniques routinely fool trout. A beetle is always a good option to throw over selective and troublesome quarry. The best beetle fishing in the world is probably in New Zealand, where visible trout of two to over ten pounds pick them off the surface with regularity. Now that's amusement!

Jan's Ant Caddis

Hook: Style 1, #16 to #20
Thread: Black or claret
Body: Two distinctly separate balls of black dubbing
Wing: Light fine elk hair

    One of our past guides tied this up and caught lots of trout on it. I used it a lot myself, especially at the tail end of massive Trico spinner falls, and on into the afternoon in pursuit of occasional risers. The ant silhouette is topped by an elkhair-caddis-type wing of conservative proportions that's visible to anglers. I often substituted a claret, red, or even bright orange thread to, theoretically, imitate some of the more reddish amber ants. One can vary the dubbing color, too. The visibility of this ant, or perhaps more correctly, flying ant, pattern is what I like, plus it works. There are plenty of effective ant patterns around, and fish eat them all.

Cressbugs

Hook: Style 5, #16 to #20
Thread: Pale olive or gray
Tail: Pale olive or gray stripped goose biots
Rib (optional):
    Fine silver wire or pale green monofilament
Body: Pale gray or pale olive dubbing, thick and picked out at sides

Dubbing blends of angora, otter, Hairtron, or rabbit are meant to capture the translucency of the natural, with picked-out guard hairs acting as legs. Of late, these sowbugs, or cressbugs, have become popular on tailwaters and spring creeks, having been transplanted from East Coast spring creeks. These are tied shorter and a bit fatter than the shrimp or scud patterns that preceded them in popularity and are little more than a wad of pale gray dubbing.

The more traditional scud patterns usually featured a strip of clear plastic as an overback, which is held in place by fine copper ribbing. Hackle-fiber tails and matching antennae are often used. Shrimp dubbing colors vary from the realistic tan, pale olive, and grays to fluorescent pinks and oranges, colors only dead and steamed shrimp obtain! The latter are probably taken as egg patterns, and are popular during spawning seasons. The dubbing on scud patterns is picked out in a downward fashion to imitate the freshwater shrimp's many kicking legs.

Both sowbugs and scud should be fished dead-drift near the bottom, with additional weight and an indicator or two rounding off the rig. This is a standard method on such tailwaters as the Big Horn, and the flies are fished both out of the boat and wading. They can be slow-stripped and twitched, as well.

Water Boatman

Hook:	Style 4, weighted #16
Thread:	Olive
Tail:	Single strand of pearl Krystal Flash, long
Back:	Wide silver mylar or tinsel
Rib:	Fine silver wire
Body:	Peacock herl or olive marabou
Legs:	Olive goose biots, center-shank

Water boatmen are common in lakes and slower river eddies. They travel back and forth to the surface to breathe. They also leave a little trail of bubbles behind when they descend, which is what the long Krystal Flash tail imitates. They are wide and flat, with large eyes, and the fly's shape should reflect this. These can be allowed to sink before stripping and twitching them back toward the surface. Conversely, they could be tied with a foam body and be fished with a heavy split shot halfway up the leader, which would create an imitation of the diving behavior. Water boatmen are decidedly secondary for most stream fishermen, though lake anglers use them with some regularity. It never hurts to consider all the lifeforms in a river, though, and this is a good part of what makes fly fishing such an interesting lifelong pastime.

There are countless variations on small-fly patterns, but most anglers agree that having the right *size* fly is often the most critical criterion for success when trout are being picky. Shape and silhouette are next in importance, followed by color. No doubt you will find fish that adhere to no rules and have ways of dealing with humanity on their own terms. Defeats are usually more inspiring than successes when it comes to fly tying, though we certainly like to win in the end!

The Small-Fly Battlefields

Most premium fisheries that support good numbers of large fish and abundant small-fly hatches have common habitat denominators. Rich waters plus steady flows equal many trout. Good river management is of course desirable, and when it comes to maximum numbers of rising fish, a low river gradient (or drop in feet per mile) makes it easier for trout to casually surface-graze.

Water rich in nutrients kick starts the building blocks of aquatic life. Spring seepages are much more productive than snowmelt. Vegetation, crustaceans, fish, and aquatic insects reach population highs in spring-rich rivers.

Steady flows, the lack of severe runoff in the spring and drought conditions in late summer, promote a greater abundance of life. Rivers with steady flows tend to have moderated temperatures, too, which adds growing time to a trout's life span. Such moderation is brought about by springs or dams. Some natural lake outlets regiment river flows, too.

Low river gradient, or drop in feet per mile, means maximized holding water. Gushing rapids tend to hold less big fish than do expansive weed-bed flats, where a trout's need to fight the current is minimized. Certainly there are fast-water reaches of river that hold numerous big fish, like the Box Canyon of the Henry's Fork and the Quake Lake outlet of the Madison. Both of these receive the steady-flow benefit of being lake outlets and continuously support good numbers of trout in the swift pocket water. Such fish don't rise with the frequency that many anglers prefer, though, and must be "dredged"

217

Expansive weed-bed flats are typical of richer spring creeks and tailwater rivers. Well-scheduled hatches and high trout populations are common.

for with deep-nymph rigs much of the time. When it comes to good numbers of steady rising trout, low-gradient rivers can show you the most.

From Alberta to New Mexico and California to Colorado, premium fisheries exist where small-fly fishing can be the mainstay of success. The most prolific and enduring hatches of insect are mostly in the smaller sizes. Larger-model bugs like salmon flies or green drakes are shorter seasonal highlights. Other large-fly patterns are used as between-hatch diversions. Midges, *Baetis*, *Pseudocloeon*, PMDs, Tricos, and caddis top the list of long-duration, high-density superhatches. These appear with a regularity anglers can depend on, and for months at a time. Skilled anglers prepared to go small catch fish. Those that don't adapt just spend more time.

The list of small-fly battlefields reads like a *Who's Who* of America's best-known western trout streams: Oregon's Fall and Metolius; California's Hat Creek and Fall and Owens Rivers; Montana's Big Horn, lower Clarkfork, Missouri, Big Hole, and Kootenai Rivers, and Armstrong's and DePuy's spring creeks; Wyoming's Yellowstone, Firehole, and upper Madison Rivers in Yellowstone Park; Idaho's Henry's Fork and Silver Creek; Colorado's Frying Pan

Small-fly battlefields —some well known, some not so well known—are to be found year-round on western waters.

and South Platte; Utah's Green and Strawberry Rivers; Arizona's Colorado below Glen Canyon and Hoover Dams; and New Mexico's San Juan.

It's not just these famous rivers that can show consistent rising, bulging, and nymphing fish, for even swifter and lesser-known freestone rivers have low-water pools and flats where trout habitually sip small flies. This might only be a July-through-September incident on some rivers (when Tricos, Pseudos, PMDs, and small terrestrials can prevail), but that is just the period when many touring anglers fish them. Other streams have larger insect types mixed in and dominating action from May to August but become considerable midge and tiny BWO fisheries in late fall, winter, and early spring. For those who find the sight of steadily rising trout entrancing, such low-water small-fly scenarios offer the true essence of the sport.

Those practiced at fishing small, both on surface and bottom, find that they are now trained for almost any fishing situation that's likely to arise. The fine tuning and control mastered in this learning process lay the foundation for any other direction of fly-fishing growth. The mechanics of casting and line control become completely understood. The respecting of trout as wild animals and masters of their element replaces that "fish in a barrel" approach that you might have had in your angling youth. The need to imitate hatches teaches you more about river life than does the plunking of a spinner or lure in midstream. Consequently, your enjoyment potential goes way up.

It doesn't take long before you can glance at a stream and have a pretty good idea of its framework of aquatic life and fishing potential. Your improved skills of observation find you more fish, too. The ability to fool additional visible trout on light tackle is the greatest thrill of all, and there is no food source that you can't imitate when well prepared. The spreading rings on a quiet bankside eddy spark your inquiry. Knowing what's going on increases your confidence and ups your odds. Will that big speckled nose partake of your fly on the first drift? Perhaps, if your knowledge, nerves, and skill all come together on that initial presentation!

Index